THE PATCHWORK NATION

THE PATCHWORK NATION

re-thinking government — re-building community

DON EDGAR

HarperCollins*Publishers*

HarperCollins_Publishers_

First published in Australia in 2001
by HarperCollins_Publishers_ Pty Limited
ABN 36 009 913 517
A member of HarperCollins_Publishers_ (Australia) Pty Limited Group
http://www.harpercollins.com.au

HarperCollins_Publishers_
25 Ryde Road, Pymble, Sydney, NSW 2073, Australia
31 View Road, Glenfield, Auckland 10, New Zealand
77–85 Fulham Palace Road, London W6 8JB, United Kingdom
Hazelton Lanes, 55 Avenue Road, Suite 2900, Toronto, Ontario M5R 3L2
and 1995 Markham Road, Scarborough, Ontario M1B 5M8, Canada
10 East 53rd Street, New York NY 10022, USA

National Library of Australia Cataloguing-in-Publication data:

Edgar, Don, 1936– .
    The patchwork nation: re-thinking government – re-building community
    Includes index.
    ISBN 978-0-7322-6610-3 (pbk).
    1. Social institutions – Australia. 2. Social change –
    Australia. 3. Technology – Social aspects – Australia.
    4. Globalisation – Social aspects – Australia. 5. Community
    life – Australia. 6. Australia – Social conditions – 20th
    century. 7. Australia – Politics and government – 20th
    century. I. Title.
306.0994

Cover design by Luke Causby, HarperCollins Design Studio
Cover illustration: _Australian Landscape 1970_ by James Barker

Dedicated to our grandchildren, who *are* the future: Adrian, Luke, Emily and Oliver Ace.

Contents

Introduction . . . . **ix**

Section 1 : *The changing global context*

1. *Transforming the industrial economy* **2**
2. *The impact of structural change on Australian society* **21**
3. *The growing complexity of family life* **31**
4. *The new nexus of work–family–community* **42**
5. *A business paradigm shift* **59**

Section 2 : *The new tribalism — perils and possibilities*

6. *National identity and sense of place* **78**
7. *Globalisation and social movements* **83**
8. *Finding a more intelligent role for government* **93**

Section 3 : *Linking the patchwork — finding an Australian Way*

9. *Building human and social capital* **100**
10. *Redefining regionalism: the way forward* **106**
11. *Workable models of community-building* **113**
12. *Servicing the community patchwork* **140**
13. *Education — the driving force* **155**
14. *Conclusions — driving culture change and linking the future* **189**

Notes **195**
Index **216**

Introduction

GLOBALISATION NOT ONLY CHANGES THE nature of work, it strikes at the heart of our personal relationships, our community life and democracy itself.

This is a book about the re-building of Australian democracy, the reinvention of business and community in a global age, and the re-engagement of government in its task of serving the common good of all Australian citizens.

Its starting point is a belief that the social contract should be accountable to a human view, not just to economics, and that a massive shift of culture is required to bridge the chasm that has been cut by neo-liberal economics between people and government, between citizens and the political process, between the privileged and the excluded.

But the book is not intended to be an ideological tirade against government or so-called economic rationalism. Instead, it argues for a clear-headed reassessment of our core institutions — in government, in the workplace, in education and in the wider community. It recognises that technological change and the global free market have changed forever the ways in which people will relate to one another but it focuses on changing those institutions that involve people directly rather than indirectly.

Australia's future is inextricably linked to other forces outside our complacently happy shores, and if we are to thrive, we must forge new links that both break down the dangers of isolation and make our institutions work together for communities, not as silos ignoring the interdependence of life in the coming centuries.

We cannot go back to an outmoded welfare state, or to the rigidities of our former industrial relations system, or to the post-War myth of idyllic suburban family life. Nor can we allow our schools and universities to operate in denial of the changed work and family situations of their students, or allow our community welfare system to deliver services top-down to those deemed needy enough for their misguided paternalistic interference.

Above all, the book argues for a shift in the processes of government, calling for a revitalisation of local and regional communities, a deepening of democratic participation in decision-making, and a winding back of what is perhaps the most paradoxical outcome of the push for smaller government — an ever-stronger central managerialism, which is inimical to democracy and the common good. Government in the new information age has to become clever, not clumsy, must lead but not control, and must focus on the nation's quality of life not just its economy.

The image I have of Australia and its future is one of a patchwork quilt. Made up of regional and local patches, each with its own unique colour and well-loved history, it is linked loosely by the networks of government services, workplaces, schools, community agencies and families. That may sound too benign for a wired future, but it strikes the right note of government concern for all, universal coverage in a loose-knit way, without smothering or imposed uniformity. Each region and locality preserves its own integrity and makes its own decisions about how it operates, but every patch gets its share of the quilt as a whole. No-one is left out in the cold. Australia in the knowledge era must discourage uniform, top-down solutions. It must not offer a green square for everyone when some need a red triangle or a yellow circle to suit their unique situation. We have to restore a respect for place and encourage diverse, more innovative solutions to social problems and community needs.

The book cannot cover every aspect of change that might be necessary or desirable, but it tackles those aspects of Australian society that most affect people's lives — the place of government, the family, the workplace, the schools and further education, and of what are broadly called community service organisations.

In each of these life arenas, we need a new approach, a new culture better suited to the complexity of a technologically sophisticated global market. In each of them, the task will be to suggest practical ways of re-engaging people, encouraging diversity and flexibility, and aiming for positive solutions, rather than simply plugging the dam wall with a desperate finger or two.

My aim is to explain in the simplest possible terms the nature of global change and its implications for the Australian way of life (Section 1), and to outline a blueprint for institutional change that our political leaders might embrace and on which they can expand (Sections 2 and 3). If they do not, it is likely that the voters will.

The book calls for a culture change already presaged by the complex links of postmodern society, a shift towards a culture of belonging, a culture of respect for others, who may be unlike ourselves in terms of ethnicity, education level and values but whose common humanity requires respect and the encouragement of inclusion. It sees some hope in social movements that demand more accountability not just from government but also from business, while at the same time recognising the dangers inherent in what I call here 'the new tribalism'.

We have become too much the victims of professionalism, specialisation and elitism, to the point where many citizens feel they are denied respect from those in positions of power. As a result, people lack respect for those core political institutions on which democracy is based. They reject the powerful and become 'a nation of spectators', in a standoff situation that benefits nobody. Alternatively, they take action, via the new technology, to lobby for change in a more positive direction.

Our institutions are out of kilter with the context in which we now live — an information/knowledge society where every individual's unique input is potentially of value and must be given the recognition and respect it deserves. To belong is to have respect and a stake in what happens beyond your own fragile psyche.

Let me begin by asserting what seem to me to be some self-evident truths:

- Every individual wants and seeks happiness, a sense of wellbeing and a sense of control over their own life.
- Most people locate wellbeing less in money and physical possessions than in their personal and family relationships.
- Without some minimal assets, however, it's pretty hard to be happy either with your material lot in life or with your personal relationships. Governments must, therefore, be concerned about exclusion and inclusion, both financial and social, if the nation is to have cohesion of any kind.
- Most people also locate wellbeing in a sense of belonging, of connectedness, of being a valued part of a whole larger than themselves, whether that is a family, a workplace, a friendship group, a football club or some wider community. They enjoy common membership, have a stake in the survival of the groups to which they belong, and have some say, some control, in the actions and decisions made by the groups to which they belong.

   Those who lack such a sense of belonging and having a say suffer depression, alienation from or hostility to the society from which they feel apart or which rejects them and gives them no respect. The survivors — those who cope and have resilience in life's struggle — are those who have someone that gives a damn about them, and who give a damn about themselves. To achieve that resilience across a community, we need a politics of inclusion and institutional structures that give a damn.

National identity, therefore, lies in pride in the 'Australianness' of our own suburb, city and region, in its quality of life, its openness and fairness, its opportunities and its immediate preoccupations. The national symbols of mateship, Gallipoli, the Sydney Opera House and Harbour Bridge, our sports heroes and our artists may trigger national pride, but our identity grows and is embedded in the reality of everyday life; it is situated in place. Policies and programs must recognise and cater to that if they are to prevent alienation from the core institutions of society, a decline in civility and reduced cohesion (Section Two).

- The role of democratic government is to maximise the greatest good for the greatest number of citizens. The goal is not equality as such, but some equity, some justice, in the way goods and opportunities are distributed across society. By definition, democracy is made up of all the people, is structured for all the people and is determined by all the people. Though the ideal is never quite the reality, a sense of belonging, inclusion, involvement and ownership is integral to any functioning democracy.

Nor is the goal total participation by people in every decision made on their behalf but, rather, a sense that those decisions are being made for the common good and with clear knowledge of what the people need and want. Even the Internet will not return us to the Athenian *plaka*, where every citizen (then only male and free, not female or slave) could discuss public affairs and vote actively on each decision being made. Modern democracy may well develop closer and more frequent polling links with citizens who won't attend meetings in the local hall, but it is the density of relationships, the connections we make in whatever form, that make a difference, not some idealised form of active participation.

- There is no common good if some groups are systematically excluded from the fruits of good governance or from their right to contribute to decision-making that affects the quality of their lives. We have to resource citizenship through the education of children, through the forms of political and social action we devise, and through a culture of belonging based on respect for the rights and responsibilities of every individual.

The following further set of assertions is also central to the argument of this book:

- Ordinary people live their lives as whole human beings. They do not separate their personal relationships and family lives from workplace problems and they do not see public policy as being separate from their own private activities and options. Most of us understand the larger issues only through the reality tests of our own everyday life.

It follows that government departments and service providers cannot operate as silos, dealing separately with bits and pieces of people's lives. For example, education happens in myriad ways apart from schools. Youth programs cannot focus only on youth without considering family matters, job training, and physical and mental health issues. A family fronting up to welfare authorities for child neglect or abuse in most cases has other problems, such as housing, employment or drugs, so the presenting issue cannot be dealt with in isolation from the rest. Perhaps the clearest example is the unrealistic notion that job performance is not — or, at least, should not be — affected by the private family lives of the workers. Employers who turn a blind eye to work–family balance or to work–life balance fail to see the inevitable and natural interconnections, fail to integrate their various policies and programs, fail to see that the bottom line they so love is multiple not singular.

So a central theme of this book is the need to link up the disparate threads of government, business and community action. My argument is that the future is so complex and interdependent that no central planning authority, no one government department, no expert professional organisation, no 'one size fits all' solution can adequately meet the needs of people in the new knowledge economy. We have to reconnect, work together, draw on the complementary expertise and diverse perspectives of one another, if we are to become a truly clever country.

- We have to do this through the locations in which people live their lives: their families, their workplaces, their local schools and their regional communities. We have to reinvent the notion of community for a new age, go back to more local and regional control over what affects our lives, and destroy the top-down, managerial approach of government that assumes one size fits all and only the experts (or the bureaucrats) know what is good for us. Moreover, because the quality of collective life both reflects and sets the limits for business enterprise, corporations have a responsibility not only to their remote shareholders but also to the people and communities within their sphere of action, to the broader common good.

It is important to stress that I am not calling for some sentimental return to a communal past that never existed in reality. My view of community is one fully aware that local control can be very parochial and nasty. It can ignore the national interest, discriminate against those defined as outsiders or undeserving (witness Pauline Hanson's One Nation appeal against interest-group favouritism), and it can operate very inefficiently and ineffectively (as in some of the local government authorities closed down in Victoria during the Kennett Government era.)

It is also clear that community is a concept defined variously as geographic locality, common interests, value consensus or the civil society, and is too often seen as a goal rather than a process of debate and discussion. A community can be a toxic environment as well as a positive one in which to live.

As will become clear, I believe that community is based as much on conflict over scarce resources as it is on value consensus or shared identity. Most community feeling arises from shared goals, but those goals and interests often are in opposition to those of some other group. Democracy is about debate, discussion, negotiation and compromise. It's not a perfect system, but its value lies in the public discussion of competing ideas, policies and programs and the common acceptance of the consequences, at least for a limited period of time, of a vote by all citizens.

In a decently civil society, people do not have to love one another or agree with everyone else, but they do have to be civil to one another, accept their equal right to an opinion and put up with a majority vote that goes against what they themselves would have preferred. They show their respect by accepting that other people belong, not by agreeing with them, but by listening to and discussing issues with them in a civilised manner. Too much of the literature about community, about civil society, about social capital and participatory democracy, is sentimental pap, ignoring the reality that groups have competing interests and can get very nasty.

The distinguishing feature of democratic government in its Australian form is that we confine most of the nastiness to parliamentary debates and electoral campaigns and we delegate to a group of quite imperfect people the right to make policy decisions on behalf of the common good. Once they go beyond the bounds of what the Commons feels is actually good for them, we vote to throw them out and try some other lot of imperfect representatives.

But in the free-market push towards economic efficiency, corporatisation, privatisation and the contracting out of many government services, we have lost much of the sense of active participation and involvement in influencing the delegated decision-making that happens in communities between elections, the fabric of social life that can be delegated only partly to outsiders not involved in the everyday life of real communities. We have to restore the quilt.

- A real community is an ever-changing thing, as groups shift and change position, as people age, workplaces disappear and local leisure pursuits shift in parallel with popular interests. But every such community is rooted in time and place. As John Ralston Saul puts it, 'Free speech and democracy are closely tied to an active, practical use of memory — that is, history — as well as an unbroken sense of the public good.'[1] And most people's sense of history centres around their own family, the intergenerational links that give meaning to the wider events of the public arena. It is interpersonal relationships, work life and neighbourhood or regional place activities that make for a sense of community. Shared values 'are generated in intimate settings in which people deal with one another face to face.'[2]

Argue as we might about whether the Internet is creating new forms of virtual community or about whether there is any meaningful community in a sprawling outer urban suburb, the word community has little meaning without a sense of active interaction on behalf of some cause that has common or shared significance. So democracy has always relied on community action on behalf of common interests and needs that cannot be or have not been met by the democratically elected side of government.

In the global shift to corporatisation, it is this sense of common caring about life-as-it-is-lived that many Australians feel has been lost. And governments must play a more active role in resourcing vital communities, in restoring the thickness of democracy, the density of relationships that make people feel they belong and have some stake in the common good.[3] Government and other public institutions provide the stitching that is so vital to holding the patchwork together.

In the end, people live their lives in a location, with other people, eating meals, having to relate physically with others, making decisions that affect others directly and dealing with presently actual emotions and behaviour. The majority of people are concerned with issues that directly affect them, their children and their wider families. Politically diverse Internet activists may lobby governments and attack the World Trade Organisation and big corporations, but most of us are hard-pressed to attend a local school meeting or even to lobby for better street lighting in our own parks.

People interact with a family (however broadly that may be defined) and they exist within a community. We know the nature of that community, the quality of neighbourhood relationships and physical facilities, makes a huge difference to people's sense of wellbeing. Children who grow up in toxic communities, just like adults who struggle to survive in neighbourhoods with few support systems or few social contacts, become isolated and alienated. They become the abused and the abusers, the violent and the victims of violence, powerless and in despair. Research on child abuse, family violence, drug abuse, delinquency, vandalism, health, youth suicide and ethnic conflict comes together around the interconnections of a physically bounded community and neighbourhood.

- Effective solutions never come from separate programs or services tackling the problem in isolation from the surrounding community. They come from integrated, wrap-around, linked efforts across a whole range of community agencies aimed at improving the quality of life and support. They target the toxic environment as a whole, not the individual or group with the problem. What that requires is a whole-of-government approach.

The sad thing is that Australian political leaders have lost the plot. They have little understanding of this research, and react only when they think votes are at stake, as in the current scramble to pay attention to rural and regional issues. Community disenchantment with the political process is not focused just in rural and regional Australia; it strikes at the heart of an arrogant, centralist, managerialist ideology that has lost touch with the felt needs and concerns of all Australian citizens. Pauline Hanson's One Nation Party draws life from that broad public hostility.

Australian voters deserve better than knee-jerk rejection of whatever the other party says, and it is a shame that only the threat of votes going against them will drive either major party to listen to what people feel they have lost after two decades of neo-liberal ideology.

This book argues for a re-voicing of democracy, for valuing active citizenship and for making the formal political-administrative system more accountable to the citizens who pay the taxes. On the other hand, it rejects a naive call for a return to community, a concept open to many meanings, often sentimental and blind to history and the dark side of community control.

· So the task of linking the patchwork is to work out how to regenerate a government and a set of political and social institutions that keep in view the common good, to work out how best to link business aims with community wellbeing, and how best to link the new institutions of the global age with the everyday processes of communities in place, ignorant, prejudiced and busy as people may be.

The People Together report *The Power of Community* reminds us of Thomas Jefferson's words back in 1820: 'I know of no safe depository of the ultimate powers of society but the people themselves: and if we think them not enlightened enough to exercise control with a wholesome discretion, the remedy is not to take it from them, but to inform their discretion.'⁴

That is a powerful argument for stepping back, in a global age, from corporate governance in both politics and business affairs, and educating people in active engagement, starting with children in our schools, permeating every workplace and community service organisation, so that the very skills needed to compete globally in a service and information economy are engendered from birth and sustained to old age.

My call is for a change of culture in the way we do things, not simply in the words we use, and this involves, essentially, a redirection of financial control away from central governments to local and regional decision-makers accountable both to their citizenry and to the broad policy parameters set by government. A culture of belonging and mutual respect will not be achieved by exhortation; it has to grow out of action. If our institutions keep people out of the action, citizens will never feel they belong, nor feel the mutual respect that gives life meaning.

- The global age, contrary to what many writers have suggested, will make accountable governance more, not less, important. And while my proposals will push further towards smaller government at the centre, they will hold firm to the principle that an elected democratic government is vital to setting the goals and strategies for achieving the common good.

The book is not an argument against central planning, goal setting and the need for governments to set priorities and ensure optimum inclusion in the benefits of a democratic society. We must counter any trend towards negative local tribalism and narrow interest-group politics, but the structures of applying government finances to public programs must be more responsive to local and regional variations than they are at present. We need new tribes working together for the common good, within their unique geographic and social boundaries, but all part of the patchwork that makes up the country we call Australia.

Section 1 of the book gives a brief overview of how globalisation is driving the change in the way Australia operates. The old industrial economy and its once innovative institutions are now too rigid for the needs of what has become a knowledge/service economy (Chapter 1). The impact of structural change on Australian society has been profound (Chapter 2), with very unequal regional effects. But Australia is also part of the massive demographic and value shifts of the post-War Western world. Family life is now much more complex, the Singles Generation seeks new goals, and the Baby Boomers form a large and very different cohort of the aged from the conservative oldies of the past (Chapter 3). These shifts in the complexity of work and family life are already increasing the diversity of Australia's patchwork community (Chapter 4) and forcing a much-needed rethink of the dominant business paradigm (Chapter 5).

Section 2 argues that Australia faces a perilous future in the global information age, that national identity is always based on our sense of place, our locality. It suggests that a distorted sense of tribalism could drive us apart (Chapters 6 and 7) unless government adopts a more flexible and more locally responsive approach to how it operates in diverse communities (Chapter 8).

Section 3 develops in detail the implications for Australian society and offers some workable models for institutional change. We have to find an Australian way which builds human and social capital (Chapter 9) by encouraging new approaches to regional diversity (Chapter 10). Chapter 11 describes several projects which demonstrate that a less managerial government can stimulate local development and innovation. Chapter 12 outlines the need for new, more locally responsive community services for families that are based on networking through schools and workplaces, and that encourage a more healthy work–life balance. Chapter 13 then extends the argument for revamping the role of schools in community-building, making them the hub of family support, giving young people a sense that they are stakeholders in the wider society, and developing an awareness that lifelong learning is the key to success in the knowledge economy.

Chapter 14 sums up the argument for breaking down the barriers created by competing government departments, and for decentralising and properly resourcing community development. It is an argument for valuing and enhancing the very diverse nature of our patchwork country, for abandoning top-down, bureaucratic solutions, in favour of an Australian way of trusting people to find solutions best suited to their own needs, and regional and cultural differences.

Section 1

The changing global context

Chapter 1

Transforming the industrial economy

TOO MUCH OF TODAY'S POLITICAL debate is framed in outmoded contrasts. It's big versus small government. It's the free-market ideology versus the welfare or corporate state. It's unions and centralised awards versus enterprise agreements and individual workplace agreements. It's rights versus responsibilities. And it's public services versus private contracting.

These are the outmoded contrasts of a dying age, and the new creatures emerging on the political and social landscape will have to be much more adaptable. We are living through the end of the old industrial system, a system based on mechanistic, top-down planning and processes, both in government and in the management of business.[5] We are also witnessing the end of traditional patriarchy in family structures, where the male is breadwinner and the female is housekeeper-carer. In their stead, we face increasing complexity and division, requiring ever more sophisticated networks and methods of cooperation.

The essence of postmodern society is complexity and diversity, where no lumbering, centrally controlled system can cope. Adaptability is the name of the game. The new global service-communication economy, now being called the knowledge economy, is one in which neither centralised government services nor centralised corporate leadership can manage the diverse and ever-changing needs of work, family and community life. One size will no longer fit all. Government will have to allow for tailor-made solutions to widely different regional circumstances. Corporations will have to deal with employees from increasingly diverse family and community backgrounds. If we can customise consumer services in the new business-to-business (B2B) economy, why not government services as well?

So the old dinosaurs of government and business will not survive; new partnerships will take their place. The new 'leadership' will be based on participation in a range of interlocking networks, building resources that make for a viable and flexible economy, not controlling the forms to which services and work procedures must conform.

But there is a problem with the jargon being thrown around about future change. The words used are, in themselves, confusing to the ordinary person.

Haven't we always relied on good communication and interlocking networks in our business dealings, not to mention in our personal relationships? Haven't services (such as accounting, legal advice, delivering supplies from factory to shop floor, architectural design, health care, etc.) always been essential to the production of goods and the growth of the economy? And surely information systems, knowledge, and the application of learning in practical and innovative ways have always been the basis of progress and change in every field, from industry to community programs?

We need more than the sweeping assertions of gurus if we are to change the culture to one that is adaptable, workable and inclusive of the majority of people.

The paradox is that technology has now reached the point where everything can be linked, almost instantaneously, yet our social institutions remain in their outmoded industrial-era form, separate and unlinked, or linked too rigidly, performing separate functions on separate bits of our lives, as though the human being does not operate as an entity, as though social systems do not work in interconnected ways.

We saw the emergence in early 2000 of the terms 'the new economy' versus 'the old economy', and previously blue-chip stocks had to scramble to prove they were Internet-savvy, moving into value-adding through e-commerce and the better use of technology to reduce production costs. Shortlived as many e-commerce companies were, we need a parallel shift in discussion about 'the new society' versus 'the old society'. But it will not be merely some vague combination such as Britain's Third Way.

The discontent expressed by people in voting against radical free-market change, in the trend towards jingoistic nationalism and hanging on to the monarchy, and in calls for more law and order, more certainty about the limits to change, reflects a sense of riding in a buggy strapped to a rocket engine. We know we're being dragged screaming into a new century, but the carriages in which we ride are old and creaky. The voting public's rejection in 1998 of Pauline Hanson's call for a return to the happy days of yore seemed to be a positive sign that Australians were coming to terms with the inevitability of change and their own need to adapt. But One Nation's renewed strength in state elections during 2001 suggests a more deep-seated resentment of governments in power which fail to listen. People are not voting for racism or isolationist policies, they are rejecting any party that imposes its policies and fails to involve people in the policy making process.

It is time to invent new institutions for the new age, just as the era of industrialisation saw a flurry of creativity in redesigning outmoded social structures so that they could better cope with the needs of the new world of industrial production. The nature of governance itself has to be rethought.

We have to link the future, forging new connections between business and the community, insisting on joint government and corporate responsibility for the welfare of society, building partnerships between the workplace, family and community resources in ways that cut back the old barriers and encourage a more vital civil society.

We have to stop thinking in rigid categories that limit human potential and hold back creativity — male/female roles that make no social or personal sense; age-grading that bedevils learning in our schools and divides the cultures of young and old; the artificial separation of material, emotional and spiritual wellbeing; the division of government into (dys)functional areas of activity that ignore the need for a more holistic approach to social problems and community development.

Above all, we have to think our way through to a re-engagement of government with the ordinary citizens, a reinvolvement of people in the work of democracy, and a reassertion of core values without losing the richness of diversity and individual freedom, recognising the inextricably linked goals of profit, social responsibility and environmental sustainability.

The old industrial system

The whole pattern of modern society has revolved around an industrial work system. Now we are going through a different revolution: the knowledge revolution, based on new forms of communication and information technology and the growth of a service economy. Unfortunately, too few Australians understand this or are being prepared adequately for what the future will demand.

We are trapped, like previous generations, in the 'taken for granted' world in which we grew up, wanting the security and certainty provided by existing social institutions and ways of behaving, and not being creative enough at any level to visualise new institutional arrangements that might prepare us better for a more complex and uncertain future.

In our angst about the rapidity of social change, the so-called end of certainty, it is easy to forget how dramatic were the changes brought about by the Industrial Revolution of the 17th and 18th centuries. The Western world saw the end of the feudal system, based on a monopoly of power held together by force and extortion, status based on inherited wealth and title rather than individual achievement and accumulated wealth, an end to a peasant society centred around agriculture and kinship systems that limited mobility beyond the local area.

While there is no point here in repeating a complex history of the rise of capitalism, it is important for Australians to understand how dramatic were the social changes of that era, for we have to put current change into the context of what has gone before.

Indeed, Australia's origins lie in the traumas of the industrial age. It was not just the need to transport convicts from England's prisons, prisons that were overcrowded with people now poverty-stricken in the new urban sprawl, political protesters against the new English middle class, against the excesses of industrial exploitation, a release of the social pressure points that might well have spilled over into a British version of the French Revolution of 1789.

It was also the need to protect Britain's colonial interests in the Pacific, an attempt to find new sources of wealth (not long after settlement based on the new merino wool which supplied England's textile factories) and the investment of new capital in grand ventures (Peel's colony in Perth proved a disaster; Wakefield's planned settlement in Adelaide was a slightly better prospect). The colony of New South Wales, formed by Captain Arthur Phillip and those who came on the First Fleet, was a quintessential offspring of the industrial age. And once gold was found, Australia had the wealth to begin its own investments in industrial development and new social infrastructure. Our forebears did it well then; the challenge for this generation is to do it well in the new circumstances of global change.

Whereas people in the pre-industrial era handled every aspect of their assigned task — growing their own food (ploughing, sowing, hoeing and harvesting) or making their own clothes (spinning, weaving, sewing and knitting); or being the master craftsman (melting the metal, beating it, and cutting and shaping it into a pot or ornament or cart) — industrialised labour was divided into smaller, more discrete tasks, the bits being brought together into a final product through the miracle of bureaucratic organisation. The notion of a job was a new invention. Instead of being a farmer, a tailor, a merchant, a stonemason or a jeweller as a vocation for life, people now did a job for a fixed wage. And that job was just one part of a complex process of manufacturing new products in new ways.

The invention of steel (and the humble screw which held metal together in moving machinery), steam power, the spinning jenny, the weaving loom and, later, the telephone and electricity led to the complete transformation of the world order in what we now call the Industrial Revolution. Apart from mechanical transformations, such as steam trains, factories and the growth of huge urban centres, the social transformations were no less dramatic.

Jobs with fixed wages, combined with the much more efficient machinery and techniques of production being used, meant that more and more people could accumulate capital, funds in excess of basic living requirements, that could then be spent on consumer goods or reinvested in new ventures. The rise of the middle class and a working-class proletariat is the essence of modern capitalism, the Marxist theory of class, the division of nations into rival ideologies of socialism, communism and capitalism, and free-market versus protectionist theories.

Political theory and debate had as its focus the relative merits of the state as protector and regulator versus the state as a hands-off partner with business in a free-market world. The neo-liberal ideology that holds sway in most Western democracies at present grew out of dissatisfaction with state regulation, the growing costs of the welfare state, and a resurgence of the old liberal insistence that the individual, not the common good, is paramount and that governments should not intervene unless individual actions harm the liberties of others.

And though competition between companies, nations and ideologies led to colonial expansionism, wars for territory and the battle for people's minds, industrialisation did bring about a new form of social cohesion that offered individual freedom within a more tolerant social system. The new industries were so complex that people had to specialise in their particular field, become experts in narrower domains, but in a deeper way than before.

As a result, no-one was self-sufficient; everyone was in part dependent on the skills and expertise of other people. Society thus became interdependent, people more intertwined in one another's affairs, more compelled to cooperate and profit than to compete and prevail. More complex and interlocking work processes demanded a longer period of education and preparation for work, so schools, universities and specialised apprentice training grew out of that new need. Most of our current institutions derive from the flurry of activity designed to cope with the new demands of the industrial age, particularly the institutions of commerce and the law.

Durkheim and other early sociologists saw this division of labour as the underlying cause of profound changes in the law and the way society worked.[6] Whereas mistakes or offences under the old regime could be punished arbitrarily (by death, imprisonment or ruination), in an interdependent society you can't do away with those upon whom you rely for services. Instead of savage retribution, the law moved to restitution, the use of fines and the enforcement of contracts, to the notions of accountability and mutual responsibility.

People within their own families, groups and tribes had always relied on a sense of reciprocity — the mutual trust that meant a good turn done by you would probably be reciprocated when you were in need. No social group can survive with too many 'freeloaders' who take the goods but don't contribute to the common good. Modern industrial society depended even more upon this sense of trust and reciprocity — a trust in contracts, agreements, promises to deliver on time. So there was more certainty, more predictability about agreements made between interdependent parties. The law reinforced social cooperation.

Modern society, despite all the counter-examples of conflict and war, was built on cooperation and mutual agreement. The central, underlying conflict was, of course, that between the owners of capital and their wage-labourers, a conflict built into socialist/communist theories, and enacted at many levels through the efforts of trade unions and political parties of labour to exact a reasonable degree of justice and reciprocity. And though competing interest groups are always working for their own cause, the essence of a social democratic society is that they have to operate within agreed social limits, to ensure a degree of fairness and justice for all. No modern government or business leader can afford to forget that.

Nevertheless, the very nature of industrial work altered people's lives, not just because most of them moved from agriculture to industrial wage labour but because the process itself was transformed. In today's climate of distrust of bureaucrats, and the seemingly cumbersome red tape and paperwork, we forget what an amazing organisational feat the management of complex organisational process was.

Most older people have themselves experienced jobs where their little bit of work seemed to have no bearing on the end product. It was part of an assembly line, or one step in a process of bureaucratic approval that could easily be overturned and the work made useless by decisions further up the chain of command. We have been part of the industrial system for so long, we take for granted that work has to be specialised, broken down into its component parts, with everyone's separate effort coordinated into a final product. We have been sensitised to the numbing alienation of repetitive tasks by films such as Charlie Chaplin's *Modern Times*, Weber's critique of 'the iron cage of bureaucracy', and novels such as Kafka's *The Castle*. But if you think of the incredible coordination required in a large airport, you see the advantages of bureaucratic organisation over a system based on personal power and favouritism.

Peter Kellner, one of the originators of Tony Blair's Third Way in the UK, argues that the early image of socialism as a cooperative ethic (as in the Lanark textile mill of Robert Owen) was corrupted by Karl Marx into an anticapitalist ideology that implanted the notion of society as a machine.[7] It replaced cooperation and mutual responsibility with public ownership and state control, and though the economic doctrine of socialism has been discredited, its doctrinal 'smell' as 'an outdated way of regarding power, society and the state' lingers on. Even the term 'social democracy' smacks too much of large government, running society in a mechanistic manner.

Kellner calls for a more 'organic' model of society for the new age, what he calls the 'New Mutualism', in which individual and collective wellbeing is obtainable only by mutual dependence. The New Mutualism calls for a more organic image of society, one based on the increasingly complex interdependence that information technology brings about. In some senses, Kellner is right. But in fact, the image of society as a machine, planned from the top, with state power, workers' control through unions, and planned welfare services, grew out of the very methods of industrial production. And it was not, for the times, a bad thing; the image reflected the reality of the industrial age.

Industrialisation was a triumph of the human mind, a marvel of organisation that opened up new choices and opportunities for specialisation and job satisfaction for the masses. Nor is it likely that the principles of bureaucratic organisation will disappear in the new knowledge economy.

Tasks still have to be broken down into their component parts, even if they are to be done by robots instead of human beings. That is, essentially, what computer programming and industrial design do. What is happening instead is that the human elements of networking and sharing information and knowledge are becoming more, not less, important.

At the personal level, too, industrialisation had profound effects. Though we have built up myths about the extended family and how the industrial system drew people away to work in urban factories, thereby creating the so-called nuclear family, we now know that the nuclear family has always been the core social unit, with young couples always having tried to establish some independence from their kin. The difference lay in control of land ownership by the patriarch. Until he died, sons had no financial autonomy, and many of them moved away into service on other estates, as did girls, early in life. In fact, the nuclear family unit preceded the Industrial Revolution, which in turn made it possible for young families to earn a living, gain financial autonomy from their parents, and establish separate lifestyles of their own, away from the rigidity of a peasant, agricultural village system.[8]

It was their separation from the extended family that fed the needs of industry for labour. Instead of being confined to the place you were born and the status assigned you within a feudal system (peasant, freeman, nobleman, etc.), skills became transportable, labour became a tradeable commodity, and social status could be achieved through work and the accumulation of capital, not simply assigned at birth.

Also for the first time, for many families, the father (and often, the mother as well) was removed from close contact with his children, his work no longer an integral part of private family production but performed at a distance, physically and psychologically, from the daily lives of children. The early years of industrialisation saw children and women being exploited as waged labour, too, but reforms gradually separated childhood off as a separate entity, putting children to work in schools, both to protect them from parents and unscrupulous employers and also to teach them the basics they would need once they, too, became 'factory fodder' for the new industrial system.

A global economy demands greater flexibility and adaptability throughout people's life course. Work is less likely to be confined to one job in one place, men and women will both have to have paid employment, children will be cared for in new ways, and the very nature of family and community life will shift.

What is globalisation?

We are told constantly that computers, the Internet and advanced communications technology are shrinking the world into one interlinked entity; that the nation state is under threat because multinational corporations command bigger budgets than many nations, and the unrestricted flow of capital instantly around the world undermines national sovereignty.[9] Australia seems a small and insignificant player in the new global economy.

To an extent that is true, and it will change the way we think about government and the regulation of trade. Witness the 'Asian meltdown' of 1997, when the withdrawal of foreign capital and the interventionist policies of the World Bank and the International Monetary Fund brought countries such as Indonesia, Korea, Thailand and Malaysia to the brink of economic failure. Or witness the 'strike of capital' that occurred during the Whitlam years, as international business expressed its doubts about the Labor Government's management of the economy, particularly its overspending on wages and social infrastructure. The threat of sanctions against military coups replacing democratically elected governments (such as that in Fiji in May 2000 and in Pakistan in October 1999) or the withdrawal of diplomatic contacts to express political disapproval (such as with Austria following the formation of a right-wing coalition government with neo-Nazi overtones in February 2000) are indicators of growing global control, as opposed to a policy of letting countries manage their own affairs in their own way.

Even at the level of taxation, it is increasingly difficult for nation states to collect revenue from companies and individuals whose money is earned, banked and/or moved around in other countries. The problem of how to tax consumer purchases made on the Internet grows as e-commerce shifts purchasing patterns beyond national borders, services can be downloaded via computer and regulation of the Web proves elusive. Attempts to control access to pornographic sites, and China's efforts to control people's overall access to the Web, are doomed to failure as the Internet democratises information in the global age. But this is only part of the picture.

The Canadian Trade Minister, Pierre Pettigrew, made an interesting distinction in his address to the Australian National Press Club in Canberra on 1 June 2000.[10] He claimed that people confuse globalisation with internationalisation, the latter being a phenomenon that is not new. He contrasted the traditional international economic order with the new global disorder, turning the tables on those critics of globalisation who, in Seattle, Davos and Melbourne, were protesting the free-trade policies of the World Trade Organization, carrying posters and banners against globalisation.

Pettigrew asserted that the real significance of the new technologically driven globalisation process is precisely that it questions the role of government and gives new power to non-accountable transnational bodies such as Greenpeace, Amnesty International and Oxfam, whose membership is not elected, whose finances and procedures are not transparent and who are not accountable to anyone outside their own organisation. These non-government organisations (NGOs) are among the chief beneficiaries of the new globalisation, able to mobilise quickly, ignore national borders and state accountabilities to their electorates, and argue for their own view of the world.

As Diana Bagnall also points out, similar non-government organisations within Australia (Australian Council of Social Services, Australian Council of the Ageing, Mission Australia, etc.) exercise enormous influence on government and business decision-making within the nation, though they, too, are non-elected and therefore are not accountable in the way governments of any kind have to be.[11]

Pettigrew contrasted the traditional economic order, which is rules-based, with 'the global disorder', which is not rules-based, and is neither codified nor predictable. Whereas internationalisation respects the role of the nation-state in political and economic matters, and relies on governments to implement agreements, globalisation ignores borders and gives power to transnational actors and institutions. What Pettigrew did not acknowledge in this presentation, of course, is that the NGOs are targeting less the national governments who agree to rules-based international trade (or other agreements) than they are targeting those transnational corporations that aim to benefit their owners and shareholders at the expense of both national, whole of economy, interests and the interests of disadvantaged workers, those exploited and excluded within an economy or within the global trade order, whose wages are pushed down despite the efforts of governments or unions to resist. Many are disturbed by the growing gap between haves and have-nots.

But it is useful to be reminded that global interdependence is not a new phenomenon; it is, simply, happening more rapidly than anyone could have envisaged. And it is important to remember that the essential difference between internationalisation and the current globalisation is that the latter is no respecter of national boundaries or government authority. Globalisation does require a rethinking of the role of government at every level.

As soon as city states and the later nation-states began trading beyond their own borders, we were on the path towards more limited state control — trade deals forge alliances whose interests may run counter to those in temporary power. The 'world' may once have been confined to the Mediterranean, or the Middle East, but the Roman Empire stretched across the known universe, its systems of communication and control highly sophisticated, until distance and corruption from within attenuated its power too much.

Once exploration proved that the world was a sphere, not a flat slab, huge global empires were forged by the Spanish, the Portuguese, then the British, Dutch, French and Germans. Colonisation of the new lands was a battle for supremacy in a global market, and the lines of communication of such vast conglomerates as the British East India Company or the Dutch East India Company were truly global. They ran shipping, purchases, marketing, management, legal regulation, trade agreements, planting and harvesting, plus an entire naval and military complex to protect their interests. They worked in close cooperation with their national governments, in an early form of the corporate state whose reach went far beyond the geographic confines of the nation-state itself.

Since that time, globalisation and the capacity to communicate almost instantaneously took a leap with the invention of the wired telegraph, the telephone and, especially, the under-sea cables that spanned the globe before the end of the 19th century. The submarine cable across the Pacific was completed in 1902, the same year as the first trunk telephone line was laid between Mt Gambier, in South Australia, and Nelson, across the border in Victoria. The Sydney–Melbourne trunkline was completed in 1907. Trade deals, commercial and military intelligence, corporate spying and money-shifting are not inventions of the last couple of decades. Indeed, as O'Rourke and Williamson point out, the first great wave of globalisation was even more dramatic than what has happened since World War II.[12]

Between 1840 and World War I, transport costs and trade barriers fell, international trade expanded to the point where Britain's exports rose from 10.3 per cent of GDP to 14.7 per cent, and Germany's rose from 7.4 to 12.2 per cent. Both capital flows and migration across national borders were far greater than they are today. Some 60 million Europeans left for the Americas between 1820 and 1920, 60 per cent of them to the United States, while within Europe itself, intercountry worker mobility was high. Prices across the world converged, and the foreign debt of the United States in 1894 was equal to 26 per cent of its GDP (even Brazil's debt in 1980 was only 19 per cent of its GDP).

These writers argue that globalisation on such a scale created losers as well as winners, and the same theme emerged at the World Trade Summit held in Seattle in December 1999 and at the Davos meetings of world business leaders held in Switzerland in early February 2000. The backlash against globalisation began to spread as early as the late 1870s, when cheap grain imports from America and the Ukraine threatened farmers' jobs and Europe closed its agricultural markets. Only Britain and Denmark kept their agricultural markets open; the United States raised its tariffs to help finance the Civil War and later raised protective barriers against imported manufactures competing with its infant industries and began to restrict the hitherto free flow of migration from Europe.

Indeed, what the Canadian Trade Minister calls internationalisation is an outcome of attempts following World War II to stimulate productivity and growth by once again removing national tariff barriers to free trade, or more precisely, trade interdependence guided by some agreed rules. The General Agreement on Tariffs and Trade (GATT) forged at Bretton Woods arose from trade restrictions that had led to the disaster of the Great Depression and World War II. GATT was soon (and still is) undermined by the USA trying to protect its own farmers and industries. The Cairns Group, led by Australia and Canada, was a coalition formed by small nations trying to break into the US market, and the battle still rages over the huge subsidies paid to farmers in Europe and the USA, which keep prices high and harm the less powerful trading nations. It must also be noted that the IMF and the World Bank have contributed in no small measure to 'global disorder', often insisting on financial policies that work against national interests, damaging even the global economy, as in the Asian crisis of 1997.

Quite clearly, globalisation is not in itself inevitable or desirable. But what is new is modern information technology and the way it facilitates communication and new alliances. On the one hand, it encourages a democratisation of information, making it possible for any individual to access education, specialised knowledge and advisory services from anywhere round the world, reducing the tyranny of both distance and time. Those countries and individuals without access to the new technology will remain, of course, information poor, but global entrepreneurs such as Microsoft's Bill Gates are busy breaking down those barriers, through donations to disadvantaged areas as well as through trade deals opening up new areas. Self-interest combines with apparent altruism in much of this.

A knowledge economy, with its emphasis on free-thinking science and adaptable citizen/workers, demands intellectual freedom and open political institutions; it is anathema to political tyranny. Education becomes the key weapon to encourage development, to extend the bounds of inclusion in economic progress as against the exclusion of disadvantaged groups.

On the other hand, global mergers, such as that between Time-Warner and America Online early in 2000, threaten a monopoly of access to content that was unknown in any previous age. Many companies are now more powerful, at least in terms of money power, than many governments. *The New York Times* reported this shift in dramatic terms, by comparing company stock values to the GDP of various countries. It is worth noting that a company's market value can change daily, unlike GDP which is an annual measure of a country's total output in goods and services. As the *Times* put it, 'forget price-to-sales ratios ... it's price-to-fantasy'. But on this comparison, the following companies represent new megaliths in the global economy and political spectrum of power relations.[13]

Company	Stock Value	GDP Equivalent
Microsoft	$593 billion	Spain
Hewlett-Packard	$107 billion	Greece
Wal-Mart	$227 billion	Argentina
General Electric	$456 billion	Thailand
IBM	$201 billion	Colombia
Lucent Technologies	$227 billion	South Africa
American Express	$66 billion	New Zealand
America Online	$194 billion	Philippines

One has to wonder what sort of notice these companies will take of a small nation such as Australia and its concerns about internal jobs, trade prices, the environment and the social impact of trading decisions taken in company headquarters.

The international agenda has to move beyond the notion of free trade to that of fair trade, beyond legislating against exploitation to capacity-building for both nations and individuals, and from an ethic of justice/equality towards an ethic of care and broader social wellbeing.

That shift will mean, as we shall discuss later, that governments must not, and will not, become powerless in the global age (Chapter 8). A country's political institutions and value systems will still have a profound effect on how global corporations can operate and on the way the new knowledge economy impacts on its own people. We need to remember as well that today's developing countries will be the developed countries of the future and that global power shifts may see the end of the like of those companies listed above. Whereas in the past 25 years, China's output per head has risen an average 5.4 per cent a year and India's by 2.7 per cent, the West has increased by only 1.8 per cent. Such countries have not yet reformed their institutions in the ways that gave the United States such an advantage over the past 100 years — institutions friendly to markets, trade, innovation, science, learning and the rule of democratic law (not to mention its giant natural resources and trade protectionism). India is today as well off as were Italy and Scandinavia a century ago, and China and India are already the second and fourth largest economies in the world, so 'the next century could be theirs'.[14] That, too, will depend upon how well their governments handle the problems of overpopulation, water supply and inequality.

The new knowledge/service economy

People are confused about the changes taking place, and much of the technical language used obscures rather than helps. Terms such as the information age, the knowledge economy, the service economy and post-modern society have little resonance with the everyday citizen who is directly affected by obvious changes in the workplace but does not read the economics pages or the books of futurist gurus.[15]

At the simplest level, this is what the 'knowledge economy' means: brains replace brawn; freed from the long hours of agricultural and manufacturing work, people must now use their knowledge in applied problem-solving and more innovative ways if they are to progress. We can produce more using machines than with hands and backs; value is added by creating new and more effective ways to enhance productivity. Applied knowledge is now the most central service of all.

This does not mean that everyone will be working in the information and communication industries. Things still have to be made and services still have to be rendered. Nor does it mean we are freed from the tyranny of long work hours. Indeed, the contrary applies — because knowledge knows no boundaries, computer systems and the Web never sleep, and we can do our knowledge work at any time, in any place, the demarcation between work life and private or family life becomes ever harder to maintain.

The OECD has recently published a list of where its member nations sit on the scale of knowledge economies. At the top is Germany, not the USA, with knowledge-based industries accounting for 58.6 per cent of German business output in 1996; the USA, in second place, has 55.3 per cent. (Australia's knowledge economy as a percentage of business output was 48.0 per cent in 1996, only Italy being lower, at 41.3 per cent). The OECD counts in the category of knowledge-based industries not just high-tech computing and telecom industries but also sectors with a highly skilled workforce, such as finance and education. Germany tops the list because of its huge automobile, chemicals and machinery industries; even in the high-tech industries, where it is supposed to be streets ahead, the USA ranks behind Japan and Great Britain — high-tech industries produce 3.7 per cent of Japan's business output and 3.3 per cent of Britain's, but only 3.0 per cent of the USA's output.

So the knowledge economy involves more than just a simple distinction between manufacturing industries and information technology industries. It involves all those industries (including manufacturing, chemicals, heavy machinery and computers/information technology, as well as service industries such as education and health) that rely heavily on higher level skills, investment in research and development, innovation in methods, and smarter work processes. Their growth depends on investment in knowledge as well as in physical capital. Unfortunately, standard accounting systems virtually ignore such intangible assets as the education and knowledge/skill levels of employees.

The OECD tries to measure such intangibles by adding together countries' spending on development and research, investment in software and public education, and a rough measure of private education spending, reaching a figure of 10 per cent of GDP for the OECD overall, compared with 20 per cent investment in plant and machinery. Sweden invests most in knowledge so defined (10.6 per cent of GDP in 1995), France ranks second, because of its generous investment in public education, while the USA lags behind, because its government spends so little on public schools. (One might also query this, since local taxes are spent on schools, and the OECD figures ignore the high level of private investment in universities and colleges.) Japan, surprisingly, spends only 6.6 per cent of GDP on 'intangibles', while it spends a whopping 28.5 per cent of GDP on physical plant and equipment.

Simply using the proportion of GDP spent on education, Australia (at 5.7 per cent) lags behind Canada (7.2 per cent), Denmark (7.0 per cent), Sweden (6.7 per cent), and the USA and Finland (6.6 per cent).

Paradoxically, we have replaced the alienation of boring, repetitive work with the stress of long hours using our thought processes, thinking hard about what will solve a problematic new situation, bringing together whatever information and knowledge is relevant to the task. Clearly, such an emphasis gives those with a good education (not just qualifications, but the ability to think and to apply what they know to new work challenges) an advantage over those who are less literate, less numerate, less intelligent in a broad sense. The new 'knowledge worker' is the money-maker of the future — an irony, given that in the past teachers and university academics, or those wildly creative people outside the system, have been unvalued and poorly paid. (See Chapter 13 on education.)

In particular, it is not immediately obvious how we can become a service economy when traditionally, productivity and national wealth have been defined in terms of agriculture (riding on the sheep's back, producing wheat, fruit and wine) or digging up the endless mineral deposits of the land and turning them into manufactured products. We have grown up being taught about primary, secondary and tertiary industries, a distinction based on the amount of processing and conversion of raw products (animal, vegetable and mineral) that is involved.

Despite our history of protection of both agricultural products and a fledgling manufacturing industry, Australia is only just learning to value-add to its raw products, instead of exporting them and allowing other countries to gain the benefits of transforming them into much more expensive commodities, which we then have to import. Of course, without an adequate supply of human capital, of knowledge workers, and the funds to build value-adding processing plants, we have little alternative but to be primary producers relying on natural resources.

Since 1980, however, Australia's fastest-growing sector of export growth has been in manufacturing; between 1990 and 1997 the export share earned by manufacturing increased by 54 per cent; and by 1997, elaborately transformed manufactures accounted for two-thirds of all manufactured exports. This represents a major change in Australian business culture, though we still have a long way to go.

The usual claim about globalisation and the new economy is that we are moving from an industrial economy to a service economy. But how on earth do we make money from services? Many children are still taught that a real job is one where you 'make' something and sell it. A tradesman makes furniture or builds a house or engineers machinery. That's fine, but the factory cleaner, or someone who services the washing machine, is performing a service, and thus keeping the work of others going. A merchant makes money out of buying and selling other people's made products, a tangible service, dealing in real things that people need. A lawyer helps people with contracts and partnerships, or settles disputes. Teachers provide a service, yet politicians have been telling us for the last couple of decades that we have to cut 'waste' on central bureaucratic services, be more efficient, get people into real, productive work in the economy. Businesses have been downsizing, saying that a lot of those services (like a person over the counter in a bank, or a personal shop assistant to advise on goods and take our money, or all those middle managers) are redundant, unnecessary, and a drain on profits to shareholders. The declining level of service in many sectors is a major cause of public dissatisfaction.

No wonder people are confused when we claim the future lies in becoming a service economy, in leaving behind the old forms of farming, manufacturing and industrial labour.

Of course, services are essential to efficient production. A properly run organisation ensures that adequate planning and design goes into new equipment, new tasks. Design engineering, architecture, electrical engineering, ordering supplies at just the right time — these are all 'services' without which new products could not be made. New machinery, or processes, must be adequately serviced — oiled, checked for safety, properly maintained, supplied with fuel and raw material, employee safety and health maintained — again, vital services in themselves. And once a product has been completed, it has to be checked, packed, marketed, costed, distributed and sold, or the whole exercise has been a waste of time. Accounting and financial services management gain renewed importance in e-commerce. These end-services are another crucial part of the value-adding chain.

So it's not as if services are anything new to the old industrial economy. Increasingly, however, those services need sophisticated training and skills in order to add value, improve efficiency and raise profitability. A key reason for high youth unemployment is that those lower level jobs in both industry and the public sector that were once filled by young people now demand much higher skill and education levels. Employers assume that all new recruits will be information-literate, with computer skills no-one had a few decades ago.

Today's services need to be knowledge-based, drawing together in creative ways the best that is known in order to give a particular firm an economic advantage over its competitors. Many of the old services are now performed by computer, such as the automatic tallying of sales volumes and the reordering of supplies for a supermarket, once done by hand, now done automatically as groceries are scanned at the check-out counter. But still, someone has to invent the software, service the machines, develop the company's systems and market the products, and so services move from the routine to the more sophisticated.

The crucial change towards a service economy is that it becomes able to sell its services to others, thus for the first time helping the balance of trade in the same way as do material products that are exported rather than imported. Australia's foreign earnings from service industries have also increased, largely through tourism and foreign students.

Internal services are often treated as on-costs, and this is fair enough when they are, like raw materials or administration, part of the process of developing a product to be sold. But we persist in thinking of education or training or research as a cost, when they are, instead, a crucial investment in our future productivity. The smart countries in a global market start to trade their know-how for profit — they sell computer services, health services, management systems, architectural advice. Australia has been slower than others to do this, but we do now trade in such esoteric knowledge services as social security policy and administration, land care, desalination methods, wind-power electricity generation, medical procedures and educational methodology.

The more we build up our human capital, by investing in people and in knowledge processes, the less we will have to rely on exports of raw primary products that are exhaustible resources (such as coal, iron, gas) and/or environmentally contentious (such as uranium, or rice and cotton crops that deplete water levels and salinate the land). The developing countries may need better food and manufactured products, but even more crucially, they need know-how in order to become more self-sufficient, and competitive on the world market.

We must be sceptical about happy little predictions that if we become the clever country, develop our services sector and become more of a service economy than an agricultural or manufacturing one, all will be well, forgetful of the fact that other nations are busy selling the same services, in competition with us. India has a vast, highly educated workforce of young computer software programmers. They are well trained, and the industry is globally marketed. Even those US information technology companies that make headlines every day rely heavily on the skills of programmers in India and elsewhere (who are, of course, cheaper than their own US graduates). Ireland and Israel have been investing heavily in information technology, moving much more quickly than Australia to offer special tax incentives, and incubator protection for emerging business enterprises. Sweden's mobile telephone, aeroplane engine and car manufacturers have proved highly competitive on the global market, because of their investment in knowledge and sophisticated servicing.

So Australia's slow move towards a service economy is not a secure answer to the problems of declining prices for minerals, wool and other primary products. The knowledge workers of Australia are a minority, and unless we invest more in education, research and innovation, we will not be able to compete.

Nor is it correct to think that all jobs in the new service economy are mentally challenging. Think of the new call centres, staff answering the same questions time and again while stuck to a computer screen and monitored closely by a supervisor for service quality, not really far removed from the old bank clerk of Dickens's novels. Or those myriad other services such as outsourced house cleaning, food delivery, gardening, parcel delivery, garbage collection. E-commerce and Internet shopping may do away with shop assistants, but they will rely more heavily on packers, delivery drivers and accountant managers. In the new knowledge/service economy, much routine and mind-numbing work will remain.

The key to success lies in deepening the knowledge and skills base of our population. This applies as much to the adult generation as it does to those going through our schools. Whether in advanced manufacturing or in the services sector, in the global age only a deeply skilled workforce can compete. Australia faces a huge skills gap. And that process of deepening our skills base is a task as much for business as it is for government.

Chapter 2

The impact of structural change on Australian society

STRUCTURAL CHANGE REFLECTS THE changing nature of world trade and the way productivity is achieved. Usually, this is discussed in bland, objective terms that refer to the shift from labour-intensive agriculture and manufacturing to different sets of activities and services that make money on the world market. Our emphasis here will be more on the social impacts of these changes, the lack of humane concern for those whose jobs have disappeared.[16]

Manufacturing work has been hardest hit by changes in technology and the world economy. As pointed out above, manufacturing exports have grown, thus aiding our balance of payments, but this is small consolation for those whose jobs have been abolished. In February 1999, only 1,073,000 Australians were employed in manufacturing, a drop of 10,000 jobs every quarter since August 1997. This follows, of course, the damage flowing from the Asian economic crisis of that year, with machinery and equipment manufacturers having shed 40,000 jobs, 15 per cent of their workforce. All export and import-competing industries shed jobs to stay afloat, with mining and agriculture laying off 19,000 workers (four per cent of their workforce) in the same period. But it reflects the capacity of fewer workers to produce more, output per factory worker having grown by 23 per cent in the past decade. Australia has slumped more than other OECD countries, with manufacturing now making up only 12 per cent of Australia's output and employment alike, whereas between 1960 and 1973, it provided 28 per cent of jobs and 25 per cent of output.

We are importing more and producing less, our deficit in manufacturing trade being $55 billion in 1998. In 1980, Australia's total net foreign liabilities were $27 billion; by 1990, they had mounted to $170 billion and in 1999 they reached a staggering $380 billion. That represents a shift from 1.5 per cent of Australia's total income going to foreign investors in the 1970s to nearly five per cent in the 1990s. Reducing tariffs further, as recommended by the Productivity Commission, is likely to exacerbate the trade imbalance and further damage our capacity to produce those goods we need for our own use.[17]

Only the service industries added jobs — some 355,000 between August 1997 and February 1999. This employment growth included 85,000 jobs in property and business services, 82,000 in retail trade, 53,000 in health and community services and 31,000 in education. While most forecasts place hope in a growing service sector, many of the more professional services are likely also to be vulnerable to overseas competition, and schools, universities, legal and accounting firms, architecture, and even health research and diagnosis may come under threat unless they can prove the superior quality of the service they provide.[18]

The main difference will be, however, that more of even these workers will be working as their own boss, contracting out their services competitively in the marketplace, having to learn entrepreneurial and self-management skills not needed in the older, bureaucratic system. They need knowledge skills and communication skills if they are to sell their services effectively to others.

The Australian Department of Employment, Education, Training and Youth Affairs projects job growth and further shrinkage in the following areas:[19]

Fastest-Growing Occupations	Fastest-Shrinking Occupations
Personal-service workers	Miscellaneous clerks
Business professionals	Construction and mining labourers
Medical and science technicians	Metal and machine tradespersons
Social professionals	Machine operators
Data–processing/business–machine operators	Farmers and farm managers
Other teachers and instructors	Stenographers and typists
Managing supervisors	Stationary-plant operators
Miscellaneous professionals	Engineering and building technicians
Tellers, cashiers and ticket salespersons	Printing tradespersons
Other metal tradespersons	

The biggest rises in job numbers have been in areas such as property and business services (up 134 per cent since 1985); recreational services (up 93 per cent); hospitality (up 95 per cent); construction (up 46 per cent); health (up 53 per cent). In contrast, the biggest job losses have been in mining (down 13 per cent since 1985) and utilities (down 56 per cent). However, more jobs does not always mean better pay, with the losers clustered in service industries such as hotels and restaurants and the big pay-packet winners being managers and administrators, men in the computer industry, and women in mining and telecommunications.[20]

As for most other Western nations, advances in education and technology have driven a shift from productive work based largely in agriculture, mining and manufacturing to what are loosely called the service industries. The average rate of structural change has been higher for Australia during the 1980s and 1990s than it was in the 1970s, and higher, on average, than for other OECD countries, though lower than for the leading Asian economies. Between 1981 and 1996, the employment share for the services sector increased in 109 of Australia's 113 regions, while that for agriculture declined in 88 regions.

Employment in the services sector has grown from 2.6 million in 1966 to six million in 1996, while the broad 'production' industries have employed a static 2.3 million workers, a drop from 46 per cent of the Australian labour force to 28 per cent. Of these services sector jobs, 51 per cent are occupied by women; 29 per cent are part-time, though this figure varies, with over 40 per cent of jobs in hotels, restaurants and retailing being part-time. Moreover, there are reduced opportunities for blue-collar workers (from 40.6 per cent in 1986 down to 35.7 per cent in 1995) and increased white-collar opportunities, with most jobs requiring a higher level of skill than in previous decades.

Behind such bald statistics lies the brutal fact that Australian business embraced the fad of corporate downsizing in the name of efficiency gains more ruthlessly than did most other countries, our retrenchment rate being double that of the USA. By 1999, 3.4 million jobs had been snuffed out across Australia, many of them in the middle-management sector comprising men in their middle age who were the main income earners for their families. Other jobs were created, but this hardly lessened the damage done to the fabric of Australian family life and to that sense of trust on which any functioning society depends.

Nor was it only business that downsized in the 1990s. The NSW Labor Government eliminated one-third of senior executive positions in the public service; the Victorian Kennett Government slashed teacher numbers and reduced the public service by about one-quarter. One-third of Australian households have felt the pain of retrenchment, and while government can claim the creation of new jobs and sustained employment levels, the prospects of re-employment for men in their forties and fifties are very low. The old, benign career structure has disappeared, and a tyrannical bottom line creates a workplace culture in which loyalty and commitment are no longer rewarded, corporate values are distrusted and the 'cult of short-termism' seems to reign.[21]

What is significant for the broader social impact of such change is that regions with similar rates of structural change have had markedly different employment outcomes, largely reflecting the wider range of alternative employment options in metropolitan regions and the higher dependence of many rural regions on one or two core industries. As a result, the life chances of Australians now depend even more heavily on regional location. Even job opportunities vary according to which piece of the patchwork nation you live in. Inequality in incomes reflects a complex interaction between educational skill levels and geographic industry-sector concentration, and the school system (including TAFE colleges and universities) can no longer assume that one type of curriculum experience or set of course offerings will fit all students as preparation for productive labour.

This helps explain the political dilemma faced by our major political parties. Where once the Liberal and National parties could depend on the 'rural vote', and Labor on the blue-collar votes mainly clustered in the cities, the electorate no longer divides neatly into such categories. Business owners and employees alike may find their regional needs damaged by government actions or neglect, whether located in the city or in the bush. The uneasy Liberal-National coalition has collapsed not just because rural voters felt their interests were being swamped by the city-centric Liberals, but also because certain regions have been affected more severely than others by structural changes in the Australian economy. This explains the appeal first of One Nation, then of the other Independents, whom people felt would work more for their regions and electorates than for the policy positions imposed by the major parties. This new tribalism in Australian politics (see Chapters 6–8) follows from the complexity of economic and social change and its variability across different regions. The big parties can no longer take any voting bloc for granted.

While it is easy to blame global forces for undermining the certainty of the old order, we need to distinguish several related social changes. And we need to understand that national and state governments do still make a difference; we are not simply pawns of global corporations or an abstract global economy. Politics and policies still matter.

Certainly, developments in microelectronics, information and communication processes, biological technology, new-materials technology, robotics and energy-related technology all change both the type of job skills needed and the number of jobs available. So, too, does the discovery of new mineral and power resources or the depletion of other resources or resource degradation through, for example, soil erosion and salinity. Global market changes affect Australia through increasing specialisation and competition from other countries. The unrestricted movement of global capital across national borders to find cheaper labour and safer locations for capital investment also clearly affects the structure of the Australian economy.

But much structural change derives from our own policies and internal decisions. For example, successive Labor and Coalition governments have moved away from policies of tariff protection and labour regulation towards an open market economy, floating the Australian dollar, and liberalising trade and industrial regimes. They have also dramatically shifted the public sector towards a corporate, competitive model, privatised utilities and services, and driven infrastructure changes that hope to promote improved productivity, competition and targeted outcomes. Labor market reforms have introduced enterprise bargaining and individual workplace agreements in place of blanket awards, as well as reforms to workers' compensation, superannuation, occupational health and safety legislation and the rules of unfair dismissal. National Competition Policy now drives all tendering and regulatory processes, and taxation reforms aim at removing barriers to competitive industry development and broadening the tax base on which all governments depend.[22] Change in the past two decades has been massive.

Overall, such shifts towards a more open economy have increased business competitiveness and adaptability. Australians seem to have moved from a glum resentment of economic change to an acceptance that the old ways must go if we are to survive. Yet the fallout continues, and governments must ensure that their own internal policies genuinely care for those most badly affected by structural change.

Structural change is also driven by changes in demography and lifestyle, affecting both demand and supply in the labour market. The most dramatic shift here is the increased labour force participation of women, especially married women. This is partly the result of increased costs of living, with one male wage now being insufficient to support many families. But it is also the result of a remarkable improvement in levels of education for females, and a shift in community values about the rights of women to full participation in paid employment. Norris and Wooden describe this increase as so large '... as to render it one of the most significant labour developments during the last 25 years, and certainly one with profound economic and social effects'.[23] It has been assisted by demographic shifts such as the later age of marriage and child-bearing, declining family size and better provision of childcare services, more flexible working arrangements via part-time and casual jobs, and improved (though still not equal) female wage relativities. (See Chapter 4, on work–family relations, for more detail.)

At the same time, collapse of the full-time job market for young people (as much the result of public service downsizing as of the demand for fewer and more highly skilled workers in private industry) has led to a decline in the labour-force participation rate of young people, and increased retention rates in secondary and tertiary education. These trends, together with declining job opportunities for older males, have changed the social composition of the Australian workforce. Moreover, the quality of labour has improved, with the number of 15- to 64-year-olds gaining postschool qualifications increasing from only 20 per cent in 1971 to 42 per cent in 1996.[24]

It is also timely to be reminded that, although Australia's ageing population is not yet a problem, it may well become one. Between 1970 and 1997, the number of people aged 15 years and over increased from 9.3 million to 14.6 million and this group's share of the total population rose from 71 to 79 per cent. It is this shift, together with a slight increase in the overall labour-force participation rate (a modest four per cent over the period), that has led to an increase in the number of jobseekers and, by extension, the number of unemployed and underemployed. Population growth has fuelled growth in the labour force in each year since 1991/2. Current projections suggest a shift from the 'bulge' of the baby boom generation to a 'coffin'-shaped population graph, and thus the need both for increased immigration and new structures to retain older experienced workers in productive labour. One consequence of the ageing population is that the skills base of many firms is now nearing its use-by date very rapidly;

if older employees all retire together and there are no young people trained and mentored in the same skills, even viable firms with products still in demand will not survive. (See Chapter 3 for more on the impact of ageing.)

Other lifestyle and behavioural changes drive shifts in the nature of work also. Prolonged education and delayed marriage alter family and community life. A large part of the growth in the services sector is replacement of work traditionally done in the home (cooking, cleaning, gardening, repairs, etc.) by the parents themselves. Ruthven argues that this 'outsourcing' of household tasks will continue, providing jobs growth, but at the lower end of the income scale and in a casual/contract framework.[25] Parents have to support young people longer, but many of them move out to live independently. As the number of single-person households has grown to over 20 per cent, so too has the demand for small apartments, household goods, convenience food, leisure activities, exercise equipment and entertainment outlets.

My prediction is that this group of 'Sassy singles' or 'Solos' (Generation S) will become larger, working long hours, making lots of discretionary income, never marrying or having children, and demanding new outlets for energetic play and entertainment. They will be the highly mobile, footloose workers of the global economy, and they may well have less sense of loyalty to either neighbourhood 'place' or their employer — or the nation, for that matter — than do the Baby Boomers or even Generation X. They sit as a lacuna in any argument (including my own in this book) for increased government attention to the needs of children and families and for greater local and regional control of the way government funds are spent.

Job mobility in Australia is already high, with the equivalent of the entire labour force finding a new job every four to five years.[26] Of an estimated 8.4 million people employed in February 1998, 14 per cent (1.2 million people) had changed jobs during the previous 12 months. Almost two million workers (22 per cent) at that time had been jobseekers in the previous year.[27] Though much of this movement was within existing industry and occupational groups, there was sizeable movement between firms in different industries (462,400, or 40 per cent of job movers). Such figures call into question many assumptions about job tenure and the newness of 'insecurity',[28] though there was still a core of stable workers in the Australian workforce (34 per cent had been in their current job for less than two years, 25 per cent for two to five years, and 41 per cent for more than five years).

It is likely that structural change in Australian industry will increase, not decrease, in the next decades, so people need to be prepared in ways that facilitate the transferability of skills, rather than acquiring skills that are industry-specific or linked to highly specialised technologies and industry practices. As David Leser puts it: 'In the new economy, an increasing number of people will be doomed to fail in their chosen career. Life will not turn out as it was supposed to. Careers will be broken, loyalties will be severed; a lifetime of experience will be deemed worthless. The challenge, then, will be to find self-worth in other ways, through applying professional skills in other areas; through children, through partnerships, through hobbies, through a deeper commitment to community.'[29] For those middle-aged employees told they are redundant, such a task in the face of despair will not be at all easy.

We need to be careful, too, in assuming that the future lies simply in the services sector. The 'new economy' will not completely replace the 'old economy' in either jobs or opportunities for innovation and greater productivity. Australia is still a resource-rich nation, and mining and related industries, plus value-added agriculture and other primary industries, will require newly skilled employees. Our scientific and engineering base has already proved valuable in increasing exports of value-added products, so manufacturing is not a dead sector. We export leather for BMWs, braking systems for Chevrolet, wheel hubs for Harley-Davidsons, new tramcars for Kuala Lumpur, pharmaceuticals, electrical equipment, huge ferries and processed food, to mention but a few Australian manufacturing success stories.

The new age of information does not mean that trade skills, production skills of the old kind, will not be needed. Manufacturing reflects Australia's strength as a natural resource-based economy, and in every sector there will be wide variability in rates of structural change. Jobs and, thus, education and training needs, are not uniformly under threat or in high demand. For example, between 1970 and 1990, industries such as food, beverages and tobacco; paper, paper products and printing; chemicals, petroleum, rubber and plastics; and basic metal products increased in size relative to other manufacturing, but fabricated metal products declined, as did textiles, clothing and footwear.

Similar variations exist in the services sector. Whereas finance, insurance and business services have grown rapidly since financial deregulation in the early 1980s, and community, leisure and personal services have also increased, construction services declined rapidly, as did wholesale and retail trade industries. Lifestyle changes may reverse some of that, as discussed above.

In particular, the new era of business-to-business (B2B) will see further job cuts, particularly to those who act as 'middle men' in marketing, sales and distribution. What B2B does (as yet, imperfectly) is make it possible for large companies to merge their common functions. This seems to be happening first in relation to procurement, where pooling information and contact networks can reduce the amount of time businesses spend locating different suppliers, looking at what is on offer and filling in order forms or invoices.

For example, Marriott International has developed an electronic purchasing system to integrate purchases for its 2000 hotel properties worldwide; a global exchange for car parts has been formed by Ford Motor, General Motors and Daimler-Chrysler; Hewlett Packard and Compaq have formed a marketplace for high-tech firms; and Wal-Mart is now using its in-house exchange, Retail Link, to connect with 7000 worldwide suppliers selling everything from toothpaste to outdoor furniture. Such systems will cut into the work of purchasing managers, hotel housekeepers and invoice accountants, because supplies can be ordered and paid for on-line, using preferred suppliers anywhere in the world.

In Australian metropolitan regions, services employment grew by almost 1.2 million, but a high rate of growth does not always mean more jobs. Where structural change produces job growth is in regions with a wider diversity of industry; where regions rely on single industries such as mining, structural change can be disastrous. For example, Bathurst-Orange has enjoyed high employment growth because of its strong regional services activity, and Queensland's Sunshine Coast because of tourism, whereas regions such as Newcastle or Gippsland have little on which to build now their core industry has gone.

This variability in our economic fabric indicates how important it is for governments to consider the integration of education, training, community services and other planning activities. Regions vary on a whole range of factors other than their industry base. Their climate, geographical proximity to transport and markets, skills base, employee lifestyle opportunities (to attract workers with the right skills), regional economic and community infrastructure (to induce business to stay or set up there), and links with complementary activities in adjoining regions are all relevant.

Thus local and regional administrations, schools, TAFE colleges and other training institutions, community service organisations, and businesses need to act in concert to generate growth across a region. Peter Brain's argument about the 'global city' and 'new growth theory' could be extended to the integration of services within any region. This approach 'stresses the strong spin-offs from capital investment, research and development, and education and training ... [and] demonstrates quite clearly that growth rates can be increased by applying strong, wide-ranging government policies and establishing collaborative, cooperative networks between businesses.'[30]

I would suggest that such networks have to extend beyond those between businesses. Chapters 4 and 5 show how central are the links between business and education, and between schools and community services, and how important it is to better integrate the work of currently separate functional departments of government activity.[31]

Chapter 3

The growing complexity of family life

FACTUAL DESCRIPTIONS OF STRUCTURAL change in Australian industry often fail to point out that the numbers refer to real people living real lives in real families and communities. Yet, as indicated above, structural change is itself in part a result of changes in demography and in the nature of family relationships.

This chapter does not suggest that the family is one of the dinosaurs that must go in the new information economy. Rather, it hopes to describe the background against which family policy and business must operate if they are to deal sensibly with the realities of modern family life. These themes are taken up in detail in Section 3 of the book.

It has become trendy to criticise the family as outmoded and conservative of the status quo. Yet the family, in whatever form, is the foundation for every child's human capital; it is the crucible of competence. It is also the starting point for every child's networks, its connections with the wider world, its sense of trust of and reciprocal obligations towards 'strangers' in the society as a whole. Married or not, single parent or two, first family or step, based on blood ties, adoption or simply deep friendship, families are the key mediation point between individual and society, the private self and the public self as employee, voter or community group member.

I have therefore always argued for the importance of family policy, against its relegation by Labor to the scrapheap, to be left to conservatives who cannot face the realities of change in the nature and needs of modern family life. In a global age, our private, intimate connections become ever more important as an affirmation of reality and self-worth. No political party can ignore the importance of family; no community exists outside the concerns of families; no workplace can thrive without paying attention to family matters.[32]

We make our first connections with the outside world in and through the family. The extended family, and its favoured networks of friends and contacts, may share the parents' positive bias, but as soon as the child moves into school, more objective and universal standards are applied, to which children realise they must measure up. The human and cultural capital built up during childhood affects life chances in profound ways, despite modern society's attempts to create equal opportunities in education and training.

So we cannot view the future without considering how changes in family life are likely to interact with changing work conditions, changes in the nature of community and changes in the links between public and private life.

Family life has always been varied and complex, but the factual and ideological dominance of our Western nuclear-family model has hidden that complexity. In the last few decades, several factors have conspired to break that norm, and Australia has followed Western world trends in the transformation of family life.[33] There is no longer, if there ever was, one uniform unit called the 'the family'. Instead there is a colourful and complex patchwork of family relationships.

Young people need prolonged education, so stay longer in the parental home. They lead open sexual relationships that are sometimes exclusive and committed but often short in duration. They are marrying later or not at all. They are having fewer children or choosing to have none. Both partners are likely to be in paid employment, making caring for children even more problematic. And their search for personal fulfilment and mutual gratification leads them to reject conformity with outmoded social expectations about appropriate gender roles.

The typical conservative response has been to deplore the rising divorce rate, the promiscuity and casual nature of sexual behaviour, and the apparent failure of parental control of and responsibility for children. Family values seem to be under attack, and calls for moral reform repeatedly make us feel guilty and concerned.

As Saunders puts it: 'Dramatic changes have taken place in family life — most notably, the rise in divorce rates (a 300 per cent increase since the 1960s), the rise in cohabitation outside marriage (more than a 300 per cent rise since the mid-seventies), and the rise in births outside marriage (a six-fold increase in the last 40 years). Today in Australia, more than 700,000 children live solely with one parent … and many more live in reconstituted families.'[34] Barry Maley concludes that there has been 'a profound decline in parental participation in the lives of a large proportion of children, and in their relations with their natural parents, within the space of 30 years'.[35] A report from the Centre for Independent Studies blames single mothers for the apparent trouble boys have with school, health, suicide, delinquency and drugs, downplaying other key factors such as unemployment, schooling processes, the macho culture and peer group influence.[36]

The central issue is the extent to which we can or should blame parents as individuals for their failure of responsibility. Should we instead blame the social system for the pressures it has put on parents, through downsizing, unemployment, underemployment and, on the other hand, longer working hours and work cultures that ignore employees' family responsibilities? Or should we blame the political system's failure to support parents through adequate childcare, resources for parenting, family counselling and welfare services, and schools and other community-based organisations designed to support parents in the task of nurturing children towards competent adulthood?

As modern life has become more complex and demanding, the ties that bind have taken on new forms that are taking a bit of getting used to. History shows this has always been so, but we have been through an exceptional period in which one form of family life was the norm, both in value terms and in its demographic spread, and that standard family unit has now been superseded by a range of relationship options.

The future will see increasingly complex, non-standard forms of intimacy, and we need to adapt our institutional structures to better cater for a more varied set of family and personal support needs.

Consider how different our private relationships are now from those of the post–World War II generation whose marriages produced the 'Baby Boom'. This was the first time in history that close to 100 per cent of all men and women married and formed their own nuclear-family units. The couple family dates back to pre-industrial times, as young people were forced to leave home to find work, and to gain freedom from parental control and arranged marriages. Marriage and children required money. Often the passing on of property to the eldest son left other children without the means to marry and be independent. In Australia in the 1930s, roughly one-quarter of men and women never married; they were the bachelor uncles and maiden aunts of popular novels and comedy sketches.

The post-World War II years were a true watershed in several ways. First, men returning from the war were assisted into higher education, training and jobs as post-war reconstruction began a long period of growth and prosperity. Second, their wives, many of whom had been employed in 'men's jobs' during the war, were pushed out of the workforce (and often left willingly), to become mothers and homemakers in the new suburbia of Australia's growing cities. They were the generation of *Women's Weekly* mums, pressed to buy the new labour-saving devices, conform to a mould of probity and cleanliness in dress and behaviour, gain their satisfactions within the private sphere and leave the public/political sphere to men.

But something basic had changed. Many women had tasted a new freedom, acquiring skills previously considered male attributes. Their new homes and children did occupy a lot of time, but they were better educated than their parents, and the new affluence allowed them to explore activities beyond the back yard. They demanded more open and equal relationships with their men, often to be rewarded with silence, abuse or even violence.

More importantly, sexual relationships had also changed, with birth-control methods improving since the campaigns to control fertility in the 1890s. Moreover, rising affluence made having fewer children and investing more in those few a new social goal, with the inevitable consequence that husbands and wives were obliged to discuss their sexuality and negotiate how sex would be handled.

This was the beginning of the transformation of intimacy in modern life.[37] True intimacy demands openness and equality, the honest disclosure of self, warts and all, and everything then becomes negotiable, no longer propped up by strict rules and role expectations. Men could no longer define masculinity in terms of supposed gender-based superiority, while women no longer saw femininity as meaning female subservience. None of this was totally new, of course, but once the contraceptive pill became available, in the early 1960s, there was no going back. Feminist writers had long railed against the stupidity and injustice of treating one-half of humankind as inferior, but once sexuality was unshackled from inevitable reproduction, men could no longer dominate sexual politics in the same way.

Such changes affect not only our private interpersonal relationships. They spill over into our work life and the nature of community organisation. Decry as some might the loss of a stable family life, the decline of communal values and neighbourhood links, it is my view that those links may offer new opportunities that will help rather than damage society.

Ageing and the future

Perhaps the most profound change in family life that will have a bearing on how workplaces and communities operate is the ageing of the population. Decreasing birth rates and an ageing society alter the dynamics of the work–family–life balance and create new issues for management response, as well as for government policy.[38]

The facts about ageing workers should be more widely known.

Those Australians aged 55 and over currently comprise 11.2 per cent of employed males and 9.6 per cent of the total employed. By the year 2030, that figure will be about 20 per cent. Less than half of them work full-time, but they still make a major contribution to Australia's labour force. Fertility levels will have dropped to 1.65 by the next decade; life expectancy will rise by 10 to 20 years over the next century; and the years 2020–2040 will be the crucial 'ageing decades', when our population profile moves from a pyramid to a coffin shape.[39]

By 2031, the number of people aged 65 and over will be 5.2 million (triple the 1.9 million in 1991). There will be only 52 men per 100 women aged over 85 years. Because we have failed to use immigration to replenish our supply of younger workers, former immigrants are the most rapidly ageing group in Australia's population, with one-quarter of those aged 50 to 70 not speaking English very well and few culturally appropriate aged care services.[40]

The ageing group coming through in 2020 to 2040 will be the generation born in the 1960s and 1970s, who went through secondary schools in the late 1970s and 1980s, took university courses in the early 1990s, and are now in the prime of their work and family careers.

The old of tomorrow will thus be very different from those of today. Scaremongering about rising welfare dependency supported by a shrinking taxpayer base ignores the fact that education levels (especially for women) in this group are higher than for previous generations, and are already leading to higher workforce participation rates at later ages. The ageing cohort will have more experience of changing jobs and being adaptable throughout their working life than did previous generations. For them, already, it is a sign of stagnation, not reliability or stability, to stay in the same job for more than a few years. Internet-savvy, they will be much more adaptable to technological change than any previous generation has been.

On the more negative side, whereas families are currently the main carers for the old, not expecting or wanting an interfering 'nanny' state to step in and shoulder the full burden of aged care, this future generation of aged Australians will have more complicated family lives.[41] More will remain unmarried and childless/child-free, so aged care may not be able to rely as heavily on family carers as it does now. A bonus is that childcare may become less of a burden for the state, but we cannot allow the state to bow out of providing appropriate services for the aged or anyone else.

There is no evidence that older workers are any less productive than their younger counterparts, and some evidence that industries with high productivity growth are those with a smaller share of young (as opposed to mature adult) workers.[42] A recent La Trobe University study of 7000 workers aged 50 and over found 89 per cent liked their jobs and three-quarters felt appreciated by their employers, a very positive view overall. Many more older people would like to work than can find jobs, making the official unemployment rate for older people over 10 per cent — a reflection of employer bias against taking on older workers.[43]

We must think beyond the square, not stick with outdated assumptions about the old. And we must call for institutional and cultural change beyond just those areas currently defined as the province of ageing policy. We can't look only at the older person and find solutions through policies for the aged.

It is easy for glossy government brochures in the International Year of the Older Person (1999) to call for a valuing of older people and of the contributions they can make, to insist on ending discrimination against older workers, and to encourage people to stay in jobs beyond age 55 or 65, so that they gain better self-funded superannuation benefits and help keep the cost of aged pensions down to a manageable level. But the reality of ageing in Australia is not so glossy.

Australia celebrated the International Year of the Older Person with slogans like 'Still loving. Still working. Still laughing. Still making a difference.' Would that were so. Tell it to the middle-aged manager whose wife has left him because he's been downsized and they can't afford the lifestyle to which they've become accustomed. Tell it to the widowed mum aged 64 whose children have abandoned her, and with no skills she can sell in the global marketplace. Tell the couple struggling to adjust their relationship to the husband's retirement, his constant interference in how his wife runs the household, and a pay-out that won't keep them going for more than a few years.

Indeed, the year's slogan was both insulting to those unable to match the positive image of the frenetic oldie and patronising to those who *are* active and happy. People would rather grow old gracefully — or disgracefully — in their own way, than be pushed to conform to some prancing, ever-energetic, ever-smiling elder pretending they can 'still' (or would want to) do all the things they used to do at 20 or 30.

Exhortation towards changed attitudes is one approach, but we are looking at another major culture change that will be achieved only if we begin to build older people into other institutional structures as well as the workplace.

The problem with ageing is that it starts in childhood. No matter how hard we try to change the culture about ageing, we can't escape the inescapable. The symbols of youthful vitality, full-strength energy and self-control in midlife, followed by gradual enfeeblement of mind and body, then death, are embedded in both biological process and the human psyche. Our brain cells are dying off by the thousand from the moment we are born. They can be replaced and regrouped, but dying starts from birth. A Test cricketer is too old at 35; an Olympic swimmer too old in the early twenties.

A recent Queensland report by the Anti-Discrimination Commission found many workers who turn 20 are considered too old and are replaced by younger staff. Women over 50 are called 'granny', while people in their forties are considered too old to learn the new information technology. Queensland's Attorney General, Matt Foley, commented wryly, 'You can never be too young to be old'.[44] So, while ageing activists and government propaganda may be upbeat and optimistic, there's a lot of work to be done to change stereotyped community attitudes to the old.

Within the workplace, we cannot simply assume that employers will not discriminate against the older worker — they've managed to discriminate against women for centuries, despite the fact that half the population of working age has always been female. We have already made it illegal to dismiss people on the basis of age, but their chances of finding a new job after downsizing and restructuring are marred by a culture that still sees old people as slow and out of touch.

A study by Bennington and Tharenou found a range of stereotyped attitudes on the part of employers affect recruitment decisions: that older workers take more absences, are more accident prone, and have memory problems and declining intelligence; that performance declines with age; and that older workers are less creative, less adaptable to new technology, and cost more in training time than younger workers, do not fit the culture of a younger workforce and are simply not interested in work, merely biding their time until retirement.[45] The research demonstrated that none of these stereotypes is supported, but the crucial thing is that employers do hold these attitudes. This was demonstrated by a 1999 Drake Management Consulting survey of 500 senior executive and human resource managers, which found that not one would employ a worker aged 50 or over. This age group would also be (indeed, already have been) the first to be retrenched.

One might have thought common sense would urge employers to retain some of the experience and wisdom accumulated by their elders and contemporaries, but the new economy favours the young and gung-ho, those willing and able to work ever longer hours, the footloose global worker not bound by family commitments or exhaustion to one spot or one job. The future (under this scenario) belongs to the mobile portfolio worker, moving from project to project, totally up-to-date with the latest technology and able to muster the right information just in time, adapting knowledge to meet volatile and diverse situations.

There is, however, another view, one that sees great potential for workplace culture change to utilise sensibly the skills and experience not only of married women but also of older workers. It is time to stop thinking of ageing as a problem of the welfare state. It is, instead, an opportunity for us to rethink outmoded institutions and rules based on the industrial model. In the knowledge economy, brain, not brawn, is the new resource; maturity and reflexivity are the qualities in demand; and problem-solving, adaptability and communication are the core skills.

Anthony Giddens, Tony Blair's guiding academic guru, argues that: 'Old age is a new-style risk masquerading as an old-style one ... Becoming older presents at least as many opportunities as problems, both for individuals and for the wider social community.'[46] The very notion of a fixed age for retirement and a pension entitlement based on reaching a certain age are, he says, 'as clear a case of welfare dependency as one can find'.[47]

The language of discourse about ageing should become that of positive risk-management, finding ways of adding value to the older years just as we have added value during our younger years, not the final refuge of selfish individualism, but a time when we can continue to repay society for the advantages and privileges many of us have been given during our more energetic years.

The Western concept of ageing as progressive deterioration rather than increased value is a denial of the contribution every person makes in their own way to family and community.

As already noted, the most common new worker model will be the very small business, the single-person operator contracting his/her services to shifting work projects with different teams and different firms. They will have to develop for themselves a portfolio of skills, not just obtain a certificate or degree, and they will have to be capable of joining forces with a range of workers from other portfolios as just-in-time teams.

The interesting thing about portfolio work is that it requires some experience before you have a convincing portfolio. Unfortunately, many people do not accumulate a range of experience at work; they simply have 30 or so years of exactly the same experience. Now everyone must be multi-skilled, regularly retrained and their skills upgraded. The numbers of new young workers coming through will not be sufficient to guarantee an adequate labour supply, even if advancing technology continues to reduce the number of people required to produce the same output.

Employers, managers and supervisors need help in redesigning the workplace to accommodate the old — many of them do have less energy for heavy work or for working long hours but are still able to do useful work. Here, the task of linking the future is one of re-linking the generations. Using older workers as mentors and master workers in training programs for the less experienced is an obvious way to go. This would add value to the younger workforce, and also would best utilise the skills and experience of the older worker. Employers need to see it as their responsibility to guide employees in managing their financial resources over a less predictable life cycle. Time out needs to be built in as a normal expectation for every individual — time out to care for young children or teenagers, time out for sabbatical and rest leave, time out for upgrading skills and retraining. The notion that everyone has to work for a fixed period of years, then retire, must go.

As Tom Bentley points out, continuous, lifelong learning involves forgetting as well as remembering.[48] In order to solve new problems, we have to be able to cast aside the assumptions and models that no longer serve us well. This is not so easy to do, though it is more likely to happen when those assumptions and models no longer meet the reality tests of everyday life. The cult of youth has been based on the somewhat passive nature of ageing in the past. Our bodies aged, our ideas became fixed, we were removed from the mainstream scenarios of action — work, entertainment, sports (though not always politics) — so our habitual patterns of thought and behaviour continued to serve us pretty well.

The older person's resistance to change, their inability to adapt, has been challenged by the rapidity and scale of change in today's world. The old assumptions do not work, and now many older people are just as keen to learn new ways of working as are the young. Their future stretches out before them as being longer than a few years of retirement; they know they have time to relearn.

Today, ageing is a much more active process, more open to reflexive thought and active decision-making. We now don't have to stop work, stay at home and tend the garden. We can decamp and become 'grey nomads', caravanning around the continent; we can continue to work part-time or from home; we can go back to college or become active in a University of the Third Age; we can reconstruct marital and family relationships — if, that is, we have the resources and the psychic energy to design our own older lives, and if society's structures and institutions don't hedge us in and limit our options.

Nor do the aged want to be pushed by a rationalising, cost-cutting government into having to work beyond the time when it makes sense to them, shamed into a pretence of competence that is beyond them, struggling with an ageing body and mind to keep up with the more energetic and dismissive young who will continue to be favoured in the workplace.

We should not think about older adults in the workplace in isolation from other age groups and other social institutions, nor apart from other functional areas of government, health and social security.

For example, what happens to our schools and the wider education system will vitally affect the nature of work for older persons in the new millennium. We have to start preparing the young for a longer and more productive old age when they become the elders of Australian society. Any attempt to improve the quality of educational inputs now, according to 'new growth theory', will have a greater impact on our future economy than will the mere size or relative age of the workforce.[49]

There is much talk about the need for lifelong learning, retraining, and updating of our skills, given the rapid obsolescence of existing jobs as the new knowledge economy develops. But our schools remain age-graded, open only a few hours a day, for children, not older people who might have dropped out too early and need to drop back in.

The clear message is that education is for the young, that you go to school and college in order to learn something that 'qualifies' you to work in your chosen field. It's not about learning how to apply what is learned to a variety of life situations, nor about drawing on the learning resources that reside in other, older people, or outside the educational community, in other organisations and situations.

The schools also, by and large, keep adults out — even parents, who have the strongest vested interest in seeing that what children do in schools actually prepares them for life in an increasingly complex society and workplace. Schools are not geared to using adults other than formally qualified teachers to guide the learning process, to serve as mentors, or to discuss the realities of work in a factory, office or corporation. Yet the aged could be a major resource for schools in the future just as they will be a crucial resource for industry.

Australia will have an older population in the future; that is fact. We must, therefore, develop an ageing policy linked closely with such policy areas as education, family care and workplace practices. It is the only way to avoid the growth of ghettos for the aged — either walled enclaves for the elite or isolation and badly run nursing homes for the less well off. This is a key task of linking the future, and is one not just for governments, but for business and the wider community as well. The aged will be an increasingly significant part of the vast and varied patchwork that forms Australian family and community life.

Chapter 4

The new nexus of work–family–community

WHAT I HAVE BEEN ARGUING IS that several powerful forces have combined to change the way Australia as a nation will be able to operate in the future.

Globalisation in one way reduces the power of government yet in another way makes government more important in guiding and protecting the nation. The information economy is driving massive structural change in both the jobs available and their regional distribution across the nation. These forces in part drive, but are also a reflection of, marked shifts in the family life-cycle and the nature of social values. Delayed marriage and reduced childbearing make for a greater diversity of family life, with both single women and the aged uniquely new players in the social policy scene. This diversity alters forever the old assumptions about women and family relationships,[50] about how governments can best support family life,[51] and about the way work fits into our personal lives and private time.[52] Job security can no longer be assumed; indeed the new singles seem not to care.[53]

Notwithstanding concern about the social damage done by such changes, it is my contention that these changes open up some exciting possibilities for the future of Australian society. We are forced to re-examine the old separations[54] — between work and family, public and private, men and women, government and non-government, paid and voluntary work,[55] schools and the wider learning community. Such change alters forever the way private family life interacts with life in the paid workforce and points towards new linkages that could hold the social fabric together in a way that satisfies both business and the public good.

Inextricable links: family and work responsibilities

What the future requires is a new conception of the links between family, work and the wider community. No employer can ignore the links and reciprocal impacts of either family life or other personal life pursuits on workplace morale, job performance and productivity. As well, we have to start thinking outside the square and forge new links between the workplace and those other systems in the community which either help or hinder workers in meeting their family and personal responsibilities. In a networked world, it is time to stop thinking of work as a separate segment of our lives.

For many, the workplace of the future will be both timeless and placeless. But such descriptions can be misleading, because we still live in real time, in a real place, and have to pay attention to our human and social responsibilities as well as to workplace demands. Machines don't need to sleep; we do. Machines don't have partners; we do.[56]

The demonstrable shift to more flexible working times, with production continuing seven days a week, 24 hours a day, is driven by the new information technology, which gave business the capacity to operate across the global marketplace instantaneously. I can order a pair of jeans in Sydney, my measurements being transmitted to a factory in Taiwan or the USA, where robot machines will cut and sew the cloth to fit me perfectly. I can order a new or out-of-print book at Amazon.com, charge it to my credit account, and have the company locate the book wherever it is in stock anywhere in the world. Someone, however — a real person in real time — has to supervise the process, even pack the goods and make sure they are posted to the right address. And if my work is a service, involving close interaction and communication with those people in need of my services, I have to make sure our time zones are 'in sync'. Otherwise, it will not work.

We also hear much about telecommuting (the modern version of the travelling salesman); about contract portfolio workers drawing on their skills as needed for every new project; about home-based work and the small home office; about deals made via the Internet, face-to-face contact rarely needed. We have to remember, though, that every transaction, at whatever distance from central office or from the contracting employer, involves human interpersonal communication and mutual accommodation in order to get the job done. The home-based worker has to receive assignments, has to report results, has to be accountable to some performance standards. They will have to come in to some central point at least occasionally to discuss performance, show a human face. More importantly, they will have to deal with family responsibilities in a different way from those who can escape to the office and leave family, at least physically, behind.

Job-sharing, which is, in essence, just a more formalised type of shiftwork or even part-time work, demands very clear debriefing and standards of continuity; otherwise, clients and customers can be upset. The nurse coming on night duty was a forerunner of this trend, and if the debriefing provided by those on duty before her was inadequate, patients could suffer, even die. Often, employers resist job-sharing simply because it requires careful specification of duties and performance standards, as well as a protocol for handing over and briefing job-sharers on customer needs and work in progress, and some managers are too lazy to plan a sensible system. Even some of our major law and finance firms (where clients demand continuity and personal attention) are now seeing the advantages of job-sharing, especially when special leave or sickness intervenes.

Project teams brought together 'just-in-time' have to have very advanced communication skills; they must be able to adapt quickly to new co-workers, team leaders, work situations and time demands. Contractors need to draw on their pre-existing networks in order to pull together the best team for the new project; team members must learn quickly how to interact productively with their fellows; they all have to rely on adjustable linkages to achieve the result specified.

Perhaps the most efficient example of such a team is the film crew working on a feature film or a television series. There is usually a producer and a director, who choose crew members they feel will best suit their way of working. They draw on previous experience and the dense networks of the film and television world to staff the complex roles in a film crew. The actors may never have worked with this director, nor even with one another, yet they have to learn quickly how to be part of the new team.

Contrary to what Richard Sennett suggests in his book *The Corrosion of Character*, such teams do not involve or engender superficial feelings, isolated self-interest or shallow moral values.[57] Instead, they draw on a complex set of role expectations for the various tasks to be performed in any media project; they depend on a spirit of common enterprise and pride in the outcome of their cooperative effort; and they engender deep commitment and mutual support amongst fellow crew members. When it goes wrong, it is because someone in the team has let them down (a poor scriptwriter, an inept director, an inefficient line producer, an inexperienced actor), and there is a real sense of regret, even if they still put their hand out to be paid. In the competitive environment of the digital age, where teamwork, not just individual talent, will be at a premium, there may well be a deeper sense of mutual respect, trust and dignity in the quality of work than there has been under the hierarchical work structures of the past.

Indeed, the secret to building effective modern work systems is to improve the linkages both within and outside the organisation. The keys will be optimum communication, clarity about expected outcomes, information systems that actually work strategically, and effective, accessible networks inside and outside the company. And the sensible entrepreneur will be looking in both directions all the time.

The words 'public' and 'private' make little sense, though they lie at the heart of the political divide between liberal individual-ism and social-ism in the widest meaning of those terms. The division of labour between men and women that came to characterise the industrial system both reflected and exacerbated this false distinction, pushing women into the private domain of the home, reserving the public world of work and political action to men. Already, that distortion of natural abilities and social justice has broken down. In the new economy, talent knows no boundaries of gender, race or creed, and the blurring of private and public becomes both an economic necessity and a social prerequisite for the good society.

This means that one of the most significant linkages to be addressed is the interplay between workers' job performance and their private responsibilities and interests. There has been a marked culture change already in this regard, partly because of the increased workforce participation of women, but also because many of the younger generation (dubbed Generation X) are insisting that they have a life outside the workplace and will not accept the notion that loyalty to one employer or job is the be-all and end-all of their existence.

We need to be careful in the terms we use, because it is easy to blur the distinction between those aspects of private life that are obligatory, or clear responsibilities that serve important social functions (such as raising children, caring for a sick partner or an aged parent, or working on a school committee), and those other aspects of private life that may affect job performance but which are for our private benefit and are not social obligations (such as playing sport, drinking alcohol, gambling, or taking a day off when stressed out).

Most of the former examples come under the heading of work–family policies and programs, while most of the latter are work–life issues, matters of concern to a healthy workplace in which people can balance, within reason, their personal needs with their work responsibilities — but there is considerable overlap. Indeed, there has been something of a backlash against work–family programs, as young singles claim they are discriminated against by being asked to do more of the weekend work, the overseas travel and the non-standard work shifts because they do not have children, and yet children are, they say, a private choice some people make.

Work–family policies compared

With more married women employed in the workforce (increasing from 36 per cent of wives in 1966 to 67 per cent in 1999), demands grew for workplaces to be more accommodating to family-related responsibilities. The debate was, predictably, framed in the context of the conventional nuclear family, where it was expected and normal for the female partner to carry major responsibility for child-rearing and housework. It was conveniently ignored that, by 1987, some 42 per cent of male employees were the fathers of dependent children, compared with the 41 per cent of female employees who were mothers of dependent children. The word 'family' was still confined to the female side of the lexicon.[58]

So work–family policies were at first seen as part of the equal opportunity, anti-discrimination and affirmative action agendas of the 1980s. Employers were dragged reluctantly into paying attention to matters such as work-based childcare, maternity leave and return-to-work arrangements, more flexible hours, part-time work and job-sharing. Some realised they had no choice — the demographics of a declining birth rate, together with the improved educational opportunities for women, meant there would not be enough qualified males to fill job vacancies. A few came to see that women brought new skills and attitudes to the workplace and that their desire for flexibility might actually suit the employer's production schedules better than union-negotiated award conditions. But the majority regarded women as a damn nuisance because they didn't fit the male workplace culture and because they were demanding structural changes that might be costly.

In 1990, the Hawke Government implemented the International Labor

Organisation's (ILO) Convention 156 on 'Workers with Family Responsibilities', aimed at ending job discrimination on the basis of family obligations, so employers had to comply, just as they had had to comply with the *Sex Discrimination Act 1984* and the *Affirmative Action (Equal Opportunity for Women) Act 1986*. The government also supported positive incentives in the form of a Corporate Work–Family Award, to recognise best practice, and set up an Office of Work and Family, to provide information, offer advice on implementation, and conduct research on both the process and the outcomes of work–family programs.

Australia's approach to ILO Convention 156 on Workers with Family Responsibilities is somewhat different from that of other countries. We are more progressive than Britain, which is only now, under the Blair Government, recognising that parental leave and job flexibility are crucial to reducing many people's exclusion from active work, and reducing the stress and breakdown levels for British families. Yet Australian provisions lag behind those of the Scandinavian countries and, in a different way, those of the USA. We have the unique combination of government-mandated award provisions plus private employer-provided work–family programs.

In the USA, because government-mandated services and regulations are so few, more is left to the individual employer, and the motive for introducing family-friendly work practices is more clearly based on known cost-benefits to each company (such as absenteeism, accident rates, retention levels and attractiveness to new recruits).

Historically, with the massive shift from agriculture to industry and urban living in the 19th century, American companies assumed an increasing role in the welfare of their employees and their families. Migrants were taught English, and firms offered help with housing, medical care, education, and social and recreational activities. This form of 'welfare capitalism' was in keeping with the Founding Fathers' ideology of minimal government interference with private enterprise and family life, and company paternalism reached its peak during the 1920s, when almost every aspect of workers' lives was controlled by the company.

The Great Depression shattered faith in private enterprise, and the New Deal brought about more interventionist federal policies on public welfare. Ironically, the new order led to 'a growing separation between work and family life in the workplace as employers adopted a more rational and bureaucratic management ethic. Encouraged by such works as *Scientific Management* by Taylor (1947), a "masculine ethic" and a "separate worlds" orientation between work and family life developed in the workplace and in the larger society and fuelled an increasing division of labour between men and women.'[59] The power of unions increased (though they never grew as strong as they did in Australia) and the US federal government's involvement in welfare grew rapidly through the 1960s.

Then in the 1980s, the Reagan administration cut both taxes and public social services in its attempt to stimulate the economy, at the same time again encouraging employers to assume more responsibility for the private lives of employees and their families. (John Howard's call to corporate philanthropy is a milder version of this approach.) The Clinton administration was more responsive to the needs of working men and women, introducing the *Family and Medical Leave Act 1996*, which requires employers with more than 50 employees to extend up to 12 weeks of unpaid, job-protected leave to those facing serious health problems (or those of a family member) or have responsibility for a newborn or adopted child. This, in turn, is a pale imitation of the Medicare system and other family-support systems available to Australian workers.

The assessment of how effective work–family initiatives have been in the USA varies. No more than five per cent of workplaces offer work–family strategies of any significance.[60] Companies such as Dupont, IBM and Merck are clear trailblazers, with many others offering an array of family-friendly programs, ranging from child- and elder-care assistance, alternative work schedules, fitness centres, life-education and stress-management programs, and information and referral services to paid personal days for child and family responsibilities. Yet the 'bottom line' still dictates priorities. In a 1996 *Business Week* survey, three-fifths of employees said their companies took little note of 'the people variable' in decision-making. Another survey, of parents with children under 16, found that three-fifths evaluated their jobs as 'very stressful', with over half describing their job prospects as 'insecure'.[61] Even the much-touted low unemployment rate in the USA relates less to a sound economy (US foreign debt is massive) than to a low-wage structure, the winding back of welfare payments, and the fact that close to two million people (mostly male and black) are in prison.

For the other 95 per cent of companies in the USA, work–family programs are very thin on the ground.[62] Industries still reliant on unskilled labour or other skills of which there is no shortage can blithely ignore worker demands and needs for childcare, parental leave, flexible work times and the like. If you don't like working conditions here, then leave. But in sectors where there is high competition for skilled labour, being the employer of choice is increasingly defined as having a social conscience, being family-friendly and offering conditions of work that enable a more balanced lifestyle. Some of the best examples of family-friendly corporate practice are American. It has to be said: most family-friendly work practices apply more meaningfully to the upper-echelon worker than to the lower-level worker, who is more readily replaceable. The market still rules.

In Europe, especially in the Scandinavian countries, work–family policies and programs stem from a different ideology. As far back as the 1930s, Swedish activist Alva Myrdal argued for publicly supported childcare for those families lacking the resources to raise children properly. Childcare was to serve two purposes — make it possible for women to get paid jobs and provide a stimulating environment for children. Post-World War II deliberations about social policy reflected the dominant value systems of each nation. Short of manpower, most countries in Europe had to employ women in order to recover from the war, but it was not mere pragmatism that drove reform. Germany wanted women to have more children and stay at home to raise them, so family policy offered them a range of incentives. In France, the focus was on support for families in their parenting role, so there was less emphasis on childcare and on jobs for women than there was on funding a network of local 'family organisations' that would offer help as needed and information about child-rearing.

In Sweden, there were serious public policy forums in which the shape of future society was debated — it had to be inclusive, universal, just and equitable — leading to a comprehensive view of how the new welfare state should combine the social and the economic. It was women's right (and duty) to have access to paid work; it was also their right to bear children. Therefore, the state had to make sure the two did not conflict. Paid maternity leave, followed by childcare and flexible work hours on return to work, were the result. The state's commitment was to an equal-status workplace contract and a dual-breadwinner model of the family. But sexist assumptions persisted, and researchers have commented that because the Swedish state provides so much, there has been little need for corporate culture change in the way managers treat the private-life needs of men and women. There was public concern, too, at declining birth rates, seen to reflect the priority of work over family life.

Progressively, that led to new provisions to enable men to participate more actively in the rearing of their own children, and to relieve women of the sole burden and disadvantage of taking maternity leave. Early provisions limited paternity leave to the first six months of the child's life, and cynics noted that few men took up the option. However, once it was realised that these are the months of breastfeeding, where fathers are of little use, the period of eligibility for paid parental leave was extended, and more men did take their turn at being at home with their (slightly) older infants.

The evidence suggests that paid parental leave and comprehensive state-funded childcare services can have an impact on population outcomes. These policies have managed to keep women in the paid labour force and not discourage them from having children. By the mid–1990s, one-fifth of all children born in Sweden since 1974 had had their fathers take regular parental leave to care for them. That figure has dropped in recent years, largely because the compensation pay while on parental leave (either maternal or paternal) has dropped from 90 per cent to 75 per cent of their normal wage.[63]

Australians have handled the childcare issue rather differently. Most married women with dependent children choose to work part-time rather than full-time, and studies of both job satisfaction and childcare outcomes suggest that if the mother is happy with the hours she currently works, the results are positive.[64]

The corollary, of course, is that women's rates of pay have remained below those of men doing comparable jobs, men have not been provided with incentives to take leave for child-raising purposes, and childcare remains predominantly informal rather than formal. Our birth rate continues to decline, and the debate over childcare and parental responsibilities recurs in the media without satisfactory resolution. One advantage is that, in Australia, discussion about work–family responsibilities has moved beyond the issue of women and children to include flexible provisions for other family responsibilities, such as aged care, and a much broader definition of family than the policy debate might indicate.

It is ironic that the nations with the most conservative 'pro-family' values (such as Italy, Spain and Germany) have the lowest birth rates of all. Today's couples will not be exhorted to have more children when that means keeping the mother at home, which restricts the family income to one wage, and with few social-support services available for families in general. They want more support for the few children they do have. While it is true that countries such as Sweden and Norway have found the costs of their welfare state an increasing burden, with high taxation no guarantee against unemployment or an increasing aged-pension debt, they have shown that state-encouraged family supports in the workplace can have a positive impact on the birth rate.

In Australia, federal industrial relations legislation entitles parents to share 52 weeks of unpaid parental leave to care for their newborn or newly adopted child. To be eligible, the employee must have completed at least 12 months' continuous service with the company before the expected date of birth. Only one partner can take leave at any one time, even where they are working for different employers. Some public- and private-sector employers do offer paid parental leave, such as the Australian Taxation Office, which offers 12 weeks of paid leave to a woman with 12 months' continuous service, plus 40 weeks' unpaid maternity leave. Private companies offering paid maternity leave have risen from 14 per cent in 1995 to 20 per cent in 1997, but paid parental leave, open to men as well as to women, is very rare. Only three per cent of enterprise agreements include paid parental leave, which is available in only 18 per cent of all Australian workplaces.[65]

The Australian Government's own 1998 report *Work and Family, State of Play* shows that only two per cent of certified agreements offer paid paternity leave, and just seven per cent offer paid maternity leave.[66] The figures for individual Australian Workplace Agreements (AWAs) were 27 per cent for paid paternity leave and 30 per cent for paid maternity leave. But those figures conceal the fact that 11,493 of the total 11,532 AWAs including paid paternity leave give only one week's pay, in stark contrast to the generosity of the Swedish arrangement. An irony of the Australian system is that because we have one of the world's highest rates of casual employment, most casual workers are women, and eligibility for parental leave does not apply to casuals, more men (more of whom are in permanent jobs) than women are eligible for parental leave.

As well, there is scepticism about the extent of real culture change in relation to family-friendly work practices. Many employers, managers and supervisors still fail to realise the degree to which family life has changed, operating on the old stereotypes that a woman's place is in the home and that every male worker has a female partner at home, looking after his needs and those of the kids. Or they know that things have changed, but hold on to the equally outmoded view that private matters have nothing to do with work and should be kept out of the workplace. They fail to see that nothing can stop private family concerns and responsibilities from impinging on job performance; they always have and always will. But there is evidence that employees who access family-friendly policies do find that their careers stall, and the 'glass ceiling' now seems to affect men on the 'daddy track' as well as women on the 'mummy track', if they pursue more active involvement in child-rearing by taking parental leave.[67]

What is required is a massive culture change in the way men and women see themselves in relation to both work and family life, plus major changes in the way work itself is structured. If the workplace is designed on a male model, demanding long hours and constant presence in the office, no amount of attitudinal change will alter the problems faced by men and women with children (or disabled or ageing family members) to care for.

Even in Sweden, where there was large-scale public consensus in the post-War years on the need for equal workforce participation and where government legislation has mandated paid parental leave, carers' leave, and full childcare provision to back up the goal of equal status, the male-oriented work culture has continued to interact with the female-oriented culture of family life to keep women as the main homemakers, men as the main breadwinners. A 1992 Goteborg study found that nearly two-thirds of men had made some sort of work change because of their children (24 per cent had reduced work hours, 35 per cent had sought more flexible work hours, 17 per cent had refused promotion, 16 per cent had found a more family-friendly employer and 36 per cent had reduced overtime). But the figures were higher for employed mothers. As well, only 11 per cent of unions had done anything to encourage men to take parental leave; many corporate leaders were still unsympathetic, even though they had to comply; and more women are now reluctant to take full advantage of leave provisions, for fear of career damage. Bjornberg suggests: 'the policies of employers regarding work and family will be more important in the future than will the formal rights mandated by the government.'[68]

Haas and Hwang feel, in contrast, that the resistance of unions and employers still needs to be addressed by government action: 'As the older generation retires, younger workers are likely to have different priorities and interests that will shape a new, more family-friendly organisational culture.'[69]

I doubt it. Until there is absolute parity of pay, until the skills and experience of women match those of men, until men see the role of father as being equally important and rewarding to them as the role of mother is to women, and until the structure of the workplace changes, such a culture will be hard to shift. Some would say pigs might fly! Nevertheless, the evidence remains that government-mandated work provisions can be very effective in shifting that culture; it should not be left to piecemeal change and the gradual enlightenment of male employers and managers.

Australia, as noted above, has quite a good record of combining government provisions with private initiatives, but the present conservative government is adamantly opposed to compulsion in preference to individual action. They resource (through the Office of the Employer Advocate) the active consideration and inclusion of work–family provisions in both Certified Agreements and AWAs; they continue the information side (though not the research side) of the Work and Family Unit; they remain supportive of the Corporate Work and Family Awards; but no new policy initiatives have been forthcoming. The Labor Party has threatened to remove AWAs completely if elected, going back to collective agreements that may well not be flexible enough to suit many employees.

Sydney Water Corporation, one of the winners of the Corporate Work and Family Awards, offers maternity, paternity and adoption leave, yet only two per cent of its staff have taken advantage of part-time employment, the most obvious way of combining paid work with childcare responsibilities.

Employers baulk at the cost of maternity leave, though most of it is unpaid. Small firms, in particular, find it difficult to manage their workload if one or two women are on maternity leave, and they must train someone new, yet hold the job open for the return of the woman on leave. Those who do the actual costings find it is nonetheless cost-effective to bring back employees with experience. Westpac, for example, estimates that it costs them $40,000 to replace a staff member with eight years' experience and $60,000 to replace a senior manager. It costs about $80,000 to $85,000 to replace a solicitor with two years' experience who does not return from maternity leave, but only $15,000 to pay her maternity leave.

Companies such as Esso, Mobil, AMP and NRMA have improved their rates of return from maternity leave by keeping in touch with the women, bringing them in for retraining, and allowing them to come back on reduced hours and more flexible schedules. AMP has introduced a range of family-friendly leave provisions, including six weeks' paid parental leave to the primary caregiver and expanded opportunities for part-time work, job sharing and working from home. Some three-quarters of AMP employees agree that 'their manager is considerate of their life outside work', the retention rate after maternity leave has increased from 52 per cent in 1992 to 90 per cent in 1997, and the resignation rate has dropped for all employees (from 18 per cent for women and 15 per cent for men in 1993 to 11 per cent for women and 12 per cent for men in 1997). This is sensible practice, and saves the cost of lower productivity while new employees gain experience in a job vacated by someone who leaves because the workplace is an environment hostile to family responsibilities.

Nevertheless, it has to be said that the work–family issue has gone the way of most other management fads. Like equal opportunity and affirmative action, many companies took action because of public pressure in the 1980s and early 1990s, complied with the requirements of legislation, even appointed senior women (usually not men) to the position of Equal Opportunity Manager or Work–Family Coordinator, and then failed to do much about changing the workplace culture which continued to operate against their stated policies, goals and values. Unless changed values are driven and exemplified by senior management, unless they themselves 'walk the talk', the old ways will persist. Add to that the fact that so many companies entered a mania of downsizing, restructuring and re-engineering through the 1990s, and it is not surprising that the structures of work have failed to shift in the direction of more family-friendly work practices.

This is a failure of management, a failure to appreciate the real implications of a mission statement that includes the sentiment, 'Our people are our greatest resource'. Competition in the open market should mean ensuring that the best people are recruited, that workers are given the right conditions in which to perform at their best, being treated as human beings whose lives as a whole are worthy of consideration.

Human resource management has come to mean considering people not as whole human beings but as time resources. An employee is a lump of time to be worked. The more hours that can be screwed out of him/her, the better the investment-output ratio. This is despite all the evidence (from the Mayo Clinic to the Tavistock Institute, to Drucker's theory of the learning organisation) that people can perform optimally only when their other needs and interests are taken into account. This is despite all the evidence that presence in the office does not equal performance. This is despite proof that long work hours and a work culture that ignores private responsibilities and causes burnout and stress in turn lead, to poor performance, mistakes, accidents, absenteeism and lower productivity.

The Government's 1998 report on the state of play in work–family programs shows that the emphasis has shifted from culture change based on a real understanding of human needs to a focus on flexibility of work hours. The most common category of family-friendly provision is listed as 'flexible working hours', now included in 52 per cent of all Certified Agreements and 56 per cent of all AWAs. Yet of all Certified Agreements, only 18 per cent offer regular part-time work, two per cent offer job-sharing and one per cent offer home-based work. Of AWAs, 44 per cent allow regular part-time work, eight per cent job-sharing and eight per cent home-based work. This is touted as a huge breakthrough in support of family-work balance, yet the total proportion of AWAs with 'at least one flexible hours provision' is still only 56 per cent, and most of these (42 per cent of all AWAs) are 'time off in lieu' provisions, which cost the employer nothing. Some 24 per cent allow an averaging period for hours of work, six per cent allow a compressed working week, only 22 per cent have flexible start and finishing times (surely, the most helpful form of time flexibility for workers with children), 24 per cent make flexitime available, 12 per cent have negotiable hours of work, and nine per cent allow make-up time when family responsibilities call people away during normal working hours.

This is some progress in employer flexibility, but it is still nothing like universal recognition of the enormous diversity in private family needs. Several commentators have suggested that time flexibility is a benefit for the employer, not necessarily for the employee, and there have been cases, such as the Steggles factory worker ordered to start work at six even though she had children to get off to school and had arranged suitable after-school care, where sacking is threatened if the employee refuses to be flexible in the way that suits the company. Part-time work may well suit many married mothers, but for those in need of a full-time wage and a secure job, casual labour and changeable work hours can cause major stress.

Indeed, job stress is a rising phenomenon in the Australian workplace. Of all those surveyed in the 1995 Australian Workplace Industrial Relations Survey (AWIRS), one-quarter reported that their satisfaction with the balance between work and family had decreased in the year prior to the survey. With the average number of hours worked having risen since 1995, that level of dissatisfaction is likely to have increased. Part-time and casual employees are more satisfied with their job overall than are full-time workers, and females make up the majority of both casual and part-time groups.

Three strategies that seem to improve job satisfaction are ensuring that workers are working the number of hours per week that they prefer; that employees have a future in the organisation; and that there is a telephone available at work for family-related reasons.

In the AWIRS study, 41 per cent agreed that their job was 'very stressful'. Of note is the finding that having caring responsibilities is associated with feeling job stress, and male carers (the group that works the longest hours in the economy overall) are more likely to associate the two (46 per cent) than are female carers (42 per cent). Rates of job stress rise for women, too, as hours per week rise. Having no influence over start and finish times was also associated with higher levels of job stress.

The ILO report on working hours in 1997 found that American workers spent longest on the job, an average of almost 2000 hours a year, two weeks more than their Japanese counterparts. Hours worked by Australians have stayed fairly stable since 1980, when we worked 1869 hours a year, four weeks longer than in the UK and three days more than workers in New Zealand. European workers, by contrast, have been working progressively fewer hours on the job, particularly in Scandinavian countries. As the ILO's director-general, Mr Juan Somavia, said: 'The number of hours worked is one important indicator of a country's overall quality of life. While the benefits of hard work are clear, working more is not the same as working better.'

The usual employer response to such findings is that time waits for no man, the job demands time input, customers demand that employees be present when needed, and if you want to work fewer hours, it must signify lack of commitment. Yet good management can ensure that customer needs are met (through job-sharing, for example) or can change customer expectations. Far from lack of commitment, allowing workers to decide on their own working times (start, finish and total number) could engender greater commitment. Ricardo Semmler in Brazil certainly found his workers fully capable of and responsible in making decisions about their own work times and even their own pay levels.[70]

My own position is that Australia should continue to build on the public–private partnership model of work–family policies and programs that has been in place. Government should take the lead in shaping the culture in a direction that values children and family life, values equal opportunity in employment for women, and values the contribution of fathers as well as that of mothers to the nurturing and socialisation of children. But employers and other groups in the community have to realise and accept their own responsibility for the quality of family and community life and for the environmental conditions that make for optimum child development and human quality of life.

It is still a novel suggestion that companies, employers, managers and supervisors have been responsible for much of the stress, family conflict and marital breakdown we have seen in Australia over the past 30 years. There are three key arguments in favour of family-friendly workplace policies. When I speak to groups of employers about work–family issues, I play off three complementary themes.

First, family problems and responsibilities have an inevitable impact on job performance and, thus, on the employer's bottom line. Managers must consider how efficient employees are at work after a major row with their partner or when a child is seriously ill. There is now plenty of Australian evidence on the cost-benefits of family-friendly work.

Second, they must understand that the new economy puts a premium on communication skills, interpersonal competence, empathy, and the ability to work adaptively in a team. In the information age, the authoritarian boss, the angry, dogmatic manager or supervisor is anathema to creativity and the ability to change direction quickly as conditions shift. Interpersonal competence becomes a core skill in the new economy, and there is already evidence that men who take parental leave, for example, return with more mature personal skills, self-confidence and depth, which enhance their productivity. As one personnel manager said, 'Really, it is a step in manager development that a person is at home and takes care of children, for it means a new situation, and every new situation a person handles is development.'[71] Amazingly, it has taken employers decades to recognise that women who have raised children and managed a household might have gained in the process valuable skills and adaptability which enhance rather than hinder their productivity on return to paid work.

But the third angle is often more surprising to many corporate leaders. That is, that inflexible and unreasonable work-time expectations, a workplace culture that ignores or dismisses family matters as irrelevant to performance, place people under such stress that it not only adversely affects their performance but also increases the likelihood of family conflict, separation and divorce. The cost of this to society and to the company itself is unconscionable. As well, the damage caused to children by inadequate parenting is a blight on future development.

The parallel is with environmental damage. It is obvious that un-sympathetic land use, chemical pollution and waste disposal damage 'the common good', and that companies have a responsibility to society beyond their shareholders or employees to ensure that the commons is not damaged beyond repair, either now or for future generations. But it is less obvious to them that they have a responsibility to the quality of private life that can be led by the commons, to the fabric of social life, which constitutes a sane (and profitable) environment for business itself and, in particular, for the wellbeing of children, who will be their future employees, consumers and critics.

In a recent Relationships Australia survey, 75 per cent of Australians admitted to having major relationship problems.[72] The main causes were financial difficulties, work pressures and child-related problems. The work issues that cause most angst are coming home from work stressed out (53 per cent), changing work hours at short notice (34 per cent), coming home late from work (27 per cent) and pressures from work deadlines (25 per cent). This leads to poor quality family relationships (45 per cent), an inability to plan family life (17 per cent), relationship difficulties with a spouse (17 per cent) and a high level of conflict (six per cent). The stresses are worse for senior managers, and younger men with young children.

Whilst it is necessary to have that sort of hard data on cost-benefits of work–family programs to even start to get through to some male managers, an appeal to the corporate bottom line plays into what Bellah has called 'the commodification of family life'.[73] Auerbach feels it is dangerous to argue for cost benefits without also stressing the benefits of work–family policies for women, children and families. The typical American economic discussion stands in stark contrast to the language of 'solidarity', 'universalism', 'the gender contract' and 'the common good' that informs public discussion about the work–family balance in Sweden.[74]

The problem is one of workplace culture operating out of kilter with the realities of modern life. But it stems from a failure on the part of business leaders to apply economic theory in the context of a rapidly changing society where human values and networks will be more important to the bottom line than ever before.

Chapter 5

A business paradigm shift

THE FAILURE OF WORK CULTURES TO adapt to changing family conditions stems in large part from the inability of business managers to make the link between economic theory and social policy. We currently suffer from the failure of economic theory to incorporate knowledge from the other social sciences.

Indeed, it's almost a contradiction to call economics a social science, since it has managed to extract the human and social element from its theories and formulae. Notions of supply and demand are partly linked by what is vaguely called consumer confidence, and progress is measured by how well consumers can be manipulated or motivated to increase demand for products they didn't know they really needed. But no account is taken of people as citizens, as sentient human beings more interested in the quality of life than in the corporate balance sheet and shareholder profits.[75]

There is not even a recognition that human beings are often not rational — they will do things that are not in their own self-interest, they are often emotional and illogical in their choices. The market is seen as some supra-human entity that operates along rational lines, in near isolation from any human or social consideration, apart, that is, from so-called rational choice theory. It must, we are told, be left free to operate as it will, unencumbered by too many government rules and regulations. In the other social sciences, this is called the sin of reification, treating an abstract concept as though it were real, sentient, motivated and active. The market is not an entity in itself; it is a concept used to describe the complex and often confused best-guesses of human beings who are at one and the same time self-interested and other-directed.

Even the neo-classical economic theory of the firm, and its belief that price is the sole determinant of competitiveness, on which the argument against market regulation by government and unions rests, is logically flawed. The so-called 'invisible hand' of perfectly competitive markets stands in direct contradiction of a reality in which 'the centrally planned and coordinated mini-economy called the firm actually exists'.[76]

Since, in reality, the firm's management cannot control prices, the only way it can see to maximise profits is to minimise costs. That is what lay behind much of the downsizing and restructuring of the past two decades. It is what also lies behind much of the present government's drive against union power and the right of workers to collective bargaining. No matter what our criticisms of excessive union power may be, we should remember that the recognition of legally protected trade unions (1871–75) was part and parcel of the democratisation of British society, the voting franchise having been extended in 1867. It recognised the need for representative bargaining to strengthen the weakness of separate individuals. Compulsory trade unionism follows the logic of compulsory voting in a democracy, where those who benefit have both a right and an obligation to be involved in decision-making. It removed the individual worker from the old master-servant relationship, in which power was unevenly balanced, and began the long move towards worker participation and a concept of the firm as a partnership between owners and workers for mutual benefit.

We are in danger of losing that sense of partnership, with both bosses and unions having lost touch with the central ethos of reciprocity and trust, as well as with the reality that no firm sits outside its wider social and community environment. In the global information age, profitability and competitiveness come not simply from driving down costs, but also from enhancing the skills and know-how of labour, and from the uniqueness and reliability of each firm's products and services. To do that requires greater cooperation and trust between workers and employers, and greater worker involvement in decision-making and direction-setting.

You cannot achieve a productive working relationship on the basis of coercion and exploitation; the whole history of research on morale, commitment, discretionary effort and productivity/profitability proves the point.[77] A recent study of the relative productivity of 1600 US firms over a period of six years found that unionised factories had significantly higher productivity rates than non-unionised plants, even where the latter had the same self-managed teams and profit-sharing arrangements as the best unionised plants.[78] The evidence from Australia Post (see Chapter 11) also shows that where quality is emphasised over mere cost-efficiency, and where workers are empowered to set their own performance and quality standards, the result is, in fact, better performance, greater efficiency and improved profitability. The way forward, then, is not back to arbitrary union awards and demarcation disputes, but in the direction of union-employer partnerships based on a joint concern for quality performance and the wellbeing of employees.

Economics, unfortunately, does not see the human needs of workers as being particularly important. It does not even conceptualise the ordinary human being as potentially creative. Only those called entrepreneurs are seen as creative; the rest of us are lumped into the category of labour, like genderless draught horses, with no ambition or sense of pride, born to serve the kings of industry.

Nor does economics have an adequate concept of the family, or of community, of social labour or the labour of love. The family is the major provider of social welfare and social security, yet it is treated as outside the national accounts. Even household work is ignored in economics, not counted as part of Gross National Product (GNP), not treated as the large part of any economy that it actually is. The community is seen simply as a locale for current operations, rather than as a potentially developing resource for both productive labour and improved business opportunities.

As Muhummad Yunus puts it, 'Because of this misconstrued vision of human beings, wage employment emerged as the only legitimate form of employment ... so economics text books never had any use for the term "self-employment" which it lumped into a category called "the informal sector", thus losing the opportunity to consider every individual as a potential entrepreneur and provide opportunities (through credit) to develop new forms of productive activity.'[79] Yunus is himself the founder and managing director of the Grameen Bank, Bangladesh, which has given credit loans worth $2.4 billion to 2.4 million people, mostly women. As he notes, the denial of credit to ordinary people creates financial apartheid — it pronounces a death sentence on the poor through no fault of their own, it stifles self-sufficiency and enterprise, rewarding only companies motivated by greed rather than encouraging social consciousness-driven enterprises which might improve the quality of social life.

Fred Argy, former Treasury Adviser, director of the Economic Planning Advisory Council, Australian ambassador to the OECD and secretary to the

Campbell Inquiry into the Australian financial system (1979–82), and thus one of the architects of financial deregulation in the 1980s, has sounded repeated warnings about extreme free-market economics.[80] He argues for a broader 'social welfare' view of economic policy, what he calls 'progressive liberalism', which has no commitment to small government per se, is prepared to intervene pragmatically to assist industry and regional development where there are broader economic and social spin-offs, and seeks to restrict the short-term flows of global investment capital which so often damage the national interest.

He is dismissive of the present government's pride in reducing government debt and having a budget surplus. Any low-geared company that shunned attractive investment opportunities simply to reduce debt would be unpopular with shareholders, and governments should be looking to the longer-term benefits of improved infrastructure and public investment in human capital. Nor is there any guarantee that lower government debt will reduce foreign debt, because falling public debt is often offset by rising private debt, to finance such dubious projects as casinos, ever more shopping centres, high rise apartment blocks and office buildings.[81]

As outlined above, in the new knowledge economy, the drive is for countries like Australia to shift from reliance on natural resources and manufacturing alone to services, communication and new applications of knowledge. 'This is where social and human capital and investments in people and social infrastructure are key. Societies cannot continue dematerialising their economies without investing in maintaining such social architecture and human capital. Knowledge, human capital, trust, cohesive values and sound management of the planet's biodiversity and natural resources are now the key factors of production.' These are the words of Helen Henderson, whose work for the United Nations and its 1995 report *The UN: Policy and Financing Alternatives* and her 1997 book *Building a Win-Win World* led to her sharing the 1996 Global Citizen Award with Nobel Peace prize winner Perez Esquival of Argentina.[82] Henderson is a harsh critic of the so-called discipline of economics, citing the absurdity of showing that the Exxon Valdez oil-spill disaster in Alaska had boosted Canada's GDP. As usual, economists counted the value of experts brought in to clean up the mess, but failed to include the damaged value of the environment and ecosystem.

Henderson calls for a new Bretton Woods agreement to move measures of GDP beyond the days when valuing bombs, bullets and war production was the aim, while setting the value of children, an educated citizenry, infrastructure, social safety nets and the environment at zero. This was particularly apposite in Australia in the year 2000, as we saw yet again the readiness with which government could find the money to expand our defence forces to manage the new East Timor commitment and the supposed threat of hostile Asian nations, yet how readily they were prepared to tell us to sacrifice spending on schools, hospitals and much-needed national infrastructure, all of which might be a better future line of defence in any case.

Why is it that spending on education is treated in the national accounts as a debit, not an asset? Why does GDP not include the enormous value of household work, or the voluntary work which adds so much to our social capital? Economists cannot get their heads around the notion of social capital at all. They are a little more relaxed about human capital, because that seems to be individual, residing in the head, the skills of measurable units that can be counted.

Henderson has devised an alternative to GDP — what she calls a Country Futures Indicator (CFI). It reformulates GDP and expands the information provided. She wants each country to measure income distribution, all informal household-sector production (unpaid work now accounts for $16 trillion worldwide per annum), energy efficiency, a capital asset account for public resources and infrastructure, the depletion of non-renewable natural resources, and deductions for social and environmental costs. She argues we should include community-based accounting to complement the focus on enterprise accounting, measure the effectiveness of government through a Military/Civilian Budget Ratio, and use a Purchasing Power Parity measure to correct for currency fluctuations.

Not surprisingly, Henderson is not well regarded by standard economists or business elites, which benefit from ignoring such matters in the national accounts. But, as she points out, without such added information, they are operating with their eyes wide shut. Japan, for example, is potentially able to wipe out national debt if they factored in their national assets of social infrastructure, education, health and national savings.[83]

As well, she calls for a concerted effort to stop the uncontrolled flood of hot money round the world (amounting to $1.5 billion per day), to be financed by a financial transaction fee of 0.05 per cent. Free traders would doubtless object, yet both the World Bank and the International Monetary Fund have now realised how costly to both Asian nations and the rest of the global marketplace was their failure to control financial flows prior to the

1997 Asian meltdown. She rightly targets the useless costs of war, and urges restored funding for the United Nations so it can act as a police force to demilitarise high-risk nations, while at the same time mustering non-government organisations to create and rebuild social and public infrastructure in such war-ravaged countries.

Doubtless such proposals are seen as fantasy in a world where tribal localism rises in counterbalance to the forces of globalisation, but the days of the military-industrial complex must surely go. The USA does not want to remain the global policeman, and the only alternative, notwithstanding Australia as its supposed deputy sheriff in Asia, is a properly funded international police force coupled with community-building taskforces in the United Nations.

The moral failure of business leadership

It must be stressed that Australia's tardy embrace of the new knowledge economy is a business failure, not simply a failure of political imagination. It is a moral failure because it has damaged the fabric of social life and leaves Australia open to being left behind in the global future.

One problem is that many 'Australian companies' are owned by overseas corporations which invest heavily in research and development in their home countries but don't bother to do so here. Companies in the USA in fact employ more PhD graduates from universities than do the universities themselves, and much of the 'pure' research, not just applied business development research, is conducted in corporate research laboratories. We are the losers here as well.

The Ralph Report recommends restitution of the business tax concession for research and development, to 200 per cent, not the previous 150 per cent, which was foolishly reduced to 125 per cent in 1997, then increased to 175 per cent from 2001. But the foreign control of our major companies is in itself an impediment to their investing money in the Australian end of what is a global enterprise. They can recruit expertise from anywhere, so why bother training Australians as such? For that, you need more of a sense of corporate responsibility than most current Australian business leaders seem to have.

In fact, in its own conduct, Australian business leadership has been singularly lacking in vision and creativity. Bring out Al Dunlap and they all follow his slash-and-burn downsizing formula. Read the new evidence that downsizing did not lead to greater efficiency, but left huge gaps in the linkages that make for an effective corporation, and they all start to change their mind. Bring out any of the latest fads — MBA schools, the lecture-circuit gurus, the Japanese catchwords — and our corporate managers rush to apply them, often without any idea of how different are their own contexts and cultures and without any insight into how they might adopt the best elements of new theories and adapt or reject others. They'll even rush to pay huge fees to hear 'experts' such as Stormin' Norman Schwartzkopf or Mikhail Gorbachev spout their incomprehensible gibberish about command systems, attack frameworks and personal motivational techniques. The latest fads seem to be 'values statements' and 'spirituality', laudable in principle, but more like icing on the cake than a deeply embedded culture change in the way businesses work. Contrary pressures to perform to impossible standards, to work long hours, push in the opposite direction, towards dishonesty and reduced ethical standards.[84]

Australia's business elite presided over the disaster of the 1980s crash of greed, the mindless elevation of efficiency over effectiveness, of profit over social responsibility, the failure of BHP to meet even its shareholders' interests, let alone the national interest, and a resistance to the funding of innovative research and new venture development that has probably left Australia well behind in the race to become a leader in the new knowledge economy. Australian business downsized more dramatically than in any other country and close to one-third of Australian families have experienced the retrenchment of a family member. Business is now launching new Internet entities that have no substance but hope to make fortunes on the stock exchange, or nervously rushing into e-commerce without fully understanding how the new information technology can really reduce costs for them.

There is growing criticism, too, of the failure by institutional investors to exercise proxy votes in corporate decision-making. Whereas the US Department of Labor requires that managers of funds governed by the *Employee Retirement Income Security Act* vote on issues that may affect the value of the funds' assets, and countries like Germany and the UK have over 70 per cent proxy votes, in Australia the level is much lower.[85] This suggests apathy about their customers' best interests and a level of collusion between institutional investors and their corporate buddies on controversial issues such as, for example, management options schemes or environmental impacts of business policy.

There are signs of growing disaffection with poor corporate management, with new networks between unions and superannuation trustees developing what is called a 'corporate campaign' via proxy votes to tackle such issues as executive salaries, employment conditions and protecting shareholders' interests.[86]

Australian business generally seems not to have woken up to the fact that ethical behaviour can pay off, let alone be a responsible way to act. There has been some talk of the 'triple bottom line' — business responsibility to shareholders, employees and the environment — but shareholder interests certainly dominate. With Australia rapidly becoming a land of small investors, that will have to change, because small investors are likely to have a broader interest in social and environmental damage to their community than do the large-scale investment funds. In the USA and Europe, ethical investment has become a thriving business in itself. Investment funds are screened for their involvement in tobacco, gambling, alcohol and weapons, and for their record on human rights, the environment, labour relations, animal welfare, and even abortion and birth control. This scrutiny affects over $3.7 trillion in invested funds in the USA, around $8.3 billion in the UK. Given that Australia's superannuation assets were estimated in December 1999 at $415 billion, growing to $860 billion by 2010, companies with a poor ethical record will have to start cleaning up.

The evidence is already in that good business management includes sensible health and safety procedures, sound environmental management and a clear consideration of social risks inside and outside the workplace. A 1997 US study found companies with an ethical approach to the environment outperformed others by up to five per cent.[87] Ethical companies are less subject to market volatility. In another study, US workers reported that illegal and unethical behaviour has soared in the workplace, largely because of increased pressure from management to meet unrealistic time schedules and earning goals. Three-quarters said they observed unethical workplace conduct in the last year, yet management was reluctant to deal with it. Whereas two-thirds of workers overall said they would recommend their company to job candidates, only 21 per cent of those who felt management condoned unethical conduct said they would do so. Increasingly, groups such as EthicScan Canada advise potential investors on which companies meet their moral standards on a range of issues. Australian business leaders have a long way to go.

We are also only beginning to understand value-adding as the key to extending our advantages in natural resources, food and other agriculture. We have allowed our educational and training systems to atrophy, because the ideology of privatisation sees government funding withdrawn but not replaced by private money; and we have only recently started to reform our taxation system and related business incentives along the lines of the obviously successful models of Israel, Ireland and Sweden.

Despite a shift in rhetoric from the language of 'restructuring' to the new buzz about intellectual capital and the importance of the new breed of knowledge workers, most human resources managers in Australia's big companies admit there is more lip service than action. Managers are aware that the so-called Generation X workers are less interested in a linear career, less loyal to any one company, than they are in their own professional development and a more balanced lifestyle. But companies still fail to see the need to protect their intellectual capital or to ensure, through their human resource management, that they become and stay the employers of choice. Moreover, many senior executives have resisted government pressure towards equal opportunity employment and work–family programs, not just because of the macho male culture that still permeates many businesses but, worse, because they fail to understand the real significance of diversity for success in the knowledge age.

Corporate plans, engineering designs, cost reports and marketing strategies all depend, in the end, on their being properly understood by the people who manage and the workers who cooperate with them. Given what is known about employee motivation, discretionary effort and improved performance, the more closely involved employees are in planning and controlling their own work schedules, the better their performance. The old industrial model, where bureaucratic layers divided up the work into discrete tasks to be done in controlled sequence, gradually building to the final product, will remain appropriate for many jobs, handled mechanically, but leaves little room for innovation, problem-solving, the design of custom-made products, or personal-service adaptability.

The distinction between 'active' and 'inert' tasks will always hold. Where you can define in advance both the process and the product — as in digging a hole or checking a balance sheet — there is no need for worker discretion; the task is inert and its performance can be evaluated pretty easily. However, with more active tasks — such as teaching a lesson, writing up a project or designing a faster yacht — there are myriad ways of doing the job and still achieving a successful outcome. You cannot evaluate the performance of an active task by checking the process followed against a predetermined list; only outcomes matter.

More and more of the work we do is of this kind. The employee has to be given more room to move and think creatively, not follow routine procedures. Teams are assigned to a new project and have to work out their own modus operandi, and no manager can usefully dictate how they should work. You still need leaders and managers who will set the goals and provide the motivation, but the old-style manager supervising every aspect of task performance is counterproductive in the new economy. Because the skills required for each new task or project vary, so too must team membership vary, so that adaptability and clear communication skills, listening, problem-solving, empathy and resolving conflict positively become the core qualifications for success. Evaluation can only be in terms of outcomes, not process, because many paths lead to Rome, and what matters is simply that the team gets there, on time, at cost and with the right product.

Growth of the new economy seems to favour those just graduating. They have grown up with computers and have no investment in existing, old-style careers. Risk and instability are no barriers, especially when stock options promise to enhance salaries, and it is not a stigma if your first job in an Internet start-up company is a failure. Half the job offers to new graduates in the USA are coming from the new economy industries, with the top four — consulting, accounting, computer software and finance — accounting for 30 per cent by themselves.[88]

However, in the USA and Europe, older workers are also in demand, if they have skills needed in the new economy. For example, since branding is crucial on the Internet to set your product and message apart from others, seasoned marketing executives are in high demand. And with the explosive growth in e-tailing (Web retailers), there is big demand for those with logistical skills in merchandising and replenishing products for commerce. Many blue-collar workers are retooling at vocational schools to learn networking and computer repair skills.

Another ongoing problem for Australia, however, is the archaic nature of much of our present educational system and the failure of business to articulate what sorts of skills are really required if Australia is to compete in the new economy.

Australia has been slow to realise that education, higher-skills training, and value-adding through the creative use of knowledge is the way of the future. We have had flurries of rhetoric, such as Prime Minister Bob Hawke's call for us to become 'the clever country'; the West Report on university reform, which called for greater competition and encouragement of innovation in higher education; and the recent Ralph Committee Report on a new approach to intellectual investment and business taxation. But we have not done enough to make it happen. Both sides of politics now talk of the 'knowledge nation', with heavy investment in education and skills training as the key. This is the only way to go.

Business success depends on building social capital

If, as I have argued, companies do have a responsibility to the wellbeing of employees and their families, it must be seen as a sensible and productive operation to support the wider social system in which business operates. The market does not operate freely — certainly not free from the influence of public values, private interests and community concerns.

People do not make rational choices between clearly delineated objectives, nor do they make rational choices only in their own selfish interests. Instead, they act on the basis of emotions and values that derive from their collective life; they make choices that take into consideration the wellbeing of others. It is the quality of that collective life which sets the limits and opens up new possibilities for business enterprise, and business is itself partly responsible for ensuring that the overall social environment is conducive to the inclusion and wellbeing of everyone.

Interestingly, discussion in the USA is now taking note of the comparative advantage employers will have in global competition if they operate in nations where both government social welfare supports and private initiatives operate in partnership. Googins argues that 'any new configuration of the social contract will not require so much a diminished role for government as a different role that would avoid the stigma of excessive incompetence and intrusiveness. Such a role would include a government willing to promote a partnership and collaboration in ensuring a common level of supports.' Partnerships between government, business and community will be the way of the future, if work–family initiatives are not to bog down in cynicism and resistance from the corporate world.[89]

Realistically, companies cannot do it all alone. Nor should they be expected to. No matter how family-friendly any individual company may be towards its employees, if the social environment from which its employees come is itself 'toxic', itself unsupportive of children and family life, there will be only limited impact from their own workplace programs.

But business leaders cannot continue with the notion that they sit apart from the rest of society, or that they already make a sufficient contribution by providing jobs and paying taxes — by running a business at all. They are an integral part of society in an increasingly interdependent world, and social issues are not just a 'third sector' to be thrown some scraps of corporate philanthropy. Indeed, the profitability of business in the end depends on being able to attract and retain the best employees and to operate in a context of private and communal wellbeing.

Fortunately, some business leaders appear to have realised how outdated and immoral is Milton Friedman's (1970) assertion that they have no obligations beyond financial ones to their shareholders.[90] Unfortunately, there are still many who do not understand or accept that they do have obligations to the wider society and that it is in their best interests to ensure that markets operate in a civil and cooperative society.

Corporate citizenship has to mean much more than a bit of charity and sponsorship; it has to represent a real acceptance of business partnership in contributing to the quality of society and the alleviation of social ills. The language of stakeholder interests has to replace that of narrow shareholder concerns, with the realisation that business can create two, mutually reinforcing types of value: commercial and social.[91]

Other countries are far in advance of Australia in developing this more inclusive stakeholder approach. In the UK, Business in the Community is involved in an array of initiatives for disadvantaged communities: the Education Action Zones, policy and research contributions from organisations such as the Centre for Tomorrow's Company, the Institute for Social and Ethical Accountability, the New Economics Foundation and the Prince of Wales Business Leaders Forum. EthicScan Canada Ltd, the European Business Ethics Network, the US-Europe Social Venture Network and the Asahi Shimbun Foundation in Japan all work towards a new culture of social responsibility in business.

Australia has some parallel embryonic organisations, such as the St James Centre for Ethics, the Epoch Foundation, Agenda 2000, and the Business and Community Partnerships Round Table, but actual examples of work on the ground are difficult to find, and the new ethos does not permeate the Australian corporate world. I once heard a senior manager from Rio Tinto praising his company's involvement with Plan Australia (an environmental lobby group) while at the same time insisting that involvement was driven by company self-interest rather than by social concern. They have since come a long way in seeing the business benefits of social action.

Perhaps the best example of lateral and forward thinking is the community work of the Body Shop in Australia.[92] The Body Shop's international mission statement is: 'We dedicate our business to the pursuit of social and environmental change.' And the Australian franchisees have been assiduous in applying a stakeholder view of business as a part of society, not apart from society. They actively involve their employees in this process, work with disadvantaged youth and indigenous communities, and use their own skills and resources to help build community strength. Voluntary work to broaden staff horizons expanded into training community organisations in good business practice. An Enterprise Development Workshop started in 1994, together with a National Indigenous Business Mentoring Program, has had a major impact on self-sufficiency in Aboriginal and Torres Strait Islander communities.

The Body Shop has worked with government and welfare agencies also, in its Speakout Ltd Project, a partnership to help disadvantaged youth in Sydney develop a T-shirt and streetwear industry that now exports its products overseas. A community management program now called Mornington Peninsula Community Connections used the Body Shop's expertise to build and support those smaller community welfare organisations, which were being neglected by the Kennett Government's move towards corporatisation and competitive tendering, a direction that expanded the power of both the central bureaucracy and the larger welfare agencies. It aims to promote the crucial role of smaller grassroots agencies and neighbourhood services in strengthening communities.

As well, it encourages them in the skills of advocacy and policy debate, in the belief that it is important to society as a whole for such groups to remain outside mainstream political processes and retain their capacity for disagreement, alternative ideas and radical action while at the same time meeting the accountability requirements of government funding. This is a crucial issue in the trend towards partnerships between government and the community sector. Co-option, the muzzling of dissent because people fear attacking those on whom they rely for funding, is hard to overcome, and any charter or partnership agreement must build in a guarantee of the right to independent critique.

That is why business itself stands to benefit from working in partnership with communities and acting as an advocate for the interests of the community. Business is not directly dependent on government funding or political favour; it is skilled in lobbying and directing its own funds towards political parties promising policies helpful to business interests. Their best interests lie in a civil society, one in which people are able to balance their work and family lives, encouraged to cooperate, but also to negotiate competing views in a civil way. The company itself can help facilitate that sort of social capital through its own initiatives within the community from which it draws and with which it trades.

A simple-minded appeal to individual companies to meet their reciprocal responsibilities, or to become part of a 'social compact' on the basis of corporate philanthropy, will never work, because it maintains the very separation of individual businesses and their particular shareholder interests from the wider community, ignoring the interdependence of businesses across regions, and between businesses and government-funded services, business and community life.

Instead, the way forward is to develop new structures that recognise and reinforce such a culture of interdependence, by getting business leaders to interact with others in the community — teachers, local government, family support service providers — whose work creates a viable economic and social environment in which business can thrive. (See Chapter 11 for more on this partnership approach.)

Networks as the essence of business

In sum, business in the global age enters a new era of complex networks and partnerships from which innovation and profitability will grow.[93]

Family networks are, as we have seen, already much more complex than in previous times. Young people stay at home with their parents longer, prolonging education and delaying marriage. This alters the old parent-child hierarchy, because children have to be treated as equal adults, making their family network thick rather than thin. People marry later or not at all, thus changing the nature of short-term relationships from casual to serial and serious, leaving behind a network of friendships that can be reactivated later on. Those who marry now usually do so because they have decided as a couple to have children, not because it is the accepted thing to do or because an unwanted pregnancy traps them into the formal state of marriage.

Inevitably, this means fewer and fewer people will marry or have children, so their networks will increasingly centre round workplace contacts, friendship groups, and the virtual networks of the Internet. Traditionally, the family networks of the working class have been closed and somewhat restrictive, those of the educated middle class more open.[94] Today, with better education and a much more open approach to sexual partnerships and marriage, the range of social networks will expand for everyone, work contacts themselves extending far beyond the one office or factory location.

As well, Western populations are ageing, and both families and the workplace will have to adapt to having closer contact, over a longer period, with their older generations. Networks are thus likely to be more multi-generational than they have been in the very age-graded 20th century.

Our work lives are also increasingly dependent on complex networks and work itself becomes a patchwork, stitched together over a lifetime of varied tasks. All the trends we are seeing now will expand. Team-based work, with group membership changing to suit the project, will demand not just individual communication, negotiation and team problem-solving skills; it will also require efficient networks of suitable contacts in order to pull together the best just-in-time team. The better your contacts, the better the team you can bring to the job.

The rapidly burgeoning field of B2B — business to business — Internet trading has already altered the way in which networks operate.[95] It is no longer enough to rely on the old boy networks. Business needs to have immediate access to the names of the best people with the right skills for each new project. Companies such as Niku are already trading in what they call 'warmware', specialising in those intangibles that make for more effective work, such as expertise and experience appropriate to a particular job. They go beyond the old-style human resource management and deal with regional and worldwide databases on knowledge management, finding for businesses that subscribe to their service 'the lowest cost person with the right talents'.

Information flow itself becomes more open in the new economy, thus breaking the traditional secrecy of business dealings. Core information has to be shared across the entire network if you are to trade B2B, and innovations are more likely to grow out of shared ideas across apparently competing businesses. Much of the success of California's Silicon Valley is attributed to the rich web of social contacts, talking through embryonic ideas with rival colleagues in bars and coffee shops, spinning off into new applications and problem-solving elsewhere.

In fact, B2B and e-commerce activity is rewriting the face of business, doing away with the slow process of meeting with potential partners, examining contracts in fine legal detail, and taking time to decide on partnerships and purchases, instead making rapid decision-making an essential element of beating your rivals to a deal. This approach, clearly, is fraught with danger — potential mistakes, fraud, lack of trust in the reliability of trading partners. But the examples already in operation — such as e-STEEL, which streamlines procurement and sales, inventory and marketing for over 2000 companies dealing in the whole range of steel products, from smelting to fabrication and consumer sales, or the planned London Internet marketplace where six world airlines will join to spend $US32 billion a year on fuel, replacement parts and maintenance services — indicate how profoundly this will alter the way businesses connect and network.

In such a world, more and more people will become individual contractors, hiring out their services to the highest bidder, having to market themselves across a range of potential employers and work projects. It's never been just what you know, but who you know that counts, and active networks will be the key to success for these footloose portfolio workers. Even the house cleaner and gardener, the small builder or concreter depend on word of mouth, their networks, for keeping up a supply of work. They rely on trust, their reputation for good work and reliability, to attract new work. But in the e-commerce future, they will need to be linked to a B2B network if they are to prosper and grow.

The Internet also gives consumers greater power over business decisions. Companies will have to tailor their products to suit individual preferences and keep track of customers in more detail than has previously been possible. Dell Computer has profited from close customer contact, while Proctor and Gamble allows customers to order cosmetics mixed to their preferred specifications. Amazon.com uses each book purchase to build up a customer-interests profile as a device for marketing other books on related topics. Banks and telecommunications companies are facing pressure to diversify their products in order to retain customers, some forming alliances to trade jointly and share customer information. Such 'b-webs' will comprise 'partner networks of producers, suppliers, infrastructure companies and customers linked by digital channels, making customers even more of a business driver than they are at present.'[96] As noted above, the spread of small investors may improve the ethics of business and their sense of social and environmental responsibility.

Other social changes will flow from the increasing numbers of workers who will use their home as a base, not leaving their neighbourhood suburb every morning to sit in a remote city office all day. While home-based work can be lonely, isolating and constant, the coincidence of work and family responsibilities will drive new (male) demands for accessible childcare in the neighbourhood, and better support services to relieve them of the burden of aged care, and is very likely to regenerate some of the voluntary community networks lost in recent years.[97]

Whilst those of us who have grown used to making our social contacts at work (complaining about the endless meetings with colleagues that waste our working time, yet valuing them for the face-to-face interaction they provide) may find home-based work lonely, the new generation is already more comfortable with working in different ways. They enjoy multi-tasking, going from the Internet to writing a work plan, from one Windows application to another, from changing nappies to preparing a meal or spending time with their partner.

And though the old-style manager still tries to impose rigid controls on presence in the office as an indicator of performance, and may continue to insist on hours actually worked instead of completion of the task itself within a set deadline, the days of the office block, the fixed desk, the peak hour chaos, have gone, like the days of the foreman, the office manager and others who need a captive audience to exist.[98]

All of this suggests that the old divisions of the industrial era are about to collapse. Instead of the old divisions between a male public world and a female private world, between city and suburb, between work and play, between old and young, we will have a high-tech world in which new networks linking family, work and community will be possible. The patchwork country becomes ever more complex.

In sum, many of the dinosaurs we inherited from the age of industrialisation and bureaucratic hierarchy have either gone or are now threatened. We face an age where new networks, new links across and between the institutions that control our lives, will be crucial. The links between work life and family life are changing, with the result that the very nature of community life and Australian society itself will change.

Change always brings about uncertainty, fear and distress. Opposition to economic rationalism has been loud, often simply calling for a return to our protected past and to institutions that will no longer serve us well in the global economy. But some of the opposition has been well informed, and is offering sensible alternatives to an ideology that puts an abstract free-market economy ahead of the human and social values on which a sound economy must rest if it is to survive and prosper in a linked future.

Section 2

The new tribalism — perils and possibilities

Chapter 6

National identity and sense of place

AUSTRALIA, IT IS SAID, IS FACING A crisis of identity. One might comment, sceptically, that there is nothing new in this apart from the surrounding factors that cause us to navel-gaze every now and again. In a global age, we must ask: what is the point of nationalism at all, and why is having a national identity still a significant drive, given the rise of what I call the 'new tribalism'?[99]

The early European settlers invaded a land occupied for millennia by the complex and adaptable culture of the Aboriginal and Torres Strait Islander people, denying them any identity as Australians until the census of 1967, yet we are still divided as a nation over the issue of reconciliation and government resistance to saying sorry for past wrongs and injustices. The first settlers were British, but soon fought for political independence from their colonial masters. Immigrants have been a constantly changing multicultural polyglot, particularly during the Gold Rush period, which saw an upsurge of rebellion against the establishment. The migrant impulse for settlement has always driven an identification with the new land and its independent future.

In each of the World Wars, the very seat of our so-called national identity (diggers, mateship, ANZAC pride), the nation 'forged in fire' has been divided over where our true loyalties should lie. Irish Catholics objected to fighting a British war, and formed a large part of the union movement, which asserted a unique Aussie-battler identity against the ruling classes, with Ned Kelly as a hero. Yet Australia produced massive numbers of volunteers, urged on by their women folk, to fight for the mother country. Post-War migration diluted the British majority, and Australia formed one of the most successfully multicultural nations in the world. Over one-third of Australians now come from a non-English speaking background. Yet until recently, public interest in the British royal family has been manifest, and few wish to deny the country's clearly British legal, political and social heritage. There were huge protests against Prime Minister Harold Holt's 'All the way with LBJ' approach to Australian involvement in the Vietnam War, yet our media are saturated with American content and our Vietnam veterans have finally been drawn into the unifying celebration of ANZAC Day.

We failed to vote in favour of a particular form of republic, though the rationale was argued largely on the basis of Australian autonomy from its British and royalist ties. The media and the masses glorify Australian sports heroes whose names reflect every ethnic group around the world, and the myths of mateship, disrespect for authority, a wry sense of humour and scepticism of any extreme cause persist. So wherein lies identity?[100]

I would argue that identity lies in our sense of place. Though migrants will always identify with the home into which they were born, their country of origin, their ethnicity and religious beliefs, that identity changes as current life situations bear down on their daily lives. Immigrants have to adapt, and adaptability is one of Australia's great strengths as we move into the complex world of information technology and new science. Newcomers now shop in supermarkets, not in rural markets or city bazaars; they now travel to and work with polyglot Aussies in Australian cities marked by suburban sprawl, not high-density housing. The backyard vegetable patch and barbecue invade the soul despite attempts to recreate the patios and columns and communal meeting areas of Europe. Their children go to school, where they learn in English, not in the mother tongue, except as a second language. Their patterns of social contact, partner choice, marriage and divorce converge towards the Australian norm, and first-generation forebears are pushed off the pedestal of respect that once was theirs by right and custom.

The news they read and hear is inevitably local, regional and national, not international or solely about their country of origin. The media may be increasingly controlled by the Rupert Murdochs and Ted Turners of this world, but economic survival dictates that journalists will write about Australian tennis, football, politics, casinos, scandals, road deaths and dramatic events.

You become Australian by osmosis, the very environment — its weather, colours, bird sounds and seasons — dictating what you feel. You live and work under the control of Australian institutions — the police, courts, banks, unions and work systems — so the old ways serve merely as comparison points of nostalgic complaint, often only until a return visit highlights the value of the new homeland. Indeed, the remarkable thing about Australia's experience of immigration has been the acceptance of our institutional framework, designed to ensure a fair go, a chance to make good, and a culture that accepted difference provided you were prepared to have a go yourself. It is both our civic institutions and such core values which hold this patchwork nation together.

And this sense of place is more than just a symbolic sense of Australia as a nation; it is pinned down to a locality, a street, a suburb, a country town, an outback sweep or a high-rise building which shapes what we do and how we think about ourselves. That is why Australian voters resist any attempt to get rid of the states, or local government, or to change the face of their streetscape in ways that will diminish the perceived quality of their lives. They value their own patch.

It is my belief that in their search for Australia as a nation, political parties have forgotten this locational sense of identity. Their current scramble to appeal to regional and rural interests is belated testimony to their new-found concern, but they make a mistake if they focus only on the rural at the expense of regional and urban issues. Most of our immigrants have settled in suburbia, and their Australian identity both develops and resides there. It needs to be recognised and nurtured by institutions that reinforce that sense of place.

Paul Keating urged us to rethink our place in the context of Asia, but his call was rejected as a denial of those things we hold dear. Some can imagine themselves as citizens of the world, as being closer in interest to our Asian neighbours than to Europe, but for most, that is too abstract a view of identity to sustain day-to-day practical decisions. John Howard's appeal to the white picket fence may be socially narrow and less visionary, but it is closer to popular aspirations.

The cause of reconciliation is difficult because most Australians have no first-hand, certainly no equal status, contact with Aborigines. John Howard's rejection of guilt again strikes a chord even with those who feel regret at past injustices done to Australia's original inhabitants. The attitudes of those who do have first-hand contact are coloured by their actual experiences of a culture they do not understand, a culture disrupted and corrupted by despair and disadvantage. Thus, appeals to social justice fall on unsympathetic ears.

City folk do not understand the concerns of rural folk, the wealthy and powerful have no empathy for the poor, and non-observing Christians still find other religions strange and threatening to their taken-for-granted world.

Local and regional loyalties are said not to mesh with national interests, and this was certainly true when it came to debates about free trade and railway gauges at the time of Federation, or when Pauline Hanson's anti-Asian diatribes hurt our image overseas. Yet in a sense, we can be Australians only at a local and regional level, because it is there that we are embedded in the culture; that is where our identities arise and are reinforced and nurtured. We can consider national abstracts such as 'the economy' and know that they are important to what we do and what we earn, but we understand the economy only when it affects our job, our home loan interest rate, our family tax bill or our access to hospitals and schools. We can identify with our Olympic sporting heroes, with the ideal of a fair go, but our actions reflect our own abilities, our own prejudices, based on the limits of our located experience. That is why the Olympic opening and closing ceremonies touched a chord with their lawnmowers, barbecues and giant thongs.

Hawke and Keating were also doubtless realistic in floating the Australian dollar and opening up industry to tariff-free competition, but the political fallout reflected the reality of private lives, not the embracing of Australia's new place in the global marketplace. That embrace took place later, reluctantly, as we realised the cold realities of global competition and the need to change. Our economic survival through the Asian crisis removed some of the cringe mentality about Japan and the Asian way, and the boom period of the late 1990s restored some confidence.

But all this is filtered through our own, localised experience. We know in general terms what 'justice' means, even what 'social justice' might mean, but such concepts come to life most vividly when our own home is burgled, or when someone we know is wrongly charged or denied access to what every other citizen has as a basic right.[101]

That is why growing unemployment is always a political threat — not because of an abstract sense of social injustice, but because the actual injustice is felt and the slur of dole-bludger rejected, since families now know how hard it is to find work in an economy undergoing major structural change. One-third of Australian households have experienced the retrenchment of a family member in the last 15 years. People do not, in general, respond to the welfare lobby's appeal for the rights of the disadvantaged; they respond when disadvantage comes in through their own front door or into the homes of their friends and neighbours. They will resist government cutbacks if these cutbacks affect their own family's wellbeing, not if they simply reduce funds for 'the poor' — an argument for universal and preventative support services, and against narrow targeting, which seems to produce a welfare backlash.

So it should be no surprise to find that underneath our so-called Australian identity, we are very tribal. We have particularistic loyalties to our own home base, our football team, our neighbourhood and its local causes, as well as to our ethnic or national origins. And we experience national identity only if and when we feel a wider sense of common interest, common feeling, common pride, a shared stake in what is happening at the national level. One of our core values since early settlement has been a rejection of ethnic or class background as a basis for social acceptance and the right to be given a fair go. Whenever the gap between our locally particular interests and the rest of the nation/society widens, we react with hostility and demand attention to our tribal needs.

It is important to acknowledge the centrality to national identity of cultural activities. Indeed, in a global age of potentially homogenised information and values, culture in its many forms becomes even more important. That is why resistance to free trade in cultural goods (films, television content quotas, music and the arts) is important. Cultural goods are not the same as other trade goods, because they express a society's unique take on the world. Artists shape society's emotions in ways economists cannot. We need spaces in which diverse identities and ideas can flourish, where the taken for granted can be challenged, the authorised world view cross-examined.

We need our own national stories, and children need their own myths and fairytales, not those manufactured by Disney. Witness the hold that Australia's mateship myth, the courage of the ANZACS and the story of the drover's wife still have on a nation of suburbanites. And don't dismiss the lessons of self-revelation contained in such popular television programs as 'Neighbours', 'Blue Heelers' and 'Sea Change', or the footy and gardening shows that rate so highly. We need more of them, and less of Seinfeld, or those dated British comedies that dominate ABC programming.[102]

In short, though we are comforted by being part of a nation with its own unique qualities, our sense of identity derives from our own local 'patch'. If our diverse interests are not adequately acknowledged, the fabric of this national patchwork can be very easily torn apart.

Chapter 7

Globalisation and social movements

THE CHANGES IN THE NATURE OF work and the structures of society described in Section 1 constitute a major shift in the way people can form a sense of themselves, in the shaping of national and personal identity. We seem to face two opposing forces: globalisation and convergence, on the one hand, versus fragmentation and localisation, on the other. Nations are forced together via technology and economic forces, yet nations are internally split by ethnic, religious and political conflict, as various interests struggle to preserve their own sense of identity.[103]

In most societies, each individual's identity is formed on the basis of interaction within the whole range of institutions making up the civil society (families, churches, schools, unions, cooperatives, community organisations, etc.). Because these institutions are legitimised by the state, change can emerge gradually out of democratic and civil processes, but that very legitimacy is based on the state's power to define the limits of identity, and there has always been resistance.[104]

Not everyone can, or wants to, conform to the dominant view of what is imposed or normalised.[105] They rebel, and seek meaning and purpose through forging a self-image that contradicts the standard mould. This drive for an 'identity for resistance'[106] leads to the formation of communes, or communities, the sort of ethnic, religious and political interest groups that resist the norm.[107] The Quakers are a famous and relatively successful example.

Such 'tribes' increase and take new forms as globalisation expands, because more and more people fall outside the bounds of what is imposed as legitimate or normal behaviour. They cannot gain a sense of meaning or self-identity in the context of global technology and the authorities that surround them. English as the dominant language of the Internet; American consumer values; Western secularism and individualism; permissive sexuality and self-exploration; economic values overriding social and environmental considerations — all work against the validation of personal and group identities which oppose them. Thus, identity for resistance becomes an ever more important type of identity-building in modern society, as alienation and resentment against exclusion from the mainstream grow.[108]

So, too, does what Touraine calls 'project identity', the attempt to create a personal history, to give meaning to one's life through some cause, whether that be religious conversion, the end of patriarchal society or the transformation of materialist values.[109] Indeed, as the power of tradition and custom declines, people are forced into choices that make identity-building an ever more personal (and more difficult) project. I can no longer be a 'husband and breadwinner', a 'housewife', a 'solid citizen', a 'Rotarian' or a 'church-goer' and expect that to form my life project, my sense of what and who I am. Modern life opens up alternatives, and I have to construct my own identity from a vast array of possible options. If there is less respect for authority, or a range of authorities vying for my attention, identity becomes even more autonomous and variable and the civil society (made up of legitimised institutions) falls apart.

Others write of this shift as a move towards a 'risk society', characterised by manufactured uncertainty and increased individualisation.[110] As I shall argue, risk is not necessarily a bad thing, and with the rate of change we are experiencing, it is unlikely to go away. Drucker, for example, has long argued that learning organisations must embrace risk, 'must constantly upset, disorganise and destabilise the community', if they are to survive and grow.[111] Latham argues that the complexity of modern society is such that top-down solutions must give way to a devolution of power and funding, thus 'introducing the concept of risk management into the work of government'.[112]

But it is this uncertainty and lack of accepted guidelines that people regret when they complain about the loss of community, declining social capital, the alienation of youth, and the lack of respect for politics, parliament and authority in general. And it results in both a transformation of intimacy and a transformation of civil society.[113]

Giddens argues that modernity transforms intimacy because we now have to negotiate everything, construct our own lifestyle, and build intimacy on the basis of mutual disclosure rather than on the basis of assumed roles. Men have to disclose their innermost thoughts to women or the relationship will not survive. Similarly, the footloose workers have to build their own portfolio of skills, know what they are best at, identify what goals they want to reach, and learn how to sell themselves to others in the global marketplace. It's all negotiable, open to self-reflection — a life that must be personally planned and lived out.

The trouble is, as Manuel Castells points out, this is impossible 'except for the elite inhabiting the timeless space of flows of global networks and their ancillary locales'.[114] Most people do not have the skills or resources to operate in such an autonomous and fearless fashion, so they construct defensive identities around communal or tribal principles, hence the rise and rise of identity politics and of political appeals to special interest groups.

Castells describes in detail the way in which 'project identity' for such people grows from communal resistance, taking a variety of forms. Some are large scale, such as the resurgence of Islamic fundamentalism and ethnic/nationalist rebellions in once-unified countries such as the USSR or Yugoslavia. Other identity-seeking movements are smaller but no less dramatic, such as the Aum Shinrikyo cult, which released deadly sarin gas in Japan's subways as a way of starting the apocalypse which its members would survive, as a spiritual community of true believers.

We see many movements developed on the shared basis of opposition to global forces: the American Christian fundamentalists who oppose the inroads of feminism, godlessness and permissiveness; the Basque movement in Spain struggling to preserve its own language and culture; the American Militia and Patriot movements of the 1990s taking up arms against central government, the United Nations and the New World Order; and the more recent coalitions of protesters at Seattle, Davos and Melbourne against the World Trade Organisation/World Economic Forum and the impact of global corporations on poverty in the developing world.

Not all of these movements are localised, however, and they point to a new form of tribalism that may have a positive effect on globalisation processes, a form of project identity formation that is not inward-looking but, rather, transformative of society. There is, for example, increasing political activity via the Internet, directed against such firms as Shell (Ethiopia), and those accused of exploiting low-paid workers, such as Nike, McDonald's and Microsoft. As Naomi Klein puts it: 'five years earlier, campus politics was all about issues of discrimination and identity — race, gender and sexuality, "the political correctness wars". Now they [are] broadening out to include corporate power, labour rights, and a fairly developed analysis of the workings of the global economy ... Simply put, anti-corporatism is the brand of politics capturing the next generation of troublemakers and shit-disturbers, and we have only to look to the student radicals of the 1960s and the ID warriors of the eighties and nineties to see the transformative impact such a shift can have.'[115]

Social movements in Australia

In Australia, the gaps between local, regional loyalties and the nation as a whole have widened, and the emerging sense of tribalism will damage the social fabric unless it can be harnessed in new ways. In a society where groups and communities are systematically denied the resources for capacity-building, where people are excluded from the benefits of progress, alienation and social division run rampant.

We only have to look at the figures on family income to see how far we have diverged from the national image of Australia as the land of the fair go. I would maintain it was never a self-image, always a product of political propaganda, given the historical evidence of wide gaps in income between different groups and the long struggle for wage and working conditions reform in Australia.

But it is true that the size of that income gap has increased and, crucially, that it varies widely between different regions and areas, driving some in the direction of social resentment, others in the direction of political action to restore the balance. It pits region against region, state against state, generating both positive and negative social effects.

While real income in Australia was 60 per cent higher in 1995 than in the mid-1960s, most of that growth took place before 1975. Since then, there has been only 10 per cent growth, and men in the lowest income third had lower real wages in 1995 than in 1975.[116]

The work-rich versus the work-poor divide translates into the income-rich versus the income-poor. Between 1984 and 1994, the gap widened, with the top 20 per cent of households receiving 40 per cent of total household disposable income (an average of $1205 per week) and the bottom 20 per cent receiving only a six per cent share (an average of $175 per week). Harding expresses this in terms of the GINI Coefficient of household inequality, which shows a rise for wage and salary earners from 0.500 in 1982 to 0.537 in 1993. In general, one-person households (the elderly and young singles) have lower incomes, whereas the proportion of two-income households has increased.[117]

The recent review of Australia's welfare system shows how unwieldy and costly ($41.36 billion in 1998–99) is our current social security system, with one in every seven Australians receiving some form of welfare payment, 21 per cent of families with dependent children being one-parent families, and a staggering 860,000 children living in households where neither parent works in a paid job.[118]

Using the Henderson Poverty Line (now much in dispute as a measure) to compare income units between 1972 and 1990, Saunders found the proportion of Australian income units in poverty had increased from 11.1 per cent to 16.7 per cent.[119] Others, such as Johnson, Manning and Hellwig, argue that the gap between income units has been kept relatively small because of the careful targeting of income security, family allowance payments and other benefits to low income families.[120] Their assessment of inequality in Australia is not so negative, but it is clear that government policies aimed at income redistribution are crucial.[121]

Current controversy over the regressive impact of a GST on food and other necessities, the inequity of bigger tax cuts for high income earners than for the less well off, and the need for a broader tax base to sustain government-funded services and transfer payments, is a timely reminder that the future could easily see the demise of the nation of supposed equals.

Not only has unemployment risen, but so, too, has long-term un-employment. In the 1970s, only a few thousand people were out of work for more than 52 weeks. By 1996, 150,000 had been continuously unemployed for over two years.

Australian Bureau of Statistics (ABS) figures show that for those who left full-time education in 1976, 74 per cent went into full-time jobs, only six per cent took part-time jobs, 14 per cent were unemployed and six per cent stayed out of the labour force.[122] In contrast, for those who left full-time education in 1995, only 50 per cent went into full-time jobs, 23 per cent entered part-time work, seven per cent were not in the labour force, and a massive 20 per cent were unemployed.

Moreover, employment opportunities and unemployment always cluster in certain geographic areas, no longer simply because those without qualifications concentrate there, but because structural shifts in the market have destroyed whole industries and employing companies. Rural regions seem to have been hit more than the larger cities, but the controversies over National Textiles and over the closure of BHP's steelworks in Newcastle are typical.

ABS figures illustrate how wide the gap has become. Small towns in rural Victoria have an average household income that is half that of households in Canberra. Between 1986 and 1996, the richest 10 per cent of areas increased their share of Australia's average household equivalent income from 13.9 per cent to 15 per cent. The poorest 30 per cent of areas saw their share fall from 24.6 per cent to 23.9 per cent.[123] The gap is almost as wide between central urban and fringe suburban regions, making the patchwork quilt very lumpy indeed.

Nor is it only the destruction of industry that makes for regional variations. A 1998 Productivity Commission Report shows that, between 1970 and 1990, industries such as food and beverages, paper and printing, chemicals and basic metal products increased in size relative to other manufacturing, but fabricated metal products and textiles, clothing and footwear declined.[124] The authors point out, too, that those regions which have experienced high levels of structural change without employment growth are typically reliant on single industries, such as mining, with fewer service-sector jobs. High structural change areas with high employment growth are more diversified, with a high share of services jobs, such as Queensland's Moreton region, Cairns, and the outer Adelaide region in South Australia.

Families are thus differentially affected according to where they live and work and the nature of the work they do. Levels of disease, general health and even life expectancy vary dramatically by region and suburban location.

The most striking effect of Australian structural and regional change is, as elsewhere, the emergence of social movements aimed at stopping or at least redirecting economic and social change.

In Australia, perhaps the most dramatic of the social movements prompted by such fear and alienation is the One Nation Party, led by Pauline Hanson. Its appeal is multifaceted — an expression of fear of global trade and multinational corporations; a resentment of what was termed 'special interest politics', directed particularly at Aboriginal people, multiculturalism and those on welfare; a call for ordinary Australians to be accorded the same rights as members of these special interest groups; a nationalistic rejection of our growing economic ties with Asia and the rest of the world; a racist and ethnically biased attack on cultural difference; and an outright cry of anger at the perceived indifference of major political parties towards the hardships being suffered in regions, especially rural and northern, as a result of the sort of structural change outlined above.

Most political analysts now agree that Hansonism tapped a common chord of dissatisfaction with top-down policy-making, a widely shared distrust of politicians seen to be out of touch with the common good, and in particular, the rich vein of regional self-interest that lies beneath any notion of national identity. The major parties have scrambled to redress their myopia, urged along by repeated victories for minor party and Independent candidates, the near demise of the National Country Party in Victoria, and a new-found awareness by the Canberra Press Gallery that what goes on in Canberra does not necessarily represent the public interest. The fact that One Nation lost force quickly as a viable political movement does not invalidate its original causes; rather, it reflects the emergence of more credible independent candidates who know their own electorates and appeal directly to their interests, the obvious ineptitude of Pauline Hanson and her key people, and the rapid attention paid by the major parties to rural and regional concerns. One Nation's renewed influence in state elections in 2001 resulted in part from the tactic of targeting incumbent parties, and also from scepticism about the real intentions of the major parties. It remains to be seen whether they can sustain their support.[125]

Several other social movements, less well publicised, have arisen in protest against the ravages of neo-liberalism. The call has been to combine social concerns with those of economic efficiency, to see the inevitable link between community wellbeing and quality of life and the state of the economy.

In Australia, the most active movements seem to have occurred in Victoria, the state led most vigorously by the conservative reform government of Jeff Kennett from October 1992 until its shock defeat in September 1999. Justifying smaller government and the rationalisation of services on the basis of a budgetary hole allegedly left by the Cain and Kirner Labor Governments, the Liberal-National Government rapidly reduced spending on schools, hospitals, police and community welfare services. Democratically elected local government was abolished for a time, with commissioners appointed by the government to revamp the administrative structures and set up systems that were more accountable to the central minister. Protests failed to change policies which saw public transport, gas, prisons and hospitals privatised; 300 smaller schools were closed or amalgamated; the ambulance service became a source of huge controversy; trams blocked the streets of Melbourne in protest.

Some of this reform led to improved efficiency and apparently lower costs, but like all privatisation action, it left the state with few assets from which to derive revenue in subsequent years. Some 37,000 public servants and 8000 teachers lost their jobs, and 35,000 employees of government businesses were made redundant.[126]

The perceived arrogance and indifference to opposing views of the Kennett Government including the muzzling of the Auditor General, use of the confidentiality clause in publicly tendered contracts, a much reduced time for parliamentary debate, and restrictions on disclosures under freedom of information, led to its defeat in the elections held in September 1999, a shock both to the incumbent government and to an Opposition not fully prepared for taking office.

The People Together group was formed by ex-Public Advocate Ben Bodna and the wife of Victoria's then-Governor, Jean McCaughey, both highly respected opinion leaders and academics. They formed a committee of interested people and started to document the impact of Kennett's privatisation and rationalisation policies on the quality of community life. Claims of political neutrality were dismissed by Kennett, and he publicly vilified these 'pseudo-lefties' as stooges of the Labor Party. But their public meetings across Victorian country centres attracted hundreds of concerned citizens, while their Melbourne forums, such as the People Together Summit on Inequality, held in July 1998, attended by over 1000 people in the Melbourne Town Hall, drew big crowds. They published People Together reports documenting the damage done to many rural centres and suburbs by the withdrawal of government offices, the closure of schools, railway stations, post offices and banks which reflected the same driving ideology of economic efficiency regardless of social impact, and the alienation of those rural populations from the centralist managerialism of the Victorian Government. No-one at the centre was listening, until the 1999 election, which returned Labor candidates in rural areas traditionally held by the National Party and Independent members where neither party seemed to be attending to local concerns.

People Together merged in 1999 with a movement called Purple Sage, which was also actively documenting the expressed wishes of suburban and rural citizens. They, too, conducted a series of community seminars round Victoria, asking what people felt was needed in place of centralising cuts to services. Their report highlights precisely the sorts of issues that had antagonised the voting public to the point where, at the Benalla by-election of May 2000, a Labor Party candidate won the seat vacated by the former leader of the National Party, while Independents again polled significantly higher than either Liberal or National candidates.[127]

Two similar groups also came to light in 1998. The New Radical Centre claimed that: 'Our political parties are ideologically exhausted. They still boast of their capacity to deliver dividends and security to voters, but in the new context of globalisation, they know they cannot deliver. A spiral of deepening alienation threatens to engulf us. Labor and Liberal remain trapped within the old ideological preoccupation with categories of individual and state. Relations between individuals, how people associate with each other for mutual benefit, is the key to survival and wellbeing in the new order, but this way of thinking remains alien to the worldview of both parties. A new social and political movement is now crucial.'

Out of this grew Mutuality, another Melbourne-based organisation, which held its first public forum in November 1999.[128] Mutuality aims to build community and social trust and to strengthen civil society. Based on the notion of mutuality, which Britain's Demos organisation describes as 'the idea of the next century', Mutuality is also non-aligned politically, seeking 'to move beyond the old solutions advanced by Left and Right in order to tap the creativity, energy and commitment that dialogue and new forms of action can create'. It hopes to establish link groups across the sectors of academe, trade unions, service clubs and other community organisations, possibly some form of local parliament or community roundtable to discuss and debate matters of mutual, common-good concern.

What is most interesting is the fact that the old boundaries are shifting. Most discussions of regionalism tend to assume that electoral boundaries, or government departmental regional divisions, define natural regions, areas of common interest. Yet if we look at the renewed lobbying for water flow to be restored to the Snowy River, or the groups concerned with salinity in the Murray-Darling Basin, we see that they stretch across electoral boundaries, across state borders, across farming lobbies to environmental activists and business groups. If we look to examples of rural centres that have managed to survive and grow, such as Orange and Horsham, it is clear that their activism and success has come at a cost to smaller surrounding towns, once rival centres of population. Such growth towns still rely on farmers to an extent, but they draw in new businesses and public servants who do not identify themselves as rural but who do identify with the common good of the surrounding area, their 'place' of work and private living.

This suggests that the new tribalism need not be a negative, anti-government or anti-city force. It suggests that regional or area-wide loyalties can be developed in places that seem not to have had any common identity before, and that attempts to rejuvenate rust-belt cities or declining rural regions will need to draw on more than just the old ties and loyalties. Modern technology can be an ally in this process, but so, too, can government, in the way they manage and deploy revenue. Intelligent government will recognise the multi-hued nature of this patchwork country and resource each area to develop its own solutions to its unique needs.

Chapter 8

Finding a more intelligent role for government

GOVERNMENT IN THIS GLOBAL AGE becomes more problematic. It has to both preserve national integrity and build local and regional communities with the strength to thrive in an increasingly competitive environment.[129]

The shape of government in a complex information age will be neither 'big' nor 'small'. Such terms are hangovers from an outmoded debate. The task is now to rethink the processes of government to suit the demands of complexity and rapid change.

The term I prefer is intelligent government, or 're-engaged government', aimed at setting the conditions in which those other forms of capital essential to our survival as a nation — human/cultural capital, social capital and environmental capital — can develop and not be overwhelmed by concerns for financial capital alone. Government will create the patchwork quilt, stitching together loosely a variegated pattern of community resources and services customised to suit the different needs of different locations.[130]

Regions and communities differ so much in terms of their social make-up and their access to jobs, education and other social resources that the role of government needs to be transformed, as does the responsibility of business. People need to be resourced by government in order to build their own capacity to thrive economically, socially and culturally. They need resourcing from government at the centre, and a new structure of local and regional institutions that can respond appropriately and with entrepreneurial imagination to the real needs and interests of the community.

Because of the impossibility of applying uniform solutions to work and community problems, government provision will have to shift towards more regional and locally responsive solutions. Top-down planning will not suffice when business is responding to regional labour market skill gaps; improved links between regional schools, workplaces and community services will be essential.

Though there are dangers in such new tribalism, as we have already seen, a shared culture of regional concern is the only way of gearing up more innovative effort, because meaningful links between different sectors of society can be forged only in a geographical community context. Government cannot finance everything, so business will have to pick up some of the tab for resourcing the community and insisting that schools, training and welfare services support their employees' (and, thus, their own corporate) needs.

Several writers have predicted the decline of the nation-state as globalisation cuts across national economies and multinational companies shift both staffing and financial resources to those areas most conducive to stability and profit. Some argue there will be less need for the military power of the nation-state once we move from an economy based on material, energy and labour to one based on information and communications. As Rifkin puts it, global corporations are temporal, not spatial, not bound to one community or locale, though he ignores the ongoing potential for conflict over resources and living space to support expanding populations.[131] Since national governments can no longer control the electronic flow of money, or collect taxes efficiently from companies and individuals who invest and trade by electronic means, the role of central government as a guarantor of market transactions diminishes, as does its power to affect the wellbeing of its citizens. Ohmae goes further, suggesting that the era of national governments is virtually dead.[132]

Such a scenario raises legitimate concerns about many of the institutions that structure Australian life. However, it is too broad-brush and ignores the central role of politics and the powerful influence on social life of diverse cultural values within each nation-state. National differences in policy still matter.

For example, the way in which a nation such as Japan is influenced by the new global economy is vastly different from the way Australia is influenced by it. Japan retains its company-as-family approach to employment, and its closed circle of business leaders resists world pressure to open up the national economy. Australia has gone too fast in the opposite direction, replacing the old economic nationalism with an economic rationalism that has damaged the social fabric. France tries to reduce working hours across the board, both to improve the quality of life and to reduce unemployment, while Germany moves more and more towards a corporate state model based on technological incentives from government.

In other words, culture influences the way different nations adapt to the new global economy, and their relative power as nation-states in itself makes for a different response. Nor is it true that a small economy such as Australia's can have no influence against the larger world powers; Australia has had a major impact on modifying world trade policies through its leadership of the Cairns Group.

Nonetheless, it is clear that the Western democracies are shifting away from the post-War model of the corporate welfare state towards a much more loosely controlled economy and an attenuated grip on those matters affecting what has been called the 'common good'. The old ideological battle between economic and political liberalism and a managed social economy has re-emerged, with the free market triumphant, individual rights riding roughshod over social responsibilities, small government replacing the mammoth welfare state. As a result, government services have been privatised, cost efficiency valued more highly than effectiveness in terms of social outcomes, government accountability for the quality of community life reduced, and the concept of government as the provider of public services given way to competitive tendering of services to private providers, whose interest, inevitably, is profit, not broadly based public wellbeing.

Many Australians have forgotten, or have never known, how different was Australia's post-Federation arrangement from the sorts of social contract forged between governments and communities elsewhere. In the propaganda of what came to be called economic rationalism, one would have thought Australia was today in necessary retreat from a costly and invasive welfare state. What were in fact minor problems (such as a few cheats on the dole), and what were failures of management, not of the system as such (like Medicare fraud, or the huge state deficits in Victoria, Western Australia and South Australia in the late 1980s) came to be characterised as basic flaws of a supposed welfare state.

In reality, Australia was never a welfare state in any monolithic sense. Our Federation agreement arose from the reality of a new nation on a huge continent having to work more effectively across state borders and survive in a world of market competition. To be a citizen, you had to be male, white and gainfully employed. In return, the new federal government guaranteed protection of Australian industries and their products, security of employment via industrial awards, and a minimum welfare safety net to tide people over in hard times. Welfare payments were never generous, and it was only in the last few decades, when the participation of women in the paid labour force became essential to the economy, that wider infrastructural 'welfare' supports such as childcare and aged care received adequate funding.

The Hawke-Keating Labor Accord used the term 'social wage' to describe these benefits, in part as a trade-off against wage rises. The welfare bill grew largely because structural changes in the labour market destroyed jobs, because the population was ageing, and because family stability gave way to the demands of women for equal opportunity and a more satisfactory deal from their male partners. Australian governments have recognised the needs of children (for childcare, adequate family incomes, decent schooling) as a community responsibility, rather than one that could be left to the whims and varied fortunes of parents, and child poverty rates in Australia have dropped, not increased.[133]

Yet we have seen a strangely schizophrenic campaign by the Howard Government about the need for reciprocal obligations, personal responsibility and a return to family values.[134] This seems, on one level, to recognise that the individual, the family and, indeed, the community are subject to the decisions and values of big business and the global marketplace and thus are not entirely responsible for their own failures, and it calls for a social coalition, a partnership between government, business, community and individual citizens, to work together for the common social good.

Unfortunately, the measures taken to achieve this all press in the opposite direction. The individual unemployed person is seen as a dole bludger, an over-choosy 'job snob'; must be required to prove several weekly applications for work, however meaningless such applications may be; and is dealt with punitively through requirements to work for the dole or do community work or undertake some form of training, in the stated belief that they are tainted by the culture of poverty, not willing to work and earn their own keep. They have to be taught individual responsibility. In contrast, the big business side is enjoined to increase its philanthropic activity, to give more generously to the poor, rather than to change either their values or those basic business practices which have produced structural unemployment and social hardship. Small funding programs such as Business-Community Partnership grants offer a bit of window-dressing in the name of reciprocal obligation, while the underlying structures remain the same.

Government in Australia has to do better than this, because the old institutional framework is out of date in a global economy and recourse to individualistic value frameworks will not suffice. Every government around the world is facing the new dilemmas of global challenge. China may attempt to regulate and censor the Internet, but it must trade worldwide and mass communications will inevitably undermine tight ideological controls. Britain may be reluctant to adopt the euro, but its fortunes are inextricably linked with Europe and its success in gearing up for the knowledge-based future we all face. Australia cannot survive on the fringes of Asia and a globalised economy unless it addresses the way internal institutions work together to meet such new demands. And our political institutions are crucial determinants of how competent we will be in joining the global marketplace without being destroyed by it.

It is not simply a matter of finding a Third Way, like Clinton's new democracy or Blair's attempt to marry a free-market economy with a social conscience, for Blair's Third Way is based on that same dichotomy of government versus private control. As *Time* magazine quotes him:

> Yes, there is a Third Way. The United States under the Clinton administration is trying to do this. For a lot of people in the first half of the century, government was the answer. For that period it was the answer. For that period it was the correct answer. Then the Right came along and said the answer was to get rid of government. The essence of the Third Way is to say that the role of government is to organise and secure provision rather than fund it all. For example, in pension reform, people will have to provide more of their own financial independence, but government has a role in organising that system.[135]

The danger of going along with slogans such as the Third Way is that we will simply develop unsatisfactory compromises between the common-good interests of government and the private interests of business, which in a global age cut across national boundaries.

Certain areas of government can never be handed over to private or community control — defence, core communications, and law and order. Others may be privatised but constrained by national interest — power supplies, health, education and transport. Government must set the policy parameters and allocate budget resources to maintain efficient and equitable distribution in these areas. Yet such areas, and certainly others like family support services, can be, and should be, under the more direct control of local and regional communities who know their own patch, their own needs, and how best to meet them.

The role of government is to ensure, as best it can, the wellbeing of its citizens within the national community. That requires a set of articulated values and policies that go beyond simply managing the economy so that it serves shareholders and ensures some degree of equity, justice for all, and inclusion in the business of national governance. This book is an attempt to outline how we might rethink some of our most central institutional structures to achieve such an outcome. It is a call for an 'Australian Way' that preserves the best of the past and guarantees a vital future.

Section 3

Linking the patchwork — finding an Australian Way

Chapter 9

Building human and social capital

THE BLIND SPOT IN CURRENT policy-making is the lack of integration between economic and social matters. Money capital and financial growth have become goals in themselves, supposedly producing enhanced wellbeing for the citizens, but operating in isolation from those other social institutions that directly affect the quality of people's lives.

Business relies on human capital and adopts the slogan that 'people are our most important resource', but in this formulation, people are still merely a means to an end, a resource (like iron ore) used to make money. There are other forms of capital that both business and government need to consider if they are to work for the nation. Above all, their goal must be capacity-building, both in terms of the capacity of individual human beings and in terms of nurturing the networks and relationships constituting what is called 'social capital'.[135a]

The term human or 'cultural capital' refers to those individual human capacities nurtured within family and community groups, the skills by which we cope with and learn to control our own environment, the knowledge and adaptability gained through education in its broadest sense — experience at work and our general adult experience — and the sense of meaning that grows from the symbolic activities of arts, sports, music, reading and cultural interaction with diverse others.

In business jargon, the old terms 'personnel management' and 'employee relations' have been replaced by 'human resource management', but few companies actually know how to measure the value of their human resources. Boston Consulting Group suggests, 'If a company were as ill-informed about its capital performance as most companies are about their employee performance, it would be in serious trouble with the investor community. In the new economy, they will have to treat their knowledge base, their human capital, as being of equal significance to their financial capital base. They will have to understand that know-how is created out of human interaction. 'It is a process, not a commodity.'[136] Human capital cannot be owned by a company, and knowledge workers will change jobs if that necessary human interaction is not encouraged and rewarded.

This makes networks and social interaction ever more central to business success, as witnessed by the flourishing and open communication between rival companies in Silicon Valley, California. They exchange ideas and information, and all benefit. The whole region benefits, because this social capital aids and abets the development of human capital, and its outcome in the financial growth of competing, but related, firms.

Social capital grows out of those social interactions and networks we experience in our daily lives. It is not a quality of individuals but, rather, a quality of a group or community as a whole. Bourdieu understands social capital as the networks that provide access to other resources.[137] Coleman describes it as those relationships and ties, the networks, norms and sanctions, that facilitate the attainment of human capital.[138] Putnam defines social capital as the trust, norms and networks that facilitate cooperation for mutual benefit.[139] It is an attribute of a social group or a region as a whole, if it has extensive networks of information and exchange based on mutual trust and reciprocity. Large extended families can benefit fellow members through their internal and external connections. Putnam's work on Italian regional differences in economic development showed the value of informal networks and extensive voluntary associations.

Social capital both arises out of and helps build a sense of social trust, the norm of reciprocity on which social exchange is based. Without trust, cooperation is impossible; without cooperation, society-building cannot happen — the freeloaders and Machiavellis take it all. Within the family or clan, trust relationships and networks are strong. Within a voluntary group, the ties may be weak and temporary, but they are based on trust and reciprocity, a sense of working together for common benefit. Social capital is, therefore, a resource to collective action, and nations that divide into warring ethnic groups, or communities that exclude those different from themselves, deny themselves optimum access to development, seeing survival as depending solely on the limited social trust and networks of their own in-group, sadly, in many cases, a realistic view.

Environmental capital obviously refers to industrial society's new-found concern for the quality of our natural environment, for the misuse and depletion of natural resources by one generation at the expense of subsequent generations. Business corporations and governments have only recently acknowledged that environmental quality is vital to economic productivity, to financial capital and to growth in the long term, and much lobbying is still focused on convincing companies that they must be environmentally sensitive and that being so can also improve their profitability.

Since I am no expert on environmental issues, I leave that discussion to others. But it is worth noting that groups such as Land Care in Australia are a vital force for building social capital, bringing together farmers, business leaders and community members to work on improving the quality of their shared environment and on devising more environmentally friendly methods of land use for the future. Oxley is probably right in saying that the key environmental issues are population density and the shortage of water in developing countries.[140] Access to electricity may be more of a solution to disease, squalor and war than a threat to the environment, and paternalistic Western attitudes do need to be examined critically.

In general, business firms do understand that human and cultural capital, in the form of education, training, knowledge and adaptability, are essential to capital growth, though it has taken a long time for them to move from exploitation of expendable labour to any real sense of caring for their workers as the essence of business ethics and the foundation for financial success. Some companies have even advanced to an understanding that they can profit, in terms of both public image and profitability, from being sensitive to the environmental impacts of 'green' policies. But they have yet to realise that social environments can also be toxic, and that social capital needs to be nurtured and developed if business is to build financial capital.

Building social capital must become a central goal of governments at every level. The outcomes would be a more civil society, where tolerance, mutual respect and meaningful relationships prevent social disintegration in the form of family breakdown, delinquency, crime, interest-group conflict and ethnic violence, and where business can thrive. Clearly, it is a goal worth striving for. Without a civil society, we have either the law of the jungle or totalitarian state control, both based on fear, distrust and deceit, both yielding highest gains to those with power — physical, economic or educational.

But how do we develop social capital? Is it a thing that can be produced, nurtured, undermined, misused? Or is it just an academic concept that serves as a catch-all for a range of other qualities that can be more clearly targeted?

In the Australian political debate, it is perhaps ironic that the Labor Party, which has in its midst people such as Mark Latham and Lindsay Tanner, who understand and espouse British Labour's notion of the Third Way, is reluctant to acknowledge any value in the government's attempts to address social capital. I am myself critical of the limited range of the Howard Government's conception of how the social contract, reciprocal obligations, family and community support should be handled. But it seems clear that the $240 million Family Fund package announced in April 2000 was a step in the right direction. It includes funding (admittedly, on a small scale compared with the UK's program tackling social exclusion) for what they call the 'Can-do community' ($5.2 million), providing new ideas to solve local problems and recognising the best examples of collaborative community action programs.

Another $15.4 million over four years was for 'local solutions to local problems', converting unused buildings for community use and setting up mentoring programs and food programs for families in difficulty. As well, $37.1 million was allocated to identify community leaders in socially disadvantaged areas and support their work on programs to benefit the community. A further $15.8 million was to promote volunteer work and to train those running services heavily dependent on volunteers. All this was coupled with new initiatives to strengthen families ($40 million) through playgroups, mothers' groups and community services; to train parents ($47.3 million), with a focus on early intervention support for at-risk families; and to provide more in-home childcare choices ($65.4 million) for shift workers, families with sick children and those who live too far from normal childcare centres.

While it is true that $240 million is a drop in the ocean compared with what is needed, or compared with the funds previously pulled out of childcare and other family support services by both federal and state governments, it does signal a move away from top-down government-provided services towards the sensible resourcing of families at the local level.

This is the only way to engage people in community work. It is far better to resource — that is, to fund and offer expert advice — the development of social capital than to leave it to chance and unequal local resources or to dictate from the top what people need to do to solve their own problems.

Community members need to define their own problems, work out the most appropriate solutions, and themselves administer the programs and processes they set up. Leadership needs to be nurtured at the local level; we can't simply assume it exists already.

As well, the aim is preventative rather than curative; it is spending on the fence around the top of the cliff, not on funding the ambulance at the bottom. It should signal a return to real family support, help ordinary people will welcome because it is timely, relevant to their immediate needs, and locally available, locally controlled and locally effective.

Instead of giving a supportive reaction (such as that of ACOSS president Michael Raper), the Opposition spokesperson, having to do the negative thing, described the government's initiatives as 'a gimmick', and the Democrats were 'a little sceptical'. Of course, any government should be criticised for increasing the costs of childcare for many families, and for economic policies that have driven thousands of families into unemployed poverty and the very welfare dependency the government deplores. But, surely, the more appropriate political ploy, and the most socially responsible policy response, would be to praise the initiative and its social capital-building goals and argue for more of the same, with vastly increased funding for every Australian community.

The UK, for example, has established a National Strategy for Neighbourhood Renewal. Its goal is to devolve services to the local level, and integrate them across departments and agencies to produce a more holistic approach to family and community problems. There is a clear recognition of the challenges to be faced: a change in culture and career structures for government bureaucrats; a willingness to give locals power and responsibility and a consequent need for suitable performance measurement, regulation and audit mechanisms; building into the equation community-owned assets so that it is not totally dependent on government funding; offering training and employment opportunities for local, non-professional residents within the public service; and above all, embedding a long-term perspective in local-governance processes. Taylor suggests that these problems will be overcome only by setting up Regional Development Agencies and a Neighbourhood Development Fund to train more community development workers and to shift the balance of power away from the centre and towards the regions themselves.[141]

To me, this is the way to go. Families operate at the local and regional level, yet family support services are controlled by central authorities and non-government agencies who have little idea of the diversity of local needs or even of the diversity of family types that would benefit from positive resourcing and empowerment.

For years, Australian family policy has suffered from the knee-jerk political Labor response opposing whatever the Liberal-National coalition suggests, with the result that preventative family support services have declined, community development has dropped off the agenda, and central managerialism, with its top-down, targeted services approach, rides rampant over the diversity of approach needed to build a truly civil society and to encourage the growth of those skills and attitudes that form both human and social capital.

The following chapters attempt to show how more intelligent government and business processes might operate to better link the future within a patchwork of diverse regions and localities.

Chapter 10

Redefining regionalism: the way forward

I HAVE BEEN ARGUING FOR A more locally responsive approach to community concerns on the part of both business and government. But nostalgic reference to the good old days of close-knit communities misses the fact that the nature of family, work and social life has changed.

As I have already indicated, the family as we have known it is no longer as central as it once was, and many people no longer make their social contacts through churches, sports groups and voluntary clubs, so new linkages have to be forged. Many of the new linkages will come through the workplace, with colleagues being a significant reference group. Such ties may be looser or weaker than some would like, but new connections with the local community are possible and a resurgence of regional and local identity is on the cards. Most voluntary activities have always involved loose rather than close personal ties, and they are no less valuable for that in the task of building social capital across a region or area.

Indeed, we have to address the value of loose ties in our global future. At the first conference held by Mutuality, in Melbourne in July 1999, several scenarios focused on this issue. Terms such as 'connectedness in diversity', 'corporate-citizenship alliances', 'community bio-zones', 'common-good roundtables', 'steps across the chasms', 'natural capitalism', 'communities can' and 'resourcing citizenship' give some flavour of how people want to proceed. One participant challenged prevailing social values by asking, 'Are we lions or hyenas? Lions kill and eat only what they need to live; hyenas will get in and rip for the sake of the hunt, leaving much waste behind.'

Another image I liked was that of 'loose ties', where a bundle of threads of different colour and thickness are tied together loosely at different points. Whereas you can break any one thread by pulling hard, you can't break the bundle of loose ties, because they hang together. The ties represent the rules, the guidelines set by small government to tie diverse people and communities together for a common social purpose. This is close to the image of the patchwork quilt used in this book — unique sections joined together by a common thread and agreed purpose.

Recent political interest in rural and regional Australia may be driven by political opportunism, but it is a move in the right direction. As outlined above, far from becoming more united in terms of identity or social cohesion, Australia is in danger of splintering into 'tribes' — unequal, competing for scarce resources, and wasteful of emotional and creative energy. Rather than let such division simmer and grow, governments would be wise to harness this mood to restructure the delivery of government resources in ways that engender productive outcomes.

The central aim of government should be to replace political and social disempowerment with community-based economic development and social wellbeing. Government needs to reconceptualise its role as one of facilitating community-building through a range of genuine partnerships with business and community organisations, not as providing (or even purchasing) services top-down.

Political parties must value citizenship and democracy and make the formal systems of government more directly accountable to the community of citizens. Each region across Australia needs to be resourced so that it can, in its own way, restore economic resilience, enhance the physical environment, protect social vitality and 'thicken' the democratic process. The 'new democracy' demands more active involvement in the services traditionally 'provided' to the 'needy' by government and non-government agencies. The role of business in developing this new network of community infrastructure is vital.

Political interest in regional development is not new. The history of the National/Country Party is one of special pleading for the interests of rural versus urban. In the early 1970s, the Whitlam Labor Government tried to decentralise and revitalise the diverse regions of Australia through community development schemes such as the Australian Assistance Plan, community medicine, regional economic assistance, and the Disadvantaged Schools Program. Paul Keating's 1994 'Working Nation' White Paper on Employment and Growth led to a subsequent paper on 'Business Investment and Regional Prosperity: the Challenge of Rejuvenation' in March 1994 and the McKinsey report, 'Lead Local Compete Global', in July 1994. Bill Kelty chaired the Labor Government's Task Force on Regional Development, and other reports were produced by the Industry Commission and the Bureau of Industry Economics. The Howard Government has continued this interest, and has established a number of Area Consultative Committees in each state to stimulate regional leadership and a more integrated approach to regional development. One might well wonder why the rural and regional sector felt so disenchanted and rebellious that it flirted with Pauline Hanson and led to a subsequent panic reaction by the major parties.

The way Australian political and business leaders interpreted neo-liberal theory led them to make some major mistakes. Companies downsized unthinkingly, government and business reduced services that were the lifeline of local, especially rural, communities (including schools, hospitals, post offices, banks, railway stations, welfare centres), and economic theory ran rampant over a focus on the wellbeing of ordinary people. Self-congratulation, seeming indifference to human concerns and rapacious business leadership, especially in the late 1980s, added to the unrest of people who felt increasingly ignored, increasingly disenfranchised.

A common thread in all of this was the agreement by Australian governments (April 1995) to adopt a package of reforms known as National Competition Policy, which aimed 'to encourage competition, not just in particular sectors, but across the whole economy'. The *Trade Practices Act* was amended, the Australian Competition and Consumer Commission (ACCC) was set up, and the states and territories enacted legislative changes to reform all restrictive practices by the year 2000. An important principle was that of competitive neutrality, which meant that government businesses should not enjoy any competitive advantage simply as a result of their public sector ownership. Though local councils were not signatories to the Competition Principles Agreement, it has also been applied to local government. Public monopolies such as Australia Post were thus pushed to operate as commercial businesses, though not necessarily privatised, with provision for third party access to infrastructure facilities, such as gas pipelines and phone cables, so that competitors could sell gas or Internet access without duplicating the facilities themselves.

It is important to understand that National Competition Policy was not intended to apply to community services such as education, health and welfare services, but because the ethos of competition as the answer to society's ills was so strong, state governments, especially that in Victoria, moved to apply the same principles to services that were not strictly businesses at all. Simply by changing grants to welfare agencies into contracts, business assumptions were introduced.

Moreover, despite the assertion that the goal was not competition in itself but, rather, 'creating the right blend of economic and social responsibilities', public interest tests designed to exempt certain functions from competition rules were left vague and open to dispute. The intention was to apply public interest considerations to matters of ecologically sustainable development, social welfare and equity, and economic and regional development, including employment and investment growth, the interests of consumers and the efficient allocation of resources. The benefits to the community of such legislation or programs had to outweigh the costs.

But it is not so easy to define public interest or to measure costs and benefits. There was little notice taken of how, for example, the closure of an industry in a country town might impact on other public interest activities, such as the relocation of other industries or the demise of community-based services because of population reductions. The effect was that social goals and public interest issues were relegated to being secondary or residual welfare considerations. Within government itself, administrators rushed like lemmings to apply competition principles inappropriately to community services and the non-government service providers, ignoring other publicly stated goals such as community development, social justice and reciprocal obligations within a so-called social compact.[142]

On the plus side, tariff reduction, more flexible industrial relations and technological innovation prepared Australia well for what Oxley predicts will be the third 'golden age'.[143] But it also made rust buckets out of states such as South Australia and Tasmania, Victoria being rescued by a Kennett Government which arrogantly put economic progress ahead of social and community development and the essence of democratic processes.

Regional development became a commonly accepted goal, but it was undermined in many ways by competition policy and the arbitrary slashing of government services in the name of efficiency. As the ACOSS paper discussing competition policy puts it, 'The Agreement does not allow for the fact that different goals or outcomes might be given different weightings in different locations or circumstances. For example, in a country town, closure of an industry is likely to have a direct impact on employment and be a trigger for other services and industries to close or relocate.'[144]

The key impact of globalisation and competition policy combined is to make regional interests increasingly important. As noted in Chapter 2, structural change in Australian industry has not been uniform, making regions reliant on one dominant industry alone more vulnerable than those with a variety of markets to exploit or those luckily focused on what the new economy needs. Every government must take note of this in the way it handles expenditure on services, whether they be for health, education and training, family support or industry assistance. In the global world, regions within nations are largely on their own, but governments have a responsibility to help them make the adjustment to increased competition.

The McKinsey report comments: 'We are witnessing an historic shift in our global economic landscape ... businesses compete with businesses around the globe. Likewise, regions compete with other regions from around the world to provide the best environments for their existing regions to grow and attract relocating businesses ... Automobile manufacturers in Geelong and Elizabeth compete with each other and with those in Mexico City and Stuttgart ... regions control much of the agenda.'[145]

However, reporting on economic change has focused on the decline of rural regions and has developed a sense of panic not justified by the facts. The McKinsey study found that while some regions were indeed in decline (41 per cent of regions, but only 12 per cent of the non-metropolitan population), many were growing faster than the capital cities (24 per cent of regions and 36 per cent of the non-metropolitan population).

The factors explaining the difference were, of course, complex: the impact of structural change in Australia's industry generally; the mix of industries in a region; the quality of infrastructure, such as transport and communication; the quality of regional leadership, both governmental and business; a lack of red tape; and the effectiveness of networks across a region (as in Putnam's Italian study of regional development). More than two-thirds of investment in regions came from local, already-existing businesses, and the more effective regions were those able to attract new investment, expand the range of regional infrastructure and invest in the training of skilled people.

Another process of forging new links is emerging in the form of business alliances across the global marketplace. This is an alternative to the usual merger and takeover activity, which involved $US650 billion in the first four months of 1998 alone, and carries with it the advantages of drawing on the local knowledge of firms already in place and access to extra resources without the risks of going it alone. Samsung, for example, has built itself up over the past two decades through hundreds of licensing agreements and joint ventures with such firms as Sanyo, NEC, Hyundai, Sega, Microsoft and Motorola. Australian companies such as Cochlear and Southcorp are using alliances as part of their growth strategy, and Orica is negotiating a joint venture with the South African chemicals, explosives and fertiliser group AECI.

Of course, there is danger in forming an alliance that is one-sided, but cooperation with related industries and local institutions can obviously pay. Gettler points out the problems of trying to marry unequals, and when different ownership structures, goals and management cultures get in the way. But modern manufacturing is now about managing the entire value chain, from raw materials to the end consumer, and many of the new manufacturers see themselves not as wholly independent companies, but as part of an interdependent chain of suppliers and downstream customers, with alliance partners, focused on a win-win outcome for them all.

Population size is important if a region is to reach a critical mass of activities and services, so a local government focus or a focus on one town alone is unlikely to be adequate for effective development. Success stories like Mandurah in Western Australia, Horsham in Victoria, Broken Hill and Orange in NSW, or Cairns and Darwin depend in large part on their links to regional networks of productive businesses and social contacts. Regional development depends vitally on the links between economic and social development.

In fact, as the recent work of Putnam, Ostrom and Brain shows, the most economically viable regions (whether they be in northern Italy, Silicon Valley, Seattle or Sydney) are those that build an intense network of cooperation and interchange.[146] They are those areas with manifest social capital, but they have that because people are well educated, highly skilled and creative, share their information and exchange ideas, and network on a regional basis.[147]

The key factors in successful regional development appear to be:

- partnership, not competition, between business leaders across an area, working together to reduce red tape and improve regional infrastructure;
- collaboration across sectors, with the formation of new alliances between schools, training colleges and industry, between business and community services, and between welfare agencies, schools and firms;
- all levels of government — local, state and federal — working closely with business and community organisations to avoid wasteful duplication, facilitate innovation and develop a shared vision of regional development;

- authorities acting as facilitators, enablers and consensus-builders on social and economic priorities and goals, not as final arbiters of what can be done and how it must be done;
- a decentralisation of public authority, not central control from state head office;
- thinking laterally about resources, both physical and human, and pooling those resources across regions and localities, as in the Country Education Project (see below), paring back the narrow rivalries of smaller, less viable units of organisation;
- the capacity to harness those resources to bring about needed change (as Putnam puts it, 'the local transformation of local structures', or as Ostrom puts it, 'institutional action learning'), which requires government and business funding of community-building and leadership skills;
- a focus on long-term planning, with an eye on results and outcomes, not just processes;
- agencies being licensed to work entrepreneurially, not rule-bound and restricted to narrowly defined categories;
- a focus on citizens, their views and needs, not just the service providers, and a focus on customers beyond as well as within the region; and
- wide participation by citizens in ways relevant to their interests, in order to build up the social capital on which new initiatives across the region can be developed.

The following chapter describes projects in which I have been involved, where new alliances have been formed successfully across regions or areas that formerly had little sense of common interest or cohesion. They might serve as Australian examples of how future governments could reform the way administrative silos at the centre operate, so that a more integrated, more holistic, better linked and more place-based system could build communities that are viable both socially and economically. The political debate has to stop talking about the social and the economic as if they were separate and unequal. One sphere cannot operate without the other.

Chapter 11

Workable models of community-building

IT IS MY OWN EXPERIENCE THAT THE culture of workplaces, the culture of narrow community prejudices, and the culture of education and other community services can be transformed. It can be done, in fact, at little direct cost, but is most effective where the direction of government funding shifts from a top-down, administration-heavy approach to service delivery towards a more decentralised, less strictly controlled system that trusts local and regional communities to know best what is in their own interests and to spend government money in more accountable and more efficient ways in their own regions.

The following case studies give some flavour of how government, working in partnership with business and other community organisations, could proceed to rejuvenate regional economies and build more trusting and innovative communities for the future.

The Country Education Project: new tribes

The judicious handling of resources can help develop new regional loyalties and actions. It can create positive new tribes out of disadvantage and dissent.

In the 1980s, I chaired a project which developed a new approach to funding rural schools which still serves as a model for the future — the Country Education Project.[148]

Some readers will remember the days of the Australian Assistance Plan (AAP), established by the Whitlam Labor Government in the early 1970s. Some will insist that it was a failure, a costly administrative shambles that had no lasting effect. I disagree, because it did generate a remarkable growth in the number of non-profit organisations providing community services, and because it was based on a principle with even more relevance to social conditions today: that communities need to be resourced by government so they can themselves identify and plan the services they need in order to survive in a global economy.[149] The example that follows is not from the AAP, but it does show how sensible government intervention can generate new 'tribes' that enhance the common good and strengthen the civil society rather than dividing and disrupting it.

Back in the late 1970s, the then Schools Commission had been funding disadvantaged schools across Australia as separate entities, based on a database which measured the proportion of children who came from poor homes, single-parent homes, and non-English-speaking homes. The aim was to better resource those disadvantaged schools, mostly in the cities and the poorer suburbs, to ensure more equal educational opportunity for such children. A great deal of innovative work was done, but the system tended to be arbitrary because of the measurement categories used to qualify schools for extra funding.

The Commission wanted to find a new approach to addressing rural disadvantage, assumed to lie in the schools' geographic isolation, small size, lack of specialist teachers, lack of access to libraries and so on. In Victoria, we argued against funding separate small rural schools on a submission basis. We felt the focus should shift from a deficit model to one of building on resources and existing strengths. We argued that clusters of rural schools should work together, pooling their resources, sharing the new funds available through the program, finding more innovative ways of addressing rural educational problems.

We also argued that education did not happen in the schools alone — parents, the wider community and business were all involved — and that the disadvantage of rural children could not be effectively addressed unless we tackled the quality of inputs from their parents and other community members. The philosophy was one of building on existing resources, cooperation rather than competition between schools, and developing a whole-of-area approach to tackling educational disadvantage. This would require active involvement on the part of the schools and their wider communities, and a change of culture in the way people thought about education.

That change of culture was not easy to produce, but the answer lay in a combination of top-down guidelines combined with locally autonomous decision-making about how those guidelines would be implemented. The first requirement was that country areas be designated for funding. The usual indicators were used — distance, poverty, social disadvantage — but with an overlay of potential networks for joint activity between and across schools. Railway and road links, primary feeder schools to secondary schools, and existing community networks were studied.

Our guidelines specified that Catholic and private schools had to work with state schools, primary with secondary, and any program they devised for funding had to be shared across the entire area, not just run in one school alone. We said we would not fund separate schools for equipment, but were looking for innovative ways of addressing the educational disadvantages each Local Area Committee saw as most pressing for its area.

This led to the designation of groupings that were not 'areas' or 'regions' in the normally accepted sense. For example, the Mallee Tracks Area brought together schools as far apart as Murrayville and Patchewollock; the Gippsland Area linked tiny schools in the forests such as Tubbutt with Orbost; the Western Wimmera Area combined places as far apart as Casterton and Horsham. Schools in other areas were closer geographically, such as those in the King-Ovens Valley Area, with a heavy concentration of non-English-speaking families.

The local people exploded in protest, saying they never had anything to do with that town, had rival footy teams and different local shire councils, didn't get on, were rivals economically. Schools were too far apart to work together on shared programs; we didn't know what we were doing. I was called first an 'academic', then a 'bureaucratic academic', then a 'bloody bureaucratic city academic'. At meeting after meeting in cold halls and tiny schools, we explained the philosophy and aims of the project. We stuck to our guns and proved that we meant to have them control the implementation of the program, not have us impose top-down solutions on them, but insisted the broad guidelines had to be followed.

The next step was even harder. We said that half the members of the Local Area Committees had to be teachers, the other half members of the community. Each would select its own coordinator, who would be paid out of Schools Commission funds, but this person was not to be a teacher. Some school principals and inspectors objected, arguing that teachers and parents should dominate, but we stressed that educational disadvantage had to be addressed by the whole community. The Area Committees found very creative people as coordinators — one a hippy activist, one a farmer, one a single mother, others who were involved in community development work already — some choices surprising ones.

Then we told them we wanted a survey done, by them, to identify both needs and resources. The needs they could understand, but 'resources'? The project executive officer and I spent hours explaining that resources could be either physical or human: a farmer who had engineering skills, a woman who was an expert in rose-pruning, an older person with musical talent, a disused hall, a craftsperson working alone, old sports equipment or musical instruments.

The Committees organised school children to ask their parents what they knew that might be helpful in teaching others and what 'stuff' there was lying around that might be useful to the schools; the committee members and teachers interviewed parents and other community members about what they had to offer and what areas of disadvantage they thought were priorities. All of this was done with full knowledge that the Central Planning Committee had limited funds and that funds would be available only for projects shared across the Areas and between schools. There was no cargo cult bottomless pit for special pleading by any one school.

The wealth of community activity and enthusiasm generated by this approach was amazing. People found they were suddenly empowered by a system traditionally managed from the city, rigid in its supervision, bureaucratic in its procedures. The Central Planning Committee had most trouble, in fact, with the Education Department bureaucrats, who wanted to see every invoice, with all purchases to be made through the city office. We appealed to the minister of the day, and had a strong ally in the head of the planning division, who had helped develop the philosophy of the Country Education Project with us, and got these demands overturned.

That removed the hostility of the country people; they now saw us as allies against the central bureaucrats, and trustworthy in delivering what we had promised them — local control of the processes. We also had trouble from the Schools Commission itself, which told us we could not spend money on parents or other adults, because it was a schools project. We held out against this, pointing to the wording of the program guidelines, which stated that funds were to be spent 'in relation to' the education of rural school students, not 'on' them alone. As we had argued from the outset, if an Area came up with a proposal for parents to be involved in reading skills, that was just as likely as a students-only program to help students. The scheme became more legitimate with each victory on process, and the groundswell of support grew.

This was the very essence of community development. We had an executive officer and local coordinators explaining the philosophy, guiding each Local Area Committee's work, making links across schools and other local organisations, reporting back to us and to the schools. Teachers were now working with parents and with others who had resources to offer. Members of the community were being recognised for a wide range of talents — ideas, practical skills and knowledge. Schools once far apart were talking with one another, and these arbitrarily defined 'Areas' were becoming 'communities' in a sense no-one had thought possible.

We had, in effect, created in each Area a new tribe, a new grouping with a common interest in the educational wellbeing of children, with access not just to additional Schools Commission funds, but also to a range of resources no-one previously had known existed. Out of conflict (with us, and over access to scarce funds) had arisen a cooperative community that now went beyond old parochial rivalries and saw development occurring because of the new links they had made, following the guidelines set down by the Central Planning Committee.

To give a flavour of the process and the outcomes, the following examples may suffice. In the Mallee Tracks Area, both teachers and parents said a major problem was the lack of communication between parents and young people. This spilled over into students' inability to discuss issues in class, argue constructively against other opinions or stand up for themselves against bullying, affecting their social development and emotional maturity in general. There was no standard educational course to tackle this.

The Local Area Committee located two key resources and built them into a new program. One was Mallee Family Care, a service organisation based in Mildura (outside the area), which they asked to visit local schools and work with both children and parents on issues of sexuality, communication and conflict management. Another key resource came in the form of two pig farmers from Swan Hill, the woman an ex-ABC compere, the man active in the arts. With a little funding from the central pool, they developed two related programs: a mobile van radio station which linked schools across the area, helping students discuss issues of common concern as well as schoolwork problems, and a drama role-playing program where adults reversed roles with children in a range of typical situations, encouraging more openness and expression. The spin-offs were evaluated as highly positive, both in the home and at school.

Several of the Areas identified a need or gap in the arts and in music education, often lacking not just music or art teachers but even a teacher who could play the guitar or the recorder. The resources surveys located many locals who were artists and craftspersons, so funds were allocated to help them run classes in the local schools, for students during the day and for parents and other adults at night; some Areas had mobile craft vans, while others relied on local help. This, too, expanded the horizons of children, encouraged the sharing of ideas between children and adults, and sparked a range of spin-off community craft activities, some of which became commercial.

Perhaps the most outstanding of these resource-using exercises was the music project in the Western Wimmera area, where over 1000 musical instruments were found in farmhouses, church halls and schools. As well, some local women were identified who had once taught music or who had outstanding musical skills. With limited funds, they were paid to teach a musical instrument to every student in the schools across the Area, leading to an enrichment of student and community life. Concerts, eisteddfods and even career ambitions grew out of this project.

Another Area said its students were receiving no technical education at all, despite living in the country. A new technical school would have cost over a million dollars, so with some thousands of dollars, the Country Education Project provided a substitute. Resources — such as farmers with technical expertise in electricity, engineering, the use of fertilisers, saw sharpening, motorcar mechanics, and so on—were found. As well, abandoned garages with safe electrical wiring and concrete floors were commandeered for classes. The Horsham TAFE college was enlisted to send additional technical teachers out into the area, and a whole technical life-skills program was developed, for schools during the day and for adults at night, often with adults and students working together on applied projects.

Most of the programs developed by Local Area Committees were specifically school curriculum-oriented, such as a new learning-to-read program that was opposed by the local school inspector but succeeded in getting children to read for the first time or the maths program that focused on showing parents how to help their children with homework problems. But because we had altered the approach to education, showing how a whole-of-community approach could enhance the efforts of school teachers, these areas developed a new culture of learning, which continues to this day. I was always a bit uncertain of our agreement to fund the building of a swimming pool in the King-Ovens Valley, for example. The Local Area Committee argued that many children drowned in local streams because they had never learned to swim, and that a pool at a centrally located school would bring together older and younger children and allow isolated teachers to discuss common problems when they brought students for swimming lessons. In fact, that is what happened, and the educational spin-offs were much wider than I could have imagined.

The lesson was that locals do know their community well, better than central bureaucrats and planners, and if trusted, they act responsibly. The usual objection to such a scheme of local empowerment is that government departments have to be accountable for the expenditure of public money. This is so. You can't just hand over funds to local communities and have no accountability. These Local Area Committees were held accountable for following both the broad guidelines of the Country Education Project and its philosophy and were required to report regularly on progress and outcomes. But we did not require them to match arbitrary key performance outcomes drawn up by us or any other central bureaucrat. Reporting was kept brief, and to the issue of overcoming educational disadvantage. And the fact that funds were scarce, not unlimited, made those committees more parsimonious and more determined to make every dollar count than any administrative accountability scheme could ever have done.

I use this example to demonstrate how future government funding might be directed towards real community-development programs, based on locally identified needs, and also drawing together existing resources to get greater value for the dollars put in. The world has moved on since the early 1980s, when the Country Education Project began, but the project still functions, with privately raised funds and lots of local initiative, now making full use of information technology to network across each area and to draw on resources much more widely ranging than those within the area itself. Since then, closer links have been developed with regional and local businesses, regional TAFE colleges, and other state resources such as youth services and Internet-available information.

The 'tribes' that have emerged in such rural areas are not negative, or antagonistic to government, but real partners in strategically linked resource use for the benefit of students and the communities as a whole. They both draw on and help the further development of 'social capital', through the re-engagement of government with local and regional resources.

The New Links Workplace Project

In 1989, ANZ Trustees, which handles a number of charitable trusts and estates, decided that its corporate philanthropy work was having insufficient impact. They had followed the usual pattern of taking submissions from various applicants, judging them on their merit and making grants of variable, usually small, amounts. Wanting to find a better focus, they called together a number of experts to outline what they saw as the most pressing issues for Australian society over the next few decades.

At this forum, the trustees heard about issues such as biotechnology, environmental damage, advances in medical research, and youth drug and suicide problems. My own presentation concerned the changing nature of family life in Australia and the apparent impact that inflexible and unresponsive work practices were having on marital stability and the wellbeing of children. The Australian Institute of Family Studies, of which I was then Director, was finding consistently in its research studies a conflict between meeting both the needs of children and the demands of work, and I argued that the community as a whole, not just individual workplaces, needed to respond, though workplaces had a social responsibility to actively generate a more family-supportive framework for those they employed. The added benefit would be a spin-off in the form of better family support services to others in the community who were not employed by the company itself.

The trustees decided that this was one issue they would like to pursue further, inviting me to draw up a proposal for research on work–family problems. This was a challenge, because we had already done several studies of the work–family balance and I wanted to be able to demonstrate practical change over time. I put forward an action research proposal to work with a few major companies, helping them to improve their internal workplace culture so that their managers and supervisors were more aware of and sympathetic towards workers with family responsibilities.

But my appeal was for them to start forging links with those agencies in the community that were supposed to be helping families cope. We had plenty of evidence that individual companies which had introduced work-based childcare, family leave and flexible work-time provisions had improved morale, job satisfaction, absenteeism rates, and the sense of trust and commitment that produces discretionary effort. But, I argued, companies could not do it all alone. They would get more bang for their buck if they worked actively to develop a family-supportive environment outside the workplace, in the communities in which their employees lived.

The next step was to find companies willing to be part of the New Links Workplace Project.[150] I presented the overall rationale to a seminar attended by 20 chief executives of major companies. When invited to participate, virtually every one wanted to be involved, but we had to restrict the experimental project to three or four. The Buckland Foundation agreed to fund the project generously over a period of three years, since you could not expect clear results in the short term, and that no-one had monitored either the process of change or its cost-benefit impacts over time. We decided to go with a mining/refining company (Alcoa Australia), a public utility (Pacific Power in NSW), a major insurer/retailer/finance company (Lend Lease) and a corporatising government service agency (Australia Post). The New Links Workplace Project thus had from the start a big business focus, one which led us to a new stage in later years to cover the different problems of small business in Australia.

As the project began, we found that Lend Lease did not feel the need to collect detailed data on their work, believing they already knew that encouraging close involvement with community organisations through their employees was beneficial both to the workers and to the company as a whole. As well, we found that Pacific Power was in the middle of privatisation, being split into several separate entities, so we monitored their work–family programs in much less detail than originally intended. But with Alcoa Australia and Australia Post, the full methodology was applied and monitored over a three-year period, with very positive outcomes identified.

Alcoa

Alcoa Australia is a major aluminium mining and refining group employing over 7000 workers. Its US owners have a good record in human resource management and responsiveness to work–family needs, but because it has been a heavily male-dominated industry, the issue had not been a high priority for them in Australia. When its CEO volunteered the company as one of the pilot New Links Workplace Project sites, he had already formed a Work–Family Committee to investigate what might be needed. The company's stated 'people value' was carried through in practice. Alcoa had a history of technological innovation, rapid adaptation to change, and an approach where employees, customers and shareholders were seen not as separate or unequal areas of focus but as integral to the rationale for work–family policy.

Nonetheless, there was still no integrated human resources plan, just the remains of an outmoded personnel/industrial relations approach to the employees, and some old-fashioned employee assistance programs, which were, apart from health services, piecemeal and handled as an add-on by industrial chaplains resistant to criticism. The dominant workplace culture was technical-managerial and very macho in nature.

Another initial stumbling block was the company's spread across several locations, making for core-periphery conflict and a resistance to any centrally driven program of action. Most of Alcoa's operations and staff are based in Western Australia, with refineries at Kwinana, Pinjarra and Wagerup and bauxite mines feeding them raw materials. But company headquarters were at the time based in Melbourne. The Point Henry refinery in Geelong had a very different profile, and the Portland refinery in western Victoria was seen as a renegade in many ways, with innovative human resource management and a different approach to workplace relations. These differences had given rise to a 'West versus the rest' mentality, and suspicion that the Western Australian locations would be pushed to implement what were seen as costly and unnecessary provisions at Portland.

A key to the Work–Family Committee's success was the clear leadership and support from the CEO of Alcoa. He wisely kept out of the committee itself, but gave his imprimatur and made it clear they were reporting to him.

In the new 'membership' company, where employees are partners in the enterprise and prized as its central human assets rather than treated as an expendable property, it may well be, as Charles Handy says, that the best will be like a club, a 'fellowship of companions', a 'societe' in the French sense of the word.[151] But a business has to answer to its shareholders and its own future by turning a profit. And Alcoa's CEO kept that firmly in mind, while recognising that more flexibility and management sensitivity around family needs is desirable in its own right as well as potentially enhancing performance and turning a better profit. The balance at work should be on the side of effective performance; at home it should be on the side of effective family relationships. The two go hand in hand, but the company's interests still come first. A business–community partnership does not mean a company has to lose sight of its basic purpose.

The CEO's choice as chair of the Work–Family Committee — a senior manager from Western Australia — helped allay suspicions about central office, and the hands-on works managers on the committee soon found they had more in common than they had suspected, so that territorialism and rivalry receded.

The committee quickly found they had no information about employees' family circumstances on which to base any action. This, too, is typical of most Australian companies. Personnel records are incomplete, 'prying' questions about family matters being taboo. Companies do not know whether their employees are married or have children, whether such children are infants or teenagers, whether workers have problems with childcare arrangements, whether partners also have jobs, full-time or part-time, or whether they have ageing parents or other dependants whose needs might draw them away from full attentiveness at work.

It was agreed to conduct a comprehensive survey of the work–family circumstances, needs and attitudes of every employee. Graeme Russell of Macquarie University was contracted to conduct this survey, and we convinced Alcoa to invite employees' partners to participate also by filling out a parallel questionnaire if they wished. Over 800 partners did so, giving us the first Australian data where male workers' responses could be compared with their female partners' feelings about how their partner's work impinged on the quality of family life. The survey was conducted location by location, with groups completing the questionnaire under supervision during work time. Confidentiality was guaranteed and the data were coded immediately.

At the same time, I conducted a 'community scan' in the Mandurah region, where most of Alcoa's Western Australian employees were housed. A similar scan had already been conducted in Geelong, by the Barwon Research and Community Development Task Force, and the Portland refinery had good data on its town's services.

The rationale for the community scan was many-sided. Action by Alcoa itself might not be necessary, for example, if sufficient childcare was available in the community. Some employees' needs may arise simply from lack of information about family support services already available; or they might not be used because they are seen as being only for 'the disadvantaged' or those on welfare. Thus Alcoa's task may simply have been one of publicising, in-house, those services and changing employee attitudes about their relevance. Beyond that, if services were lacking in the community, the company's task might be one of advocacy for improved service availability and delivery, seeking extra funds from various levels of government or providing staff, paid or volunteer, to expand such services' scope and effectiveness. On the other hand, if identified employee work–family problems were not being recognised or met in Alcoa site location communities (for example, emergency childcare, youth unemployment, aged support services), new links would need to be developed to encourage the creation of appropriate services to meet those needs.

The assumption was that meeting every employee 'need' was not the responsibility of the company or, for that matter, of governments and welfare agencies. However, where work–family interactions are seen to be affecting morale, performance, productivity, absenteeism, staff turnover and so on, it makes sense to link more effectively with external agencies and consultants whose services can be used to reduce those problems.

The findings were instructive, with the Employee Work–Family Survey data confirming many of the conclusions drawn from the community scans. Above all, it was clear that Alcoa's work–family initiatives would have to vary by location — there was no company-wide answer to the varied needs identified, and each location had its unique community context and workplace culture.

On childcare issues, 60 per cent of Alcoa's employees said their childcare arrangements had broken down once or twice; 45 per cent had missed a day for family reasons (average 2.1 days); 72 per cent put emergency childcare at the top of the list of what would most help them; 36 per cent said childcare hours did not suit their work needs; 71 per cent felt Alcoa should help with childcare; but only 37 per cent would feel comfortable asking for time off in relation to childcare needs.

The community scan suggested that there was an adequate supply of formal childcare places in the communities, but a shortage of emergency care, relief staff, and resources for mothers caring for their children at home. Many families had no transport to take their children to childcare centres, there was a shortage of volunteers, a shortage of school holiday programs, and a resistance from local government to the establishment of more family daycare houses (because of 'noise' in the neighbourhood).

In other words, the two sets of data reinforced one another. There was no need for Alcoa to set up costly work-based childcare centres, but there might well be a need for local political action to improve the situation on emergency and holiday care. The company was also surprised, because of outmoded assumptions about men's attitudes to children, to find that 62 per cent would like family education and parenting advice; 49 per cent saw the father caring full-time for children as desirable; and 28 per cent of the men planned to have another child in the next few years and were likely to use unpaid paternity leave if it were made available.

On youth issues, often forgotten in discussions of work–family programs, some 23 per cent of Alcoa employees had teenage children and 12 per cent reported that parenting problems with teens affected their work performance. One-third said that their children disliked the way job demands affected family life and limited opportunities to relate to their parents. Fifty-three per cent of workers said they went home from work stressed and 36 per cent felt work demands reduced the time they should spend with their children.

Again, the community scan worked well to suggest what action might be taken. Welfare agencies and schools reported that most youth problems in the region seemed to arise from family problems, a lack of parenting skills and a lack of recreational outlets for young people. Sports were well catered for, but for non-sporting teenagers, there were few leisure facilities, not even a cinema. The lack of public transport was mentioned again and again as a factor preventing youth from accessing services, or getting to job interviews even when jobs were available. There was a lack of youth focus in local services, and some communities lacked infrastructure — such as footpaths and street lighting — that might help with youth safety, vandalism and drug use. The schools had few counsellors, social workers or pastoral care teachers, and there were insufficient male role models (community police, mentors, youth leaders) for teenage boys. There was a clear opportunity for better parent-school cooperation, yet 34 per cent of Alcoa's employees said they would not feel comfortable asking for time off to attend a school function.

The schools in particular identified a growing burden from dealing with family-related problems. School nurses were overburdened with emotional trauma, family violence and conflict rather than straightforward health issues. Desperate for assistance, teachers identified repeatedly the confusion of parents, with the need for parent education on child-rearing, discipline and behaviour control. There was a lack of before- and after-school care services, and overcrowding was a problem in some schools, because of population drift (particularly of single parent families) into the area.

It was in this school environment that the children of Alcoa employees were trying to learn, and the spin-off in the form of problems for Alcoa parents was obvious. Sixty-two per cent saw the need for family education and parenting advice, while 68 per cent wanted more activity centres for teenagers in the community, as well as help with how to handle drug-taking.

Another surprise of the survey was that 16 per cent of Alcoa's predominantly male employees already had (and another 50 per cent expected to have in a few years) responsibility for elder care. Sixty-three per cent wanted better advice and information about what was available to help them. Another nine per cent had a disabled family member. But the community scan revealed a sad lack of community service support for the aged. There was little respite care, no bus services for the elderly, a lack of home help for the frail aged, and no all-day/evening drop-in centres for seniors needing companionship.

The release of data from this research to managers and workers at each location was thus, in itself, an important part of the culture-change process, altering manager perceptions of what were the important issues, improving self-awareness and knowledge of common problems, and changing views about what work–family programs were needed.

Two sets of action resulted from this research work. First, the New Links Workplace Project team presented the survey and community scan findings to the Alcoa Work–Family Committee and to both managers and groups of employees at each Alcoa location around Australia.

Second, though it was clear that action would have to vary at each Alcoa location, the committee did devise a set of statements of work–family policy that would apply across the whole company and that had the imprimatur of the CEO.

- Special leave would be available for family needs, ranging from a few hours to a full day or extended leave as required. Leave could be taken as part of annual leave or from accrued sick leave. The word 'family' was broadly defined, not limited to immediate household members.
- Parental leave (under the national award) was available, and the company would offer information and assistance, particularly in regard to return to work.
- Temporary changes in working hours could be made to accommodate important family commitments. The impact on other work-team members must be taken into account, with the supervisor responsible for negotiating the most mutually suitable approach.
- Active programs were to be developed to encourage respect for diversity and to remove all forms of harassment and discrimination.
- Part-time work, job-sharing, flexible hours and home-based work could now be negotiated with the location personnel manager.
- Each location was to establish a Work–Family Team, or its equivalent, to develop an

effective implementation and education strategy, communicate the overall policy, train supervisors in how to develop the new principles in practice, and make links with external agencies dealing with family issues.

This last recommendation was in keeping with the belief that the corporate centre could not and should not dictate the methods of change to those at the periphery; culture change had to fit with the unique make-up of each separate location.

Alcoa's location-based Work–Family Teams became the engine for action on the New Links Workplace philosophy, though as expected it was variously understood. Each Work–Family Team had to include a cross-section of managers, staff and other employees, whose responsibility was to analyse the location data, collect more information if necessary, identify a few priority issues for action at the local level, and recommend to management how this might be implemented.

Some programs can be described briefly. Pinjarra refinery turned its annual safety day into a combined work–family display, open to the entire community of Mandurah. Displays ranged from the usual safety procedures for fire, electricity, snakebite and heavy machinery to stands displaying information on childcare, aged care and marriage counselling services, with staff available to discuss their work. This led to the local marriage counselling service coming into the refinery at lunchtimes to run brief talks and workshops on issues such as marital conflict, avoiding divorce, talking more openly with your partner and the impact of divorce on children. The family safety days have been conducted every year since the project began, with thousands of community members apart from Alcoa employees and their families attending.

Pinjarra moved to develop a childcare register for the region, to include informal resources for childcare. The lack of extended hours care that would suit night shift workers indicated a need to work with and expand local family daycare services, and senior staff members actively lobbied local councillors who had been opposed to expanding daycare homes in the area. They established a consultative working committee with community groups such as Lady Gowrie Corporate Childcare Services, the Meerilinga Young Children's Foundation and representatives of the Family Day Care scheme. As a result, Alcoa decided to sponsor new family daycare places in the region to cater for short-term needs, up to 50 hours a week for each reserved place, with Alcoa paying an annual management fee to administer this extension of the scheme.

This has been in operation for four years, making a big difference in the lives of shift workers and others with emergency childcare needs.

At a location level, there have been many examples of outreach to the wider community.

In Portland, the same gap in out-of-school-hours care had been identified, so Alcoa forged new links with other local companies and with the local YMCA to provide a bus to collect school children after school and take them to an integrated activities program run by the YMCA. They applied for a federal grant for out-of-school-hours care, adding the company's weight to what might have been an ineffective parental or school submission. Portland also updated and extended its index of available community services, so that workers were fully informed about what help was available and how they could access family assistance.

Kwinana has recruited staff volunteers for mentoring in local high schools. They also sponsored a workshop for a whole range of community and industry groups, on parenting challenges and the need to balance work and family. Held at the Rockingham Civic Centre, the workshop raised widespread interest. Kwinana has made links with the new men's refuge at Calista, with Alcoa's employee assistance program providers on the management committee to provide expert advice and support. At Booragoon head office, a program of information sessions has covered topics such as financial planning for families, health and lifestyle, making a will, and legal issues relating to family law, bringing in experts from outside the company.

Pinjarra refinery has sponsored both on-site and open in-community workshops and seminars on early childcare, and created an innovative CD called 'Shape Your Future', which provides schools and employment agencies with information on the range of careers available in the mining industry.

In Western Australia, Alcoa staff have also been actively involved in government work–family initiatives. For example, participation in a working group of the Family and Children's Advisory Council has led to information sharing and planning activities for Western Australia's Family Week in May each year. Alcoa has promoted Family Week in all its locations, placing articles in their newsletters, and has provided sponsorship for a major work and family conference hosted by the government in Perth. Staff members presented papers on flexible work arrangements, on job-sharing and on the findings of a study by the Wagerup refinery on dependent care issues. One of the keynote speakers was Dr James Levine, an expert on the changing role of fathers, from the Institute of Family Studies in New York.

He met with 30 Alcoa managers on the subject of 'working fathers', which led, in turn, to a series of workplace seminars on fatherhood run by Professor Graeme Russell. The conference provided several opportunities for Alcoa to network with state members of parliament and the Family and Children's Council and to discuss issues of concern to the company and the wider community.

These are precisely the sorts of linking activities that the New Links Workplace Project aimed to stimulate. They derive from the local workplace culture, they move out beyond the confines of the workplace itself to forge new links with the wider community, and they recognise that the company has a responsibility to the wider community and its families, not just to their own employees.

Alcoa has also altered the thrust of its corporate philanthropy, so that it is integrally linked with work–family policy matters. In the Peel Region of Western Australia, where most of Alcoa's employees live, there is a community fund called PEACH. Management expertise and payroll system help are provided by 10 of Alcoa's managers, who act as trustees, and 10 Alcoa employees who handle day-to-day fund management. PEACH raised over $1 million in 1998, and the main beneficiaries of funding are organisations that support families in a wide range of services in the health and human care fields. Alcoa's own community sponsorship program focuses on organisations supporting families in the surrounding community, and they offer their payroll system to United Way, another fund for family-support groups in the community. Alcoa Western Australia was recognised in 1997 for its work–family initiatives by a Community Services Award in the Premier's Award for Innovation in Industry.

Because the New Links Workplace Project was funded for a period of three years, we were able to obtain data on changes over time. Alcoa has a meticulous system of record-keeping, and we were able to run a follow-up employee survey as well.

Interestingly, some of the most positive outcomes came from very small, signpost shifts in behaviour. For example, although Alcoa had successfully recruited women as part of their equal employment opportunity (EEO) policy, there was still overt hostility and harassment from many male employees towards women. At one location, the women were told to carry buckets of rock samples to the laboratory for analysis. Their struggles with heavy buckets stimulated derision and calls for them to 'go home and mind the kids'. Undeterred, the women consulted their supervisor, who checked with the laboratory technicians, who said they did not need whole buckets of rock samples in any case. Thus the problem was solved for both men and women. At another location, heavy hoses were used to clean mesh filters at the end of the day. When women could not control the high pressure hoses, male employees mocked their weakness. Supervisor sensitivity to EEO/work–family policy led them to devise an underarm holder for the hoses, so that they could be held firmly without escaping and spraying everywhere. The men then admitted that some of them had trouble with these hoses as well, and wanted the same harness, ending their derision of the female employees.

At another mine, the company agreed to provide men whose wives were pregnant with a beeper, so that an emergency call would reach them no matter how far they were from the mine's central facility. This cost very little, but sent a clear message that the company was 'fair dinkum about this work–family thing'. One man whose wife had suddenly left him and his two children phoned in to ask for emergency leave. The personnel manager agreed, and offered help with counselling and childcare. She admitted that, had this request come a few months earlier (before the Work–Family Survey and implementation of the policy), she probably would have refused and thus lost a good employee.

At a workshop for the company's senior managers, the CEO asked them to show hands on two issues. One was how many of them had taken their full annual leave; the other was how many of them took a few days off work on return from an overseas assignment to regroup with their family. Hesitant hands went up, but only a few. The CEO told them he always spent a few days with family on return from overseas, and they should too. He also said that annual leave was a health benefit, but also a family benefit, and he wanted no-one to assume they were indispensable, having to be at work to prove themselves every day of the year.

In a memo to all managers, he commented: 'The Management Group needs to drive the culture change necessary to sustain these initiatives and create a family-friendly environment where all forms of discrimination are unacceptable and where the external stakeholders see us as a benchmark in our industry and in the broader community.'

These comments spread beyond the head office, and again spoke powerfully about the company's seriousness in encouraging a balance between work and family life.

In the follow-up analysis, we were able to show clear cost-benefits for the company. Absenteeism rates dropped from the 1994 baseline figures, from 11.9 per cent to 1.55 per cent for female wage workers overall, and from 3.5 per cent to 2.6 per cent at one particular refinery. As an indication of cost savings for the company, this drop represented for Kwinana a reduction from 28,192 hours in the base quarter to 20,696 hours in the final quarter of 1995, a saving of 7496 hours or 208 working weeks.

More flexible leave-taking arrangements meant that the typical 'lying' about 'personal reasons' for time off dropped from 87,399 hours to 68,993 hours; leave declared as being for 'other family reasons' increased from 7896 hours to 15,707 hours. Annual leave entitlements were now more often used for these special family leaves, rising from 7600 hours to 9297 hours. Overall, this represented for the company a decrease in hours taken for non-holiday entitlement reasons, from 101,707 hours to 84,700 hours — also a big cost saving.

But it was the follow-up survey that revealed the most significant evidence of culture change and the reasons for such cost savings as those above — greater honesty and openness in the workplace, and a greater willingness in 1996 than in 1993 to request cooperation from workmates and supervisors when urgent family needs arose.

The remaining reluctance to seek leave for family reasons was not simply because of supervisor attitudes. Only 14 per cent said their supervisors were unapproachable or unsupportive; 22 per cent felt some matters were too personal to be broached in the workplace and 55 per cent felt they did not have the right to ask for time off for every family reason imaginable. What this reflects is the success of the company in developing a reciprocal trust relationship rather than a mentality of more benefits to be exploited.

Some 36 per cent reported that members of their own work team were more motivated as a result of the work–family initiatives. As well, the spin-off in terms of improved family relationships (as opposed to simply benefits for the company) was marked. There was also less difficulty in handling a range of related issues, such as working extra hours, training periods away from home and seeking advancement.

Towards the end of the three-year period of implementation, we also conducted a series of focus group discussions to get a more qualitative picture of how much the workplace culture had changed in regard to handling work and family responsibilities. Many comments reflected a very positive shift across the entire corporation:

- Two or three years ago, this was all thought to be pretty touchy–feely; but it's now got a lot of support, especially in relation to flexibility of hours and leave arrangements, as well as dependent care issues.
- People do not expend energy hiding things (though it's often the deepest problems that remain hidden) and the whole group dynamic is now more supportive. People stop and think, 'How does that affect that person?' They see it as their decision and ask, 'Where does it go?'
- It's not just a work–family issue, it's a question of generating respect throughout the workplace. We've maybe concentrated on respecting women and ethnic differences, but we now see it's a broader culture change that will take time ... We're in it for the long haul.
- Four years ago, it was 'lump it or leave it'. My wife left me and the company didn't help. Now it would.

On the other hand, some said that although the effect had been widespread, managers had not really focused on their own stresses. One at head office complained of how he had started coming in very early so that he could leave at around five in the afternoon and be home for his children, in line with the new policy, only to be accosted by a top personnel officer, a member of the Work–Family Committee, saying, 'Oh, leaving early? Bankers' hours, eh?'

One recurring problem, on which Alcoa continued to work assiduously, was the variability in supervisor attitudes, approachability, and the way of interpreting and implementing work–family guidelines. Some workers still felt it was better to take a 'sickie' than to explain that there was a family problem. But there was a lot of talking through of implementation issues and very effective guidance from personnel staff. The sorts of 'breakthrough' events that sent a positive message through the organisation included a worker using sick leave entitlements for a family member's illness; a social event being treated as 'family' leave; and a rigid 50–50 job-share arrangement being renegotiated to provide more scope to cover for one another and swap as needed. Organisations have to learn on the ground, and culture change is, in effect, real change in 'the way we do things around here'.

Australia Post

The second case study company to try the New Links Workplace approach offered different challenges. Australia Post was a huge government-controlled bureaucracy, just being corporatised, and threatened by competition policy with partial privatisation. Heavily unionised, Australia Post had suffered several crippling strikes, which led the new management to abandon former top-down approaches and ask employees to participate in decision-making and quality improvement. Their first enterprise agreement, called Quality Service One, had proved very successful, with each workplace location made responsible for its own procedures and performance assessment. Staff could follow a set of performance guidelines, and agree on pay levels and bonuses based on the quality improvements they had made. Morale had improved, as had the level of performance in post offices and mail sorting warehouses all over Australia.

The New Links Workplace approach was seen as part of this general quality improvement program, but we had to obtain union approval (a process that took several months, culminating in an Agreement from the Industrial Relations Commission under Section 170MA of the Act) before we could begin. It was agreed that we could use Adelaide GPO as an experimental location, with the understanding across Australia Post that any benefits they might be given would not flow to any other location unless and until the unions had assessed their value and the effectiveness of the work–family links being made.

A New Links Workplace Committee was formed on the basis of the Adelaide GPO's Equal Opportunity Committee, expanded to include representatives from the three major work groups — mail processing and delivery, retail and administration, and administration/management. As with Alcoa, we conducted focus groups with employees to identify issues of concern, devised an employee survey questionnaire, and presented the findings to the New Links Workplace Committee and staff through further focus group discussions.

As a result, the committee agreed on a range of work–family initiatives to be trialed in Adelaide, involving three sites: City Delivery Centre (CDC), Adelaide GPO, and Retail and Delivery. Four comparison sites were selected, to compare outcomes against the trends identified in the New Links locations. They would not be given access to the agreed work–family provisions and would not be subject to any work–family culture-change initiatives. The aim was to obtain pre- and post-test data from the New Links Workplace sites and from the four comparison sites.

Because of Australia Post's tradition of bureaucratic rule-making, there was a tendency to want the new conditions written down and followed strictly to the letter, rather than an understanding that this was a process of total culture change, but the New Links Workplace Committee used every means to push the message across, with articles and highlights in newsletters, in bulletins and at staff meetings.

In the event, outside award provisions overtook some of the internal agreements. Australia Post and its unions modernised the General Conditions of Employment Award, which was ratified by the Industrial Relations Commission in December 1995. Included in this award was the historic family leave test case decision, which recommended that employees be allowed to access their own sick leave credits to care for sick family members or co-residents for whom they were responsible. Such leave for Australia Post employees could be accessed after the three days' paid special leave was exhausted. The wider definition of 'family' for the purposes of special leave and family daycare leave was also picked up in the award. However, as New Links Workplace trials began six months before the new award was ratified, it is interesting to note that this provision did not increase the use of special leave among members at the New Links Workplace sites as some people had predicted.

With Australia Post, we were able to obtain hard data (as opposed to more qualitative indicators) over a period of 12 months. Clearly, changes over time could not be attributed solely to the New Links Workplace initiatives, since they were only one part of a complex work setting and an economic and social climate that was changing very rapidly. Nevertheless, we found significant differences within Adelaide's Australia Post workplace culture between the New Links Workplace sites and the comparison sites.

For example, staff turnover was lower for the New Links Workplace sites than for the comparison sites, with a cost reduction over one year of $63,700 within New Links Workplace sites and a cost differential of $216,000 between those sites and the comparison sites. The retention rate for women returning from maternity leave had been only 67 per cent for the New Links Workplace sites, 50 per cent for the comparison sites. A year later, New Links Workplace sites recorded a 100 per cent return rate, comparison sites an improvement to 86 per cent. The New Links Workplace sites in Adelaide had actively encouraged women on maternity leave to maintain contact and to undergo retraining, and had put in place a referral service for childcare both during the pregnancy and to help women plan their return to work.

The agreement with the unions involved monitoring indicators of cost-benefits such as 'delivery delays', 'cost to process article', 'customer satisfaction' and 'profit/sales growth'. At the New Links Workplace sites, business indicators represented a productivity improvement of 5.1 per cent for the GPO, and customer response cards reflected an improved attitude on the part of counter staff, reflecting a reduction in absenteeism rates. In contrast, the comparison sites reported delivery delays of 18 per cent of parcels delivered, and a rise in cost per article from 14.6 cents in 1994–95 to 15.6 cents in 1995–96.

The most popular initiative proved to be short-term absence on a make-up basis, with a significant saving on periods of absence that would formerly have been taken as full days on the false excuse of personal sickness. Total absence from work for New Links Workplace sites was 15.94 per cent in 1994–95, down to 15.05 per cent in 1995–96. Recreation leave at New Links Workplace sites decreased by 2048 hours; at comparison sites it increased by 832 hours. Long service leave taken by New Links Workplace site employees decreased by 3501 hours; at comparison sites it increased by 1137 hours. Maternity leave at New Links Workplace sites decreased by 1268 hours; at comparison sites it increased by 1505 hours. Looking at total leave taken, at New Links Workplace sites this decreased by 4020 hours, while at the comparison sites it increased by 2831 hours.

Such figures are often needed to convince companies that there is some 'hard evidence' about the benefits of becoming more family-friendly. Yet surveys take an enormous amount of time on the part of administration, and many companies do not even have the baseline data with which to compare outcomes over time. These data were the first 'hard evidence' in Australia, yet they are, in themselves, less convincing than the more qualitative comments on improvement that can be obtained anecdotally in workplaces where the culture has shifted to a more human, caring approach. Actions speak louder than statistics compiled after the event.

For example, one woman at Adelaide GPO had intended to resign after having a baby, but the new provisions allowed her to retrain and return part-time, with childcare support. A manager commented: 'From my discussions with staff and supervisors it would seem that a culture has been reinforced that management are receptive to assisting staff balance work and family responsibilities, and that staff apprehensions about approaching supervisors concerning these matters have been allayed.' Another employee said: 'There's nothing to comment on really, because work–family issues are dealt with as part of the taken-for-granted way we operate.'

Many employees taking the short-term leave option utilised the broader definition of 'family' to cover, for example, a de facto partner's illness, changes in child custody arrangements, community work, a grandparent's need for assistance, emergency childcare, care for grandchildren, helping out at school camps and sports carnivals, or attending a retirement club. Such diverse family-related reasons would not have been accepted prior to the New Links Workplace Project at Adelaide's GPO, and workers had previously had to use subterfuge to meet their real needs, causing a loss of hours and performance for the corporation. The culture of trust that seemed to be emerging is in itself a more valuable outcome than the specific hours saved. The broader definition makes policy more realistic and the positive impact on morale and performance is manifestly worthwhile.

In developing external community links, Adelaide Australia Post proved more difficult than Alcoa. Employees at the GPO did not live in the central city but were dispersed throughout the suburbs. It was not therefore possible to run a community scan to see what family problems were well supported by community services and what needed to be addressed. But the employee survey showed a gap in emergency childcare, and Australia Post contracted with the City Childcare Centre for five places to be reserved for children of their employees. Contacts were also made with a group called Nurturing Nannies, and Adelaide initiated a move to designate each Australia Post retail centre a Safety House for young children and the elderly and confused, a clear community refuge for people in need of help. Because the smaller licensed post office/newsagency outlets could not agree, the Adelaide GPO went ahead without them. As well, the central office extended its information catalogue of childcare and other family support agencies throughout Adelaide, and reported an increase in employee citizenship — a willingness to help others, both staff and customers. Their human resource managers forged new links with state government agencies, such as the Office for Children and Families, and the major childcare groups, to stay in touch with and influence new developments in service provision.

A regional New Links Workplace model

Partly because of our inability to activate the external community links process as effectively with Australia Post as with Alcoa and partly because we realised that big companies have a greater capacity to implement family-friendly work practices than does small business, we decided to trial a new approach. Many people who run small businesses, and small business provides some two-thirds of all Australian jobs, respond to the sorts of examples used above with the comment, 'That's all right for the Alcoas and

Westpacs of the world, but we can't afford to pay for childcare — we can't manage if more than one of our female staff goes on maternity leave. We operate on slim lines and every absence makes a difference.'[152]

This assessment is correct, in the sense that job-sharing and flexible work times may not lend themselves to intensive client service and small operations. But the obvious solution is to encourage small businesses to network and cooperate on work–family programs, so that the burden is shared more widely. As well, it should be possible to extend the notion of corporate responsibility to partnerships between big companies and those small businesses that supply and service them within a community or across a whole region.

The South Australian Office of the Family agreed to initiate a trial of a regional version of the New Links Workplace Project. In 1994, we met with, and obtained the approval of, the Community Services and Industry ministers. Then the government changed and the idea was dropped. It was revived after my discussions with a federal Liberal parliamentarian in 1998, but stalled as elections neared. Then in 1999, the revamped Office for Children and Families decided to give the idea another run, working with the South Australian BusinessVision 2010 Committee. The Office for Children and Families argued a case for the New Links Workplace to be the main work–family pilot within BusinessVision's program. We presented the rationale to them and to the Department of Human Services, and it was agreed to trial a regional approach in the Barossa Valley, centred round Nurioopta, where Southcorp is a large employer and many small businesses are clustered round the wine and tourism industry. This project is in its early stages, but will provide valuable data on improving the links between industry and local community organisations.

The Regional Labour Market Job Skills Gap Project

In another recent research project, funded by the Department of Education, Employment, Training and Youth Affairs (DEETYA), the Centre for Workplace Culture Change at the Royal Melbourne Institute of Technology (RMIT) attempted to redress the skills gap in its Regional Labour Market Project with the Greater Shepparton and Wangaratta regions in central Victoria. This is the 'food hub' of Australia which contains several highly sophisticated new technology firms and shows strong leadership in local government and in business. Nevertheless, the region had trouble attracting skilled workers, retaining young people and growing new business. The study conducted a community scan, and held detailed interviews with a range of businesses, school students and their parents, and community leaders. It found significant skill gaps that needed to be addressed — within schools, regional tertiary training courses, and on the job, within firms. Such skill gaps were not merely in technical and trade areas; people also identified a lack of general skills, especially communication skills in management and a failure of business to communicate accurate knowledge about the work they were doing across the regional job catchment area. The issues were complex, involving local community perceptions about job opportunities, the need to build community services that would hold young people or would attract them and others when older, a clear need for improved change management and skills development within local businesses, and a need for change in the ways vocational education was being managed within the school and TAFE systems. The project is ongoing, with a strong emphasis on close networking across regional businesses and the sharing of information on training and employment needs.[153]

Other Australian examples of community–building

The People Together report *The Power of Community* identifies a number of smaller, similar efforts to build better links across communities.[154] These include community workshops on how to influence change (Hume City Council); village committees that provide feedback on service delivery to the Kingston City Council; the Mildura Youth Centre, which links police, schools and the wider community to promote youth connectedness and a more holistic response to the needs of young people; a mosaic pathway in Orbost to foster a sense of inclusion for rural women; and environment groups such as the South Morang Active Residents Together. They point to the significance of LandCare, a vast movement of volunteers and farmers across Australia, and to the importance of the arts as a vehicle for community identity-building. And they contrast the apparent indifference of Melbourne-based universities such as La Trobe to regional educational needs and concerns with the close dialogue built up with community and business leaders by the University of Ballarat.

There have been moves also by the Local Government and Municipal Services Association of Australia to increase awareness of the need for local government to build their community of citizens, empowering them through consultation and active participation in decision-making. They point to such best-practice examples as the City of Greater Dandenong literacy program for new residents; the community banking movement assisted by the Bendigo Bank, and now emulated by the federal government's proposed rural transaction centres in small country towns; the City of Moreland's expansion of networks for community development; and the Blue Mountains Community Plan, aimed at improving resident wellbeing.

They call for proper benchmarking of community development projects, providing indicators for key practice areas such as needs assessment, capacity-building, networking, planning and coordination, and policy development. Their focus is on developing a more holistic view of local areas and regions, linking physical, environmental, economic, social and cultural issues rather than treating them separately. They also recognise that building social capital is not as easy as some might suggest, requiring concerted efforts to develop a shared understanding of key issues and future visions, to bring together the related activities of different levels of government, separate government departments and local organisations, to achieve real community involvement, and to ensure the more efficient and effective use of available resources. All of this echoes the work of the Country Education Project described earlier in this chapter.

These local government leaders suggest a list of principles for the provision of community services that could serve as a checklist for any level of government and for any non-government service provider: accessibility regardless of location, income or disability; adequacy as opposed to targeting; appropriateness to real local needs and circumstances; fair pricing; ecological sustainability; participation in planning and management by those most directly affected; non-discriminatory on the basis of sex, religion, race or skin colour; flexibility to take account of diverse needs and changing social conditions; creative and entrepreneurial ways of meeting people's needs; efficiency in using resources wisely and according to priority needs; and responsiveness to performance monitoring and best-practice standards.[155]

Chapter 12

Servicing the community patchwork

IN THE PREVIOUS CHAPTER, NEW ways of linking workplaces and community family support services were described. But a workplace focus is not the only way to link the future. Not everyone is employed; nor are all those who have a job employed by caring companies.

Many families operate on the margins of functionality, barely coping with the hardships and stresses of poverty, a bad marriage, troublesome children, disability, and physical or mental illness. The fact that 17 per cent of adult Australians have only the most basic literacy skills means their chances of getting a job are limited and their ability to cope is limited.[156]

It is the voluntary community services sector that has largely met the needs of this group, with or without government funding support. As well, governments (federal, state and local) have always funded a range of family support programs aimed both at preventing family breakdown and at improving family functioning. It is easy to forget that programs such as maternal and child health, out-of-school hours care, childcare fee subsidies, youth advisory services, drugs, alcohol and violence programs, and financial and marriage counselling services are all important aspects of a cohesive, functioning society. Australia has a long tradition of combined public and private supports of this kind.

However, in recent years, the system has been forced in new directions that have not proved healthy, either for community support agencies or for the families and individuals they aim to help. This community services sector therefore offers another chance to apply the principles of people control and accountability, the better linking of policy and action across related sections of the community.

Few of the earlier reports on regional development comment on the significance of social infrastructure, the quality of family support services, schools, medical services, youth and aged care provisions, and the links between community leaders and business leaders in the standard sense.[157]

Many people do not even know how extensive and important a contribution the community services sector makes to the Australian economy and our quality of life. In 1997–98, total expenditure on welfare services was estimated at $10.9 billion, or 1.9 per cent of GDP. This figure did not include social security cash payments, but 64 per cent of it was funded by the government sector, 25 per cent paid for by the users of services, and 11.3 per cent by the non-government service providers. Church and other non-government organisations (NGOs) actually deliver 60 per cent of all these funded services, comprising over 8000 'welfare businesses' which employ over 320,000 people. Seventy-two per cent of them are non-profit organisations. A total of about 11,000 community welfare agencies in Australia receive some government funding, and they benefit from the voluntary services of 10 per cent of the population aged 15 and over, contributing an average of 74 hours each year. This is a massive sector of the Australian workforce, making a major contribution to the quality of family and community life.

But governments have changed their relationship to the community sector in ways that damage both civil society and the capacity-building energy of the sector itself. If the social infrastructure is neglected, if social capital is not built up, no regional economic revival will be possible. In my view, we should stop calling the community services sector the 'third' sector, as if it were less important than government and business, and insist that the quality of networks within regions and the quality of social life for people who live within regions is the foundation on which business viability depends.

As background to the sort of change in government service delivery I think would better build community life and meet the challenge of loose ties in a global information age, a brief outline of what has happened in family and children's services is needed.

The distortion of family policy and family support programs

The state governments have a statutory role in dealing with child protection and share their role in childcare, infant and maternal health, aged care, community health services and youth services with both federal and local governments. It is a complex mix, in which people and families tend to get lost.

Particularly over the last decade, competition policy has driven governments to withdraw from direct provision of community services. Funding has been separated from delivery — government is now seen as the 'purchaser' of services, not necessarily the 'provider'. The key question — 'Why make something if you can buy it more cheaply?' — is a perfectly legitimate one, in itself, not a problem. The trend towards competitive tendering is not necessarily a denial of the concept of 'public services', nor a move to 'privatisation'; rather, it is a restructuring of how any publicly funded service will be provided and managed. Services may be state-funded as a public service, but not directly provided by the bureaucracy of the state apparatus. In fact, I maintain, control in the hands of the citizens is preferable to administrative control.

The problem with competitive tendering lies, rather, in the way it pits existing community services against one another, and in the way contracts are administered from the centre, instead of serving better to link a holistic range of family support services at the community level. Competitive tendering adds a huge burden to the work of small service agencies. It works against the very cooperation and coordination that would make for a more holistic approach to dealing with social problems. Competitive tendering encourages secrecy, and gives the central bureaucracy too much power both to define what services will be funded under their fixed contracts and to avoid transparency and accountability in their dealings with various agencies (on the grounds of contractual confidentiality).

In Victoria, certainly the shift to competition via tendering produced a crisis of morale within the community services sector, with some large agencies flourishing at the expense of smaller, more knowledgeable and locally responsive organisations. The new managerial system challenged the sense of mission of church and other service groups, who have always put in more work and funds themselves than they received from government. It turned such institutions as the Salvation Army into major commercial contractors for government service provision.[158]

It should be noted that cost has not been the only driving motive for governments to drive change. There was a quite justified questioning of the effectiveness and appropriateness of services designed/planned by the central bureaucracy and 'delivered' by them to the community. The theory was: 'Competition and contestability drive efficiency, whereas a public sector "monopoly" encourages complacency and waste.' An ironic outcome of this philosophy is that central bureaucratic management has become more powerful, not less, while many services themselves have reduced scope and lower budgets.

One less commonly discussed aspect of contracting out and contestability is the view that in protecting their own turf, traditional non-government human service agencies, as well as directly provided government services, have become too bureaucratic and resistant to change. Their origins lie in church pastoral services and in charity provision for the poor, and they tend to maintain a paternalistic and individualistic approach to social problems that supports the status quo. Some government policy makers (as well as some in the non-government sector) believe the only way to drive welfare sector change is to make such service providers consider their clients from a more customer-based, competitive viewpoint.

Nonetheless, free-market competition and contracting out have been applied to many aspects of government without a clear demonstration of likely efficiency or any consideration of other social costs that are harder to quantify. In similar vein, corporate management principles have been applied without much consideration of the different processes involved in human service delivery.

Governments have different functions from trading organisations — they provide for citizens, not customers or clients — though one could question whether state-provided services ever treated their community 'clients' as citizens in the sense of their being actively involved participants in the services delivered.

Another concern with the competitive approach is the likelihood that larger, city-based service organisations will dominate the market, driving out the experience and local knowledge of the smaller, more traditional service providers. Quality in service delivery is not only a matter of efficiency, but also of effectiveness in adapting to the particular circumstances and culture of very diverse regions. Civic entrepreneurship may not be the same as corporate entrepreneurship and big is not always better. [159]

Another important element in this background to service delivery is the growing community debate about the welfare of children. The traditional family values attitude is that a secure, intact, two-parent family is the foundation of good child socialisation and a stable social order. Against this view stand several factors: the historic and demographic diversity of family structures and processes; the hostility of many, particularly some elements of the women's movement, to the patriarchal basis of conventional family life; economic changes and their impact on women's work, child-raising and the marital partnership; and the increasing incidence and acceptance of divorce and de facto living arrangements, which make the best interests of children a matter of even more complex debate. The challenge is to help both married couple families and other types of families function optimally in the interests of their children.

Because of the recurring moral panic over child abuse, it is hard to challenge the current distribution of government funding within departments of human services. Suffice it to say that child protection as an issue sits at the very intersection of debate over the relative autonomy of the private family (an increasingly dominant ethic in an individualist, free-market society) and the responsibility of the state to intervene in, control or shape private family processes. Family policy becomes distorted as a result.

Funds have been withdrawn from more comprehensive forms of family support or child development. While reports of child abuse have increased dramatically and the cost of investigating those reports has escalated, barely half are substantiated and less than half of those actually result in any form of statutory intervention. Instead of primary prevention and ongoing support for 'good enough' parenting and family functioning, money is thrown at crisis intervention after the horse has bolted, so that costly and invasive legal procedures have exacerbated public misgivings about the right of the state to intervene and its frequent clumsiness in doing so.

Carter argues that family policy and child welfare policy have drifted apart. [160] Worse, she says, child welfare policy has been replaced by child protection policy. In other words, we have lost the focus on universal supportive services to help all parents bring up children to independent adulthood; we have even lost supplementary services aimed at assisting needy or incapacitated families to cope better. In their place, we have focused resources on supervisory and substitute services which either monitor the family closely in order to protect children 'at risk' or replace the family with some alternate form of care. This is both inefficient and socially unjust, because there is no scientific way to seek out 'risk' and because it focuses government resources on the few families defined in the system of child protection, at the expense of the far larger group of poor, needy and only partly dysfunctional families.

Expenditure on individual children and families under the protection system is much higher than any supportive or preventive social program might be, yet there are fewer demands to evaluate outcomes or prove cost-effectiveness for child protection programs than for preventive family support programs. The system is out of kilter.

Missing in much of the public debate (though not from the professional literature) is any consideration of the overall responsibility of the state for children, their nurturance and development as competent citizens, as compared with the state's duty to step in when things go wrong in the private domain of the family. Though there has been public acceptance of the state's responsibility to provide for public education and public health and to regulate for a clean environment and non-exploitative work conditions, somehow the child protection issue has become dislodged from the broader issue of child development and the state's general responsibility to optimise the life chances of every child through assisting parents and family-community networks in the task of raising children.

Moreover, the functional structure of government departments serves to obscure the important work of health workers, teachers, and others in 'child protection' in its broadest, UN Rights of the Child, sense. We have lost any sense of an integrated, coordinated approach to the development of children, and government departments operate as silos, in isolation from and often in costly competition with one another.

New directions for family and community support

What we need is a broader vision for state government activity in relation to the growth of children, family caring responsibilities and the healthy functioning of families, a vision currently missing from most planning documents. It would require a policy statement about positive investment in children, high quality care of the elderly and the wellbeing of families within a supportive community, a policy against which every government department would be evaluated.

The significance of language and the use of appropriate terminology need to be noted here, as they are central to the process of culture change. Though most current policy frameworks do emphasise prevention, offering support to families before serious problems can develop and lead to more costly and invasive interventions, the language of this preventive approach is negative rather than positive.

Instead of talking about which economic, community and family conditions will promote and enhance the healthy physical growth and optimal emotional and intellectual development of children, the terminology used focuses on risk factors and protective factors, targeting those most in need, and prevention of child abuse and neglect. It is a negative language of fortress-building, of moats and protective walls, not a language of hope, of building positive communities whose every institution encourages positive growth in children and the wellbeing of families.

In other words, the rhetoric of support and prevention does not match the reality of service provision. There is even a tendency to use 'risk factors' and 'protective factors' as a guide to the broader provision of so-called 'preventive' programs. The negative language overwhelms the notion of positive investment in the wellbeing of children and families.

To balance the picture, it must be said that the state does provide a range of truly developmental and supportive child and family services. The problem is, there seems to be little public policy realisation of the fact that such services are actually part of the overall system of child protection/child development.

Maternal and child health, formal and informal childcare, parenting advice, primary schools, the police and community safety programs, school psychology and pastoral care services, sports and youth clubs and the whole array of positive local community activities that characterise most neighbourhoods are all aspects of society's positive effort to nurture children and assist parents in their central task of raising the next generation. Yet they are not sufficiently recognised as such. Separate government departments and service providers rarely cooperate or communicate, and the policy debate that surrounds child protection is allowed to distort the real goal, which is the healthy development of every child within a community that supports and enhances the capacity of parents to raise their children in the best possible way.

As opposed to the present approach, a new model of resourcing the community patchwork is required. It would have to be based on the following principles:

- tailoring services to meet the needs of individuals, not inflexible program boundaries and client capture by agencies;
- an agreed core set of services, universally accessible, plus specialised services;
- addressing diverse linguistic and cultural backgrounds in service delivery;
- integrated assessment procedures that are outcome focused;
- services delivered in the places where people work and live, on a 24-hour, seven-day basis;

- health promotion, education and community education linked through community health centres and family resource centres, located perhaps in schools;
- a whole-of-catchment accountability for service providers;
- providers working with doctors, dentists, carers and other specialists;
- making catchment areas small enough to reinforce the sense of local community connection with providers, yet large enough for specialist service provision;
- good information management, to reduce duplication and to enhance good outcomes; and
- simplified funding and accountability arrangements.

Twelve propositions for family services

I offer the following propositions as a way of challenging the way we think about the provision of services for children and families.

1. The goal of government services intervention is to support or supplement (not replace or supplant) the private efforts of families and individuals to lead a decent life. In health, childcare, education, even police protection, government is a *partner*, not a sole provider or substitute for personal action. It follows that all such services should be designed with that partnership in mind, identifying gaps or specialist needs that citizens cannot always meet themselves, and matching services/resources to identified need.

2. The rearing of children has never been and can never be the sole responsibility of parents, who must rely on others outside the home (kin, non-parental carers, teachers, doctors) for expert help. It follows that you can't blame only the parents if things go wrong, and that the entire family support system should be redefined in terms of cooperative partnerships, with schooling redefined as helping parents raise future citizens, a whole-of-community task.

3. Modern society is so complex and family structures and processes so diverse that no one mode of service provision will meet the differing definitions of 'a decent life'. It follows that all services offered must be culturally competent and sensitive to diversity, must consult with those citizen clients who use them, and must adapt flexibly to diverse localities and individual needs. Human services cannot, by definition, be categorical, uniform or decided top-down by experts or bureaucratic managers; users demand and deserve close involvement in what is provided and how.

4. No family or other social unit is an island operating independently of other social institutions; in a complex society, we are all interdependent, influenced by and acting on a range of social factors. We live in a networked society, not merely a

hierarchical one. It follows that no human service system can effect change in family or individual behaviour without addressing the range of social, economic and cultural factors that impinge on people's efforts to live a decent life. In particular, economic viability and educational competence must be addressed.

5. Notwithstanding points 3 and 4, the first and most continuous influence on human development, action and effort is the family (however constituted and defined); every individual starts with a parent and thus a family, and that family context vitally affects life chances and constraints. It follows that any system of human-service delivery must address the modus operandi and quality of the child's family context, working in partnership with its wider kin membership.

6. The task of raising children is one for the whole community, not just parents, since the future viability of the society depends on those children's developed capacity to operate as competent adult citizens in their own right. It follows that healthy growth, optimal child development and social competence are the shared goals of a range of human services — the services provided by parents, health and childcare workers, teachers, child protection and other family support service providers. An integrated approach to human development and optimal social functioning will be more effective than one where such supports work in isolation from or at odds with one another.

7. The research shows that families function best, in terms of those growth and social capability goals, when surrounded by multiple networks of support — kith and kin, non-parental carers, schools, churches, neighbourhood clubs, sports groups, workplace friendship connections, and so on — where families are socially embedded rather than isolated from critical and supportive feedback or social control. It follows that human services are likely to be most effective when they identify and strengthen the links between separate families and a range of social networks that have the potential to offer encouragement and support — that is, when they resource the growth of social capital. Rapid social change may be replacing, not just destroying, some of those traditional connecting frameworks, but most will exist within neighbourhood proximity to the family, so services need a strong focus on strengthening neighbourhood embeddedness.

8. The research also shows that 'high risk' neighbourhoods are those with a high concentration of 'social impoverishment', defined as socio-economically distressed and educationally disadvantaged families with poor social integration, less positive neighbouring, and more stressful day-to-day interactions, using fewer family support services.[161] It follows that intervention efforts by service delivery agencies should address those levels of concentration at the community/neighbourhood level, not solely at the individual family level. Expanding the social mix, building

new networks, and making the physical neighbourhood safer and more congenial to everyday social interaction are likely to improve the social embeddedness of the whole community.

9. Within the family context, the research consensus is that 'authoritative parenting' — warmth and support combined with sensible limit-setting aimed at self-direction — is most conducive to positive child development and socialisation outcomes; in parallel, children are most 'at risk' in family environments exhibiting low warmth, high criticism, and arbitrary or quixotic control. It follows that, since it is impracticable to assess the nature of every child's family environment, the best form of intervention will be one that explains these key parenting outcome processes universally to all parents, the earlier the better.

10. Men are a double engine behind the child's potentiality, but often fail to act positively in the process of optimal child development because they are ignorant or not informed or absent or excluded from involvement in the child development process. It follows that family support services should specifically address the role of fathers and other men in maximising rather than damaging good child outcomes. This cannot be done only via traditional parent education and services but must be more creative and sensitive to male interests and time constraints, perhaps targeting the places men frequent (workplaces, pubs, sports groups).

11. Prevention is better than cure, early intervention better than late, positive strength-building better than negative blame; but even the concept of 'prevention' is problem-centred rather than educationally or developmentally focused. It follows that the terminology surrounding human service delivery needs to be rethought so that a cooperative, developmental growth model replaces the old continuum of 'primary-secondary-tertiary' prevention.

12. The outcomes of human service intervention, as of parenting, are notoriously difficult to measure — not all poor families are abusive or have children who fail to thrive; the best of families can have problems; good schools don't always turn out the best citizens; and quality childcare such as Head Start may appear to produce only short-term gains in IQ but produce long-term effects on other positive life outcomes. It follows that a mechanistic model of top-down, categorical services, a managerial emphasis on cost-benefits, efficiency and narrowly defined outcomes, and insistence on short-term, merely quantitative evaluation, will be an unreliable guide to policy and program practice. More attention to broad child development and family functioning outcomes is required, and longitudinal research on outcomes should be funded before large-scale changes to the system are set in stone or promising interventions written off as ineffective.

Decentralised services — Family Resource Zones

My argument is that family services are an excellent example of how intelligent government could operate in a patchwork country. Families are themselves diverse, they live in very varied communities where both needs and resources differ. And services are most effective when they build social capital.

What would an ideal model of family and community resourcing look like?

The goal of all such policies, programs and agencies would be clearly stated as that of resourcing families and promoting the healthy growth of every individual within a supportive family and community context.

Resources would be broadly defined across multiple contexts and institutions — including pre-schools and childcare centres, health centres, schools, tertiary colleges, local libraries, youth and aged care activities, information databases and networks, workplaces, sports and other recreational facilities, playgrounds, volunteers and mentors — not merely as 'services' provided to specific groups. Services are just one aspect of the resources needed by families in pursuing a positive lifestyle.

In a model system, the first principle would be local family and community participation in defining needs and developing suitable programs of action. The locus of power and decision-making must be within the community/area/zone, however designated, not with a centralised, bureaucratic department. Policies and broad procedures would need to be set according to governmental priorities, as at present, but the 'what' and 'how' of community resourcing action should be in the hands of those most directly affected — the community itself.

The first task for any system of family support provision is to identify which resources are currently available in the region and which are missing, in order to pinpoint both strengths and gaps and then to formulate priorities for action plans. This of necessity requires some finite, even arbitrary, definition of an area for action — whether it be called a region, a community, a location, a neighbourhood or a zone — as well as some locally oriented action group to assess both resources and needs.

I would suggest current usage makes 'regions' and local government areas too large, particularly in rural areas, and neighbourhoods, as defined by separate school catchment areas, too small. Since the goal should be to facilitate the sharing of information and other resources, and to maximise efficiency in whatever action programs are set up, it is probably sensible to use school and childcare clusters as a starting point. They would be a non-stigmatising and clearly development-oriented focus for planning.

Each area could be called a Family Resource Zone, and each would establish a Family-Community Forum, whose first task would be to generate understanding of the new philosophy of resourcing families and promoting the positive growth of every individual within a supportive community, through an active survey of family and community resources. Each Family-Community Forum would be set up under the auspices of a school or other community-based agency, driving leadership to properly resource family and community life in the Family Resource Zone.

The Family-Community Forum would act as a sort of 'regional parliament', debating how best to apply government funding and implement programs in the context of their particular zone. These Family Resource Zones and Family-Community Forums could be self-forming and might differ in size and coverage, but they should include all primary, secondary and tertiary institutions within the action zone, plus representatives of childcare, youth, elder care and other family support agencies, plus representatives of local government, businesses, police, churches, health groups and social action groups.

They would receive base funding from human services departments, and gradually identify areas of action for future funding. The funds would be administered by them, not via the central department, but annual public reports on spending and outcomes would be mandatory. The Family-Community Forum, not the central department, would eventually become responsible for contracting programs and services seen as best suited to the social make-up, needs and interests of their particular zone.

Schools, childcare centres and local libraries, community health centres, perhaps some churches and shops such as local pharmacies would be designated as the access points to a network of family resource centres, and thus the first points of call for families looking for information and assistance in the form of education programs or other services. Each zone could decide which and how many such centres would be viable.

Within each Family Resource Zone, such centres would be linked via computer to ensure efficiency, and comprehensive availability of all information to all families. The centres would have clearly designated and accessible space within the school or library, and could be staffed (day and night) by a rotating cadre of existing community service agency workers and school counsellors/psychologists. Such rotation would encourage the sharing of ideas and information, networking across agencies and between schools and community organisations, and would be cost-effective in terms of not requiring a new set of professional staff paid separately. An alternative might be to staff them with former bureaucrats from the department, provided they were not given any formal control over decisions made by the zone's Family-Community Forum.

Each Family-Community Forum could set up a series of Family-Community Task Forces, or Local Action Committees, to look more closely at specific areas of action such as appropriate recreation facilities for young people, local playgrounds, the range of childcare options, home-based support for the aged, carer networks, bullying in schools, business links and mentoring. These would broaden the range of people actively participating in family and community resourcing, and help extend understanding of the philosophy of reciprocal responsibility and community-building. They would help 'thicken' democracy by giving more people a direct stake in outcomes and the most efficient way of using the finances provided.

State Child Protection Officers would be active members of the Family-Community Forum but would not be in a dominant position. Their current role of assessing reported cases of child abuse and neglect would continue, but forensic risk assessment and case management would not be allowed to monopolise funds at the expense of creative, community-based, family-strengthening and broadly preventive measures.

The focus would be on building the families of child protection cases into new networks of support, dealing with the whole family in its context, and ensuring that context is itself made more positive for adequate family functioning. The notions of need and risk would be applied not narrowly to individual cases or families but, instead, to identifying 'toxic' factors in the zone, and in the neighbourhoods, schools and other specific contexts in which each family operates that should be addressed in health-promoting, growth-promoting ways.

The principle of networking across the full range of community agencies (schools, churches, welfare and health services and recreational groups, police, local government agencies, workplaces, etc.) would be kept in mind at every point of decision-making; and the parallel purpose of increasing the embeddedness of families within their zone, expanding their connectedness with others in order to reduce isolation and disadvantage, would inform the discussion of Family-Community Forums.

This, of necessity, would require respect for and the involvement of the families themselves, the starting point always being their own self-interest and practical concerns, as already occurs in playgroups, youth groups, childcare centres.

Logically, such a system would move away from centrally controlled programs, towards a much more flexible and entrepreneurial community approach. The goal would be to use government funds in ways appropriate to the self-defined needs of each Family Resource Zone, with accountability to the citizens affected by their initiatives, not just to the central government department. Funds would not always be spent on services as such, but on initiatives within the area that could combine resources from other sources such as police, schools, local government, Rotary clubs, local businesses, and the like in order to have a wider impact on the quality of life of the whole community.

The measurement of outcomes and the effectiveness of actions taken in each zone would not be short term, not involve just case-based numbers, dollars spent per family, but would instead comprise long-term evaluations of the impact of family resourcing initiatives as a whole on broad indicators of family and child wellbeing, such as school retention rates, infant and maternal health, fewer reports of child abuse and neglect, bullying, delinquency, youth suicide, public safety records, neighbouring activities, employment and training initiatives, the quality of aged care, even divorce and family breakdown statistics. As with the US organisation Children Now, a report card could be published annually on progress against an agreed set of indicators, along with reports of the most successful initiatives taken across the state.

Such a scheme could readily be implemented as a pilot, constructed on the basis of what the research already shows about using schools as access points, the efficacy of networking and cross-functional teams, and aimed at promoting the healthy development and functioning of all families and children within a supportive community context. It would break the old nexus between 'clients' and 'service providers' and could generate a new enthusiasm for innovative and democratic approaches to resolving public and private problems. It would also build on experiments already proving to be effective, such as the Families and Schools Together program (FAST), the Family and Neighbourhood Links Project, the Community Safety and Crime Prevention Board, and the Achieving Together, Communities That Care and Turning the Tide initiatives, all of which link the two major government departments affecting families and children — education and human services — and encourage sharing of both responsibility and funding across previously entrenched departmental boundaries. It is a model built on what is known and on principles that promote positive family functioning within an active civil society.

Job creation in the human services could be one of the growth areas of the new knowledge economy. Older people may not want to stay on the factory floor or at a desk or behind a counter, but could still earn their keep and be useful to society as a whole through taking on paid part-time and casual caring work.

But that, too, will require a major culture change in the work contexts of social welfare and community services. Here we are in the grip, again, of professional turf protection. The claim is that you must have a childcare certificate or a degree in psychology or social work before you can be let loose on dependent others. In my view, life experience, along with a sense of decency, commitment and trust, is all that is needed to make a useful contribution under the supervision of those with more formal qualifications. There is room for a good deal of value-adding to improve the quality and range of skills of aged care workers, who should be recruited from the ranks of experienced people, not just from the younger, formally qualified group.

It is simply a failure of imagination and management skill that keeps other non-professional people out of a helping role. In fact, the supposed drop (not, in fact, as bad as some would claim) in the numbers of community volunteers is as much related to the unwillingness of professional gatekeepers to deal with their somewhat messy time schedules and varied capabilities as it has to do with changing community values or even time availability.

As well, young people, supposedly suicidal and alienated from a meaningless world, could very well learn to be needed and valued if we reconstructed community services around an 'apprenticeship in care' for every student. You can't teach self-esteem; it is acquired by being valued and respected by others, through having a stake in the wider groups and society to which you belong. Mandated community credits as part of the education process would both improve self-esteem and build the social capital that writers like Robert Theobald have told us is in decline. It would also help the aged and others in need of care and support. We have to invent new forums for intergenerational contact, so that the young will learn to relate meaningfully with the old.

In sum, an ideal starting point for the more intelligent form of locally responsive government I suggest we need in the future is the community services and family support sector. It needs to be re-thought as resourcing, not merely servicing communities, and linked closely with the schools and other services to build social capital.

Chapter 13

Education — the driving force

BETTER EDUCATION IS THE KEY TO BOTH the economic and social viability of Australia as a nation.[162] But we have to start thinking of education in a broader sense, not just in terms of what happens in schools and universities or in the preparation for a job.

Education both develops and challenges our sense of identity. It expands parochial horizons and opens up new possibilities. In a global information age the options are enormous, but individuals can only control their life project if they acquire the capacity to sift information, ask the right questions and apply knowledge to new situations. So the role of schools becomes that of helping children to navigate their way through a range of learning sources and problem solving tasks, to identify and develop their competences across a variety of areas and to develop an attitude to learning that is active and ongoing throughout life. Without this approach to all children, inequality and social division will grow.

I have suggested in the previous chapter that schools might be an ideal location for a whole range of family support services. But this is only one part of what I see as the vital role of schools in Australian society. My argument is not that schools, and therefore teachers, should be loaded-up with more and more tasks to perform. Rather, they should transform their links with other community resources and change the way they operate so that a culture of learning permeates Australian society. The principle of partnership applies again. Like it or not, both technological and social change will force schools to revamp their purposes and processes so that they become more of a community learning centre than a place separating children from the world of adults and the wider community.

Schools will be integral to the process of linking the future because they are the central bastion of 'place', neighbourhood, a sense of grounded identity. People choose where they will live on the basis of interest, and those with children will always seek a locality where the schools are good enough for their offspring. The new 'solo generation' — Generation S — may well find it more salubrious to live in the central city area, close to coffee shops, restaurants and nightclubs, but once children come along, a bit more room, a back yard, playgrounds, parks and, above all, a conveniently located school dictate where they will live.

Primary schools draw from the various childcare centres, kindergartens and creches for their intake; secondary schools draw from the cluster of primary feeder schools around them. So the natural grouping formed by families, children's activity centres and schools is the perfect basis for planning other government services aimed at supporting and assisting families. The school as community hub is the obvious way to go if we are to link private and public interests more effectively in the future.

The schools will have to restructure and change their work culture, in part because the present system is inadequate to the needs of the future knowledge generation and partly because the place of children in society is under threat. Schools will have to offer more to the wider community to justify continuing financial support.

What is called public education — the state schools — is already under pressure. There is a lack of confidence in the quality of state-provided education (not necessarily justified by the facts) and a desire for something better. Parents are increasingly choosing to send their children to private schools that have a specific charter, a clear set of values, a declared academic focus and a supposed accountability to the parents who pay the fees. Given that an increasing percentage of the funding of these private schools now comes from government, the terms 'private' and 'public' are converging. Under a free-market ideology, choice becomes the mantra, and parents should not be penalised for making the choice of sending their children to a private school. That principle has been in place, though the funding practice has varied, ever since the Whitlam Labor Government recognised the disadvantage suffered by many children attending religious schools, and ended the 'free, compulsory and secular' basis of the Australian schools system.

This makes 'accountability' a more significant issue than ever. Schools and the teacher unions have long resisted attempts to monitor their comparative effectiveness, but those days are over. There have, of course, been good reasons for their resistance. For example, students from a socially disadvantaged area do not come to school with the same readiness to learn as those whose parents are well educated and well resourced; some schools cannot afford, and cannot raise the same levels of finance for, equipment, special support staff and extracurricular activities; you can't compare schools with a high multicultural student population with others where English is the only first language; test performance reflects a whole range of factors, not just the quality of teaching; test results are not the only outcomes for which any school should aim; and so on.

Yet none of these reasons is strong enough to justify making no attempt to monitor comparative student performance outcomes on a range of measures, or to disclose which schools are doing well or less well in their attempts to overcome disadvantage and prepare students for a very competitive and complex future. No other organisation in today's society gets away without performance assessment; no employee is free to do what they like without their productivity being measured and called to account. We can argue about what productivity means in this context, but the rights of children and of parents demand some reasonable level of accountability.

Parents have always wanted to know how well their sons and daughters are doing at school. The report card showing grades in subjects and including teacher comments on student attitude and behaviour has long been a source of angst and family conflict. But it has been too cryptic, and a short parent-teacher meeting now and then to discuss progress or, more likely, problems, has often revealed more about the teacher's lack of knowledge of the child than about the child's actual ability.

Today's parents are demanding more. They are dissatisfied with what they call schools' 'marketing', seeing much of it as window-dressing to attract the best pupils rather than a factual representation of what the school does — its real culture. They want some say in the values and behavioural standards followed by the school, expressing dissatisfaction with poor discipline and inadequate academic standards. They want parent-teacher meetings to be longer and less ritualistic, giving an honest assessment of progress in a range of areas, with earlier feedback on learning difficulties. They see themselves as partners in the education process and want teacher advice on how they can support their child's learning at home. And they do want information on how well their own child, and the school as a whole, is doing compared with agreed school, state and national standards.[163]

None of this should come as a surprise. Children today are born later, to couples who have chosen to have fewer children, and who invest more in those they have than was possible with a large family, in full knowledge of how difficult life will be for young people who do not acquire the skills needed in the new information age.

In fact, it is Australia's parents, rather than politicians or bureaucrats, who have taken action to ensure their children's learning future. They have bought personal computers and laptops for home and school use, wired up to the Internet, and have themselves shown a passion for further education. Computer ownership in Australian homes is 47 per cent, in the USA 42 per cent. Internet access is 25 per cent in the USA, 19 per cent and rising every day in Australia. One-third of university enrolment comprises adult students, and the numbers doing courses part-time and via distance education have soared.

Parents are not fooled by critiques of a vocational focus in education. They know from first-hand experience how quickly formal education and narrow skills training become outmoded; they understand the need for more generic skills — the capacity to find, interpret and apply knowledge to new problems. No matter how much educational theory urges learning for its own sake, and treating the child as a whole person in their own right rather than an incomplete being in need of preparation for adult life, the fact is that children do have to be prepared for independent adult functioning. No part of life sits for long enjoying its own essential worthiness. One thing inexorably leads to another, and children will follow either a path that leads somewhere or one that leads nowhere. Parents demand that schools spell out exactly where children are being led, how schools plan to do it, and when those goals are likely to be achieved.

Already, national benchmarks have been set for literacy and numeracy in years three, five and seven, and 'national league tables' have been published in the press. But parents want and need more than test results. In the UK, and in some Australian schools, the old report card has been replaced by academic review days; individual student mentoring by teachers has been established; progress reports include the children's social and relationship skills; individual student performance is reported against school targets.

Yet none of this is enough. The initiatives suffer from lack of school resources, lack of teacher time to do the mentoring and monitoring of performance, and a persistence of the outmoded division between school, parents and community that implies education involves only what goes on inside the school. It does not address the underlying structural issues that must be faced.

There are other factors at work, too, and the schools must escape from being captured by parental ambitions and a university-oriented curriculum or they will lose social and therefore financial support.

There is decreasing interest in and understanding of what schools do on the part of those who do not, and will not, have children. We have already seen that Australia's birth rate has dropped below replacement level. Close to 30 per cent of women now in their child-bearing years will never have children. One in every five Australian households is a single-person household. We are an ageing society, so the funding balance could well shift from the young to the old, with their needs and demands.

While the old may still be interested in what happens to their grandchildren, the next generation is less likely to have children or grandchildren or take an interest in the children of other people. The lives of these savvy singles — whom I have called the 'solo generation', Generation S — will be ego-centred, individualistic, aimed at achieving personal financial success, and used to seeking work satisfaction across a varied and mobile career rather than security and job satisfaction in one position. Their attitudes to those complaining about the burdens of raising children will be dismissive: you made the decision to have children; why should I care about or contribute to that?

It cannot be taken for granted that Generation S will accept old slogans such as 'children are our future', 'it takes a community to raise a child' and 'children are everybody's responsibility'. But each of them will have been through the school system and have some idea of the importance of quality schooling. Each of them will find themselves working with the products of our schools, and the appeal to improved standards of education is likely to carry more weight than romantic altruism about the child as a precious thing. As well, Generation S will be in constant skills-upgrade mode, demanding accessible courses, opportunities to broaden their social skills. They may therefore also be open to invitations to participate in mentoring, tutoring and guiding school-based projects, at the secondary level at least.

Perhaps the best summary of what our school system faces in the next decades is 'learning to live with complexity'. It is a challenge to become a learning society in which global forces will favour the adaptable, a society in which the key resource will be human and social capital rather than merely physical or economic resources.

Because human and social capital develop within families and through wider social networks, our schools must be reconceptualised as just one part of the learning culture, and become embedded in society in new ways.

When work was arranged into fixed jobs with fixed tasks, fixed timetables and fixed, relatively secure salaries, the job of the nation's schools was clear — to help parents in their task of raising future workers and citizens through imparting fixed bodies of information, set skills and positive social values, in ways that could be planned like an industrial production line and tested in standard examinations of performance. We needed only basic education for the masses, as the skills they needed to perform routine tasks were limited. Throw in a bit about civics, so that they could participate in a limited way in the democratic system, but not so much that they might challenge the status quo — a hope that was dashed, because people can think and question even if they have no formal schooling.

Clear demarcation points were built into the system — elementary schools were compulsory for a fixed number of years; then the more talented were streamed out via entry examinations for secondary schools; followed by university-determined matriculation examinations to select the few who would become the educated leaders of society.

Of course, capitalism spawned many entrepreneurs who were not educated formally, but as specialised knowledge became more important, the education system became the major conduit to upward mobility. Schools had to teach a more complex array of content. Competition from the more innovative universities in Germany and the USA forced the old English-style university system to open its doors to larger numbers and to teach courses more suited to the demands of modern industry.[164] Today, without a degree or higher, your chances of getting a job of any kind are increasingly remote.

The waters are still muddied, however, because Australia's old colleges of higher education were transformed into supposedly equal-status universities, all offering the same range of courses and degrees rather than focusing on their special skills or catering directly for their student catchment areas. Unfortunately, most of them adopted the view that universities should be free to pursue knowledge for its own sake, an essential for human progress, but were not concerned with vocational outcomes and national economic or business interests. A new TAFE system was created to cater for more limited skills training and general adult education, but does neither job very well — with over one million enrolled annually, only 200,000 complete their courses each year. And the universities themselves have been driven closer to a commercial model to justify their funding, losing their sense of purpose in a welter of administrative restructuring and competitive marketing.

The transition points between schools, TAFE colleges and universities are still too rigid, with movement from one to another made difficult and students often locked into courses that poorly match their own talents and interests, let alone the occupational trends of modern society. We are still bedevilled by university domination of the school curriculum, forcing the majority of students who do not need or want an academic degree to jump hoops that certify their 'preparation' for academic courses designed in rigid fashion.

Looming against this rigidity in the education system are some powerful forces. The world of work is, as we have seen, changing so rapidly that no one course or curriculum, no set of narrow vocational skills, will adequately prepare young people. No short course can develop the skills needed in the new workplace. The competitive system of individual achievement and examination performance gives no indication of capacity to work on cooperative team projects, no hint of adaptability or of ability to solve new problems and apply creatively the knowledge acquired and tested.

Business leaders who once insisted the schools and universities be more vocational are now calling for graduates with generic skills — people who can think, are able to solve problems creatively, can apply knowledge to new situations, and have good communication and interpersonal skills. Information is now global, and available increasingly on the Internet, so students have access to the best teaching resources around the world and the status of local academics as experts in their field is under threat. The days of short-course vocational training are not over, but such courses are in themselves inadequate and quickly outdated.

The need is for repeated opportunities to upgrade skills and relearn outdated theories and knowledge — the chance to drop back in as needed, without bureaucratic barriers being set up such as term-long or year-long course requirements, fixed class times and places, for what we now call 'lifelong learning'.

In a sense, education needs to be seen as discontinuous, not continuous or sequential. There are, of course, basics that have to be learned before higher skills can be developed, as much in language as in mathematics, physics or chemistry. But every individual learns in their own unique way, everyone comes to school with a different family background experience, and often the basics can be picked up at a later stage, given the right teaching. Schools face a 'new landscape of learning'.[165]

Modern technology is a particular challenge to the traditional role of teachers and must be applied sensibly by schools. Information technology (IT) allows students and teachers to draw on resources well beyond the classroom or even the often disadvantaged community in which it operates. Potentially, IT 'permits teachers to spend less time on what Oakeshott calls the communication of information and more on the heart of education, the communication of judgement.' It opens up the possibility for older students to work from home, local libraries and other workplaces, using peers and other more distant mentors to complete learning assignments. Noteworthy, too, is the fact that computer games, often derided by adults, 'both motivate and challenge; they do not lower their expectation because of the perceived background of the player. If the game is hard, the machine frustrates, but it is less likely than a teacher to humiliate.'[166]

Research on IT-based learning already suggests that it may be more motivating and may more naturally develop 'problem-solving' skills in students than conventional classroom learning methods, so it is important that children in economically disadvantaged areas have access to quality IT equipment and mentors. Gardner argues that IT might free up the teaching role so that schools could develop new roles such as assessment specialists understanding individual students' abilities and interests; student-curriculum brokers to match students to wider learning opportunities in their community; and learning navigators working closely with students to cull the pearls from the dross of the Internet.[167]

It may now be timely to implement a modified version of Ivan Illich's concept of 'deschooling', through educational networks and learning webs; the technology now allows it, and technology is, in fact, driving such a change.[168] Such networks would more likely be used by secondary students, but have potential across the education system for all students and teachers.

The obvious way to go, then, is to reconfigure educational IT systems so that they can operate across education clusters, linking schools, local libraries, TAFE and other colleges, possibly even welfare service agencies and businesses involved in work experience and job training.[169] Adequate technical servicing, support staff and budgets would be essential.

Unfortunately, the education system has been allowed to rigidify the sequence that must be followed by every student. It is set up on the analogy of a horse race or a football match, where only one horse wins or one group wearing the same uniform makes it — 'it' being determined by people who are safe in their tenure and who resist any attempt to make it easier for those who come after them than it was in their day.

Age-grading bedevils our school system, with cohort averages dictating what and how students are taught and learn. As a result, failure is defined as a fault of the student rather than the fault of the system. The talented child or student is rarely allowed to skip ahead and miss parts of the prescribed curriculum sequence. The slow learner, the child who starts with poorer readiness to learn, is not allowed to spend more time on the basics without being left behind by their age cohort. No creative leaps can be made, the gaps cannot be filled in later on if someone has missed out at the required time. The one, standardised pathway is set for every young person to follow, and if they cannot jump the barriers where and when they are set up, they have no second chance. The schools are defined as being only for children, not for adults who lack basic literacy skills or want to upgrade their knowledge and skills. College and university courses follow a prescribed sequence, demanding years of study, and only in recent times permitting part-time study, evening courses, or other options resulting in a longer time-frame for completion of a degree.

However, there is not just one race, not just one finishing line or goal post. The new information age puts a premium on knowledge, not just information acquired in chunks, and knowledge comes from the creative application of what is known to situations and problems whose solution is unknown. Our education system has to adapt to allow every individual to win their own race, in their own time, and to start out again as the barriers or goal posts change. Education has to be about learning to live with complexity, so the old rigid, simply managed system will have to go.

Re-thinking curriculum

Clearly, every individual in the information age has to acquire the tools for accessing information, sifting out what is relevant, reliable and useful from the chaff floating on the Internet, analysing a problem accurately and then applying knowledge to the problem at hand. It was always so, yet we seem to have forgotten the basics in a welter of new curriculum developments. Today's students need to learn many things their grandparents did not. Social and communication skills figure more importantly than ever before and technological proficiency is the basis of lifelong learning.

But without a thorough grounding in literacy — defined as the ability to read basic prose texts, documents, forms and maps, and quantitative numbers and data, with understanding and critical insight — it is pointless sitting students in front of a computer screen or asking them to work with others in a team. We can mount arguments for each of the traditional disciplines, in terms of culture, citizenship, vocation and economic growth, but the key question should always be whether the content and the way it is taught help children better to interpret and understand their environment and to cope more effectively with life's demands at the turn of the millennium.

To do that, we need to think creatively, but we also need to be realistic.

The keys to understanding lie in language and its uses; without literacy, we cannot understand or communicate with others, think subjectively about life and its meaning, analyse critically, or apply what we know to new situations. So every effort must be put into teaching every child to become competent in its own language and the generation of meaning. It may help to be literate about other media as well — how to read a picture, analyse a movie story line, or appreciate how music, light and colour can affect our mood and our interpretation of what we see. But reading what others have said and writing and speaking so that we can be understood by others are the core competencies, no matter what the inroads of technology.

This adds up to textual skills, not just word recognition and simple reading. We must be able to read texts and evaluate their purpose, content and effectiveness; we must be able to assemble our thoughts and express them in coherent textual form — written, numerical, oral or visual. Without this, we are the powerless victims of nonsense and propaganda. Central to such textual ability is the ability to analyse and criticise, to weigh conflicting facts, interpretations and arguments. So critical thinking, not mere scepticism or relativistic values, must be a central goal of education. The old term 'rhetoric' needs rejuvenation if democracy is to survive and innovation to thrive. Every child needs to be skilled in the powers of argument, and should have their mind sharpened in debate through the assembling and development of thoughts. They need exercise in exploring ideas and their implications, reaching conclusions based on assembled evidence and persuasive logic. Soft thinking, loose argument and easy praise are unacceptable.

You cannot think clearly without some sense of the historicity of ideas — an informed awareness of how ideas and bodies of knowledge have been developed, how science has had to compete with religion, the individual with society, paradigm with paradigm. That is why history is important — not to know the dates of wars and journeys of exploration, but to know your own place in history as it has been influenced by the clash of cultures and political ideas, the sheer push for land, the struggle for survival and the power of competing tribes and nations over time.

It follows that no modern citizen can achieve a sense of history without an awareness of other cultures, an appreciation of how other languages and cultural traditions have shaped the thinking of others and influenced the course of human development. Language teaching may help, but such an understanding is not simply a technical mastery of another language; it has to include a grasp of language within a value system, a time and a place. Values teaching — developing an understanding of how ethics can affect decisions about our social and physical environment — must be instilled in every classroom, not through some separate part of the school curriculum.

The most important outcomes will be those that show a growing sense of mastery over a child's physical and social environment; each child will learn their way around, learn to navigate a complex world, both in their own community and in the wider global context. This must not mean a narrow focus on the child as self, on individual thoughts and feelings, on the misused concept of self-esteem. Yes, we should aim to make every child feel good about themself, to have self-insight, achieve self-control and develop a sense of efficacy. But self-esteem arises only out of real competence, and most children are not fooled by the elephant stamps or kindergarten graduation ceremonies or parental praise for minor achievements. They evaluate themselves against others, and they deserve our every effort to develop the full range of competencies necessary to thrive in the modern world.

Children need to understand that their own efforts and desires are not all that matters, that society structures and constrains opportunities, and that sensitivity and interpersonal relationships are not all it takes to remove racism, sexism and injustice in the world. Historical and sociological studies, an understanding of politics and civics, are essential if students are to avoid the sense of powerlessness that results from thinking they themselves can do nothing to change what they dislike about the world. Group action and group assignments — schoolwork with a clear social impact on their local community, apprenticeships in care, for example — might help lift the depression that comes from navel-gazing and the pursuit of personal happiness at the expense of some sense of the common good and the power of collective action.

Since structural change in Australian industry is likely to increase, not decrease, school students also need to be prepared in ways that facilitate the transferability of skills, rather than acquiring skills that are industry-specific or linked to highly specialised technologies and industry practices. More and more graduating students will not enter a job in its traditional sense, but will have to sell their skills and know-how on the open marketplace, as small-scale operators winning contracts from their competitors.

Beyond these structural shifts, the processes of work are changing rapidly, with a decline in routine, repetitive labour of the old assembly-line kind, an increased reliance on project teams to complete just-in-time projects on a contract basis, and an increased value placed on what are called knowledge workers, those with the highest skills, plus experience, plus adaptability and problem-solving skills.

In the new learning organisation, rigidity of attitude and authoritarian hierarchy are the enemies of innovation and competitive edge. The security of one job for life has been replaced by the footloose worker, at these higher levels at least, moving freely between companies and projects in the global market. Telecommuting and home-based work will be more common, with the road warriors carrying a portable office in the form of computer notebooks, hot-desking providing a temporary base for several workers, and Internet meetings taking the place of being in the office all day, every day.

We must educate people to understand that they will no longer have jobs, they will simply do work[170] and that entrepreneurial skills will be essential for each individual marketing themselves in the open marketplace.[171] Schools and higher education systems must stop thinking of preparing people only for work in large bureaucracies and companies and realise the significance of small business in the future economy. Even by 1996–97, only 0.5 per cent of the 1,052,000 businesses operating in Australia were classified as public sector organisations. Since they include schools, hospitals and the like, they do make up 18 per cent of total employment, but private sector businesses employ an estimated 6.8 million people, and there are over a million small businesses in Australia, employing some 3.5 million people.

Clearly, the spectre of large-scale global corporations offers a different sort of threat to the 751,500 microbusinesses (those employing fewer than five people) or to any small business involved in service provision. Even with takeovers by big business, small-scale operators are most likely to be subcontractors, competitively tendering for work. Entrepreneurial skills are essential for survival, and interpersonal skills such as negotiation, communication, adaptability and teamwork are essential for entrepreneurial success. In the USA, one-third of all domestic companies and 40 per cent of all service and retail companies are owned by women, and they employ more workers than the Fortune 500 companies employ worldwide. In Germany, one-third of all start-up businesses are female-owned.[172] This trend will continue, because family responsibilities for women will always demand more flexibility and self-determination in working conditions than we have at present.

The point is that teachers, including vocational education teachers, know little about either business or entrepreneurial skills. They have been trained for tenured jobs within a large public employment system, and the schools have been geared to the same academic competencies that gave teachers their life chances rather than to this huge sector of employment in Australia. That gap in knowledge and targeted curriculum design needs to be filled in the planning of schools for the future. And it can be filled only if schools broaden their perspective and engage business and adults with entrepreneurial experience in the community.

Both teamwork and competitive tendering put a new priority on inter-personal communication skills, on building contact networks, on knowing which fellow contractors are most likely to work well with you as partners. Thus what is called emotional intelligence or emotional competence becomes ever more important.

Challenges to the culture of schools

As we have seen, family and community life no longer fit the industrial model of old. Women are active participants in both education and the paid labour force. They are not at home all day, ready to receive children pushed out of the schools mid-afternoon. Children grow up in increasingly complex family arrangements, with conflict and stress endemic. Part-time and casual work disrupt family routines and create insecurity.

Parents may invest more money in their children, but it is difficult to invest more time in them.[173] Having fewer siblings means that children are less subject to the rough and tumble of friendly competition from within the family; they can demand and receive instant attention to their needs and wants; they learn less about compromise and cooperation in the home than might be desirable; and their parents are less often present to serve as role models for acceptable behaviour.[174] This is not to suggest that parents have to spend every moment with their children, but it is to suggest that children need more one-on-one attention than they are now receiving.[175]

It also suggests that schools have to devote more attention, not less, to the social-emotional learning side of school, to building peer-substitute groups and family-like home rooms, and to bringing children into more regular and meaningful contact with a range of adults. Teachers alone cannot do this, but they could draw on the resources of others in the community and make schools a true gathering place for the aged, for family support service agencies, for business managers and for other mentors who could add value to the shared socialisation tasks of parents and teachers.

In the various consultations carried out by Education Queensland for its Education 2010 Project, several clear lines of action emerged that coincide with the needs of the networked society.

The schools themselves wished to be freed from central bureaucratic constraints. They already recognised that regional and local variation in student needs, parental backgrounds and work opportunities make any one way of running the schools both frustrating of school/community-based initiatives and ineffective in meeting desired outcomes. This does not mean a lack of accountability, because schools should remain accountable for helping students achieve specified outcomes, but they should be accountable more directly to their own constituency — the students, parents and employers concerned. Time-wasting managerial requirements for writing reports and accounting for expenditure divert teachers and school administrators from their central purpose — to produce understanding, both of various disciplines and of the world in which we live.[176]

There was a demonstrable lack of knowledge in the central bureaucracy about what is appropriate at the school level, a lack of horizontal communication at the regional and specialist level to spread best practice and information, and inappropriate/inadequate forms of support from the central agencies. Such stumbling blocks could be removed and replaced by IT-based education cluster support networks responding directly to the needs of the schools.

At the same time, there appeared to be a lack of understanding on the part of many schools themselves about their own market. Though teachers may dislike the word market and its connotations, competition from the private school system, Web-based open learning and industry-based training, combined with decreasing retention rates, make it imperative that they learn more about their constituents, particularly why parents and students choose particular schools. The preferred approach would be to improve knowledge of their constituents, knowledge of the learning resources of their region/community/locality beyond the school and knowledge of potential partnerships in the learning process. This cannot be managed from central office, but it certainly could be encouraged and supported. The point of learning about their community is to adapt the learning process to the varied backgrounds, needs, interests and learning processes of their students. A one-size-fits-all model guarantees inequality of outcomes.

There was an apparent need for more differentiation and specialisation of schools. To cater properly for what parents and students need or want requires an analysis of their market, using the special skills of staff to create unique programs of excellence from which learning clients may choose. Examples mentioned in the consultations included selective schools based on academic achievement, religion, ethnicity and gender; magnet schools with a distinctive approach; focus schools in specialist subject areas, such as music or maths excellence; alternative schools for students with learning or behavioural problems; virtual schools using the new technology; and work-based schools, where students combine occupational experience with more formal learning and training.

Hargreaves argues that in a plural society, there is no harm, in fact, many advantages for motivation, learning and parental support, in having smaller, philosophically unique schools, but they must also teach the 'first and public language of citizenship which we have to learn if we are to live together.'[177] The usual problems of economy of scale can be overcome through consortia on administrative and technical support, and smaller schools designed with particular needs in mind are always more likely to involve and satisfy their clients than could a larger, less personal or community-responsive amalgamation.

That is why I argue that the central education bureaucracy would be wise to encourage schools to both network and specialise — sharing resources, exchanging teachers, and linked to community-based family support systems, local libraries and other education and business organisations. Such clusters would not all be of the same size, nor coterminous with present regional boundaries; rather, they would be natural groupings to emerge over time out of cooperative initiatives across areas that make such cooperation practical.

Part of the problem is that schools have been designed to keep out other adults. Parents have handed over, in loco parentis, responsibility for teaching and learning to the professional teacher experts; teachers have asserted their professional status, as do all professional groups, by building an ethos of exclusive knowledge and keeping parents at arm's length. This loses sight of the fundamental truth that parents and teachers are partners in the child's socialisation and learning. Neither side can do it alone.

But defining education as a partnership between teachers and parents will not suffice in the global age. Teachers cannot cope alone with all the social-emotional demands of their pupils. Nor can parents. Their work has to be supplemented by bringing in help from the wider community, and doing it in ways that recognise that the nature of community has itself changed.

Mobility is high and the sense of place that once defined the neighbourhood and its school are under threat. The sense of community has moved from traditional groups such as the churches, sporting and social service clubs to the more remote and unshared groups of the workplace, special causes and the Internet. As a result, schools find it more difficult to mobilise family and community support at a time when they remain the one common meeting point for many in the community.

It is this fact that shows the way forward. Schools should build on their neighbourhood and regional centrality in new ways, to make themselves an indispensable feature of community life. They need to build links that add value to what they are doing and add value to the common good. Such a move will require a massive culture change both in the way schools view their own role and in the way they are viewed by the community. It can be achieved only if governments alter the way schools and other community services are funded and managed. The key levers will be the range and location of local and regional family support services, plus the assistance and involvement of the businesses whose work structures directly affect the lives of parents and their children. New linkages must be forged so that the schools become true community learning centres.

Such links will vary according to the level of the school and its role with children, as outlined below.

Obviously, the role of teacher in such a radically reshaped school system would have to be rethought. The notion that children are passive receptacles into which teachers, as experts, pour information has long been discredited. No teacher, however expert, can know enough to meet the needs of different students; students learn actively from a variety of sources. Self-directed learning and the application of knowledge are essential for the future need of lifelong learning, and the teacher's key role is to lead students towards applied understanding, acting as a kind of knowledge navigator, providing the essentials for self-piloting on the part of learners. Gardner defines understanding as 'a sufficient grasp of concepts, principles, or skills so that one can bring them to bear on new problems and situations, deciding in which ways one's present competences can suffice and in which ways one may require new skills or knowledge.'[178]

This form of understanding involves knowing what you need to know as much as what you already know, and being able to apply what you have already learned to the task of acquiring new knowledge for understanding new situations and solving new problems. Such an approach rejects the notion of simple task specification, instead requiring an education process based on action projects, working with teams cooperatively, solving problems, and drawing on a wide range of resources to do so. It is the school's and the teacher's job to facilitate this sort of active understanding, not just to teach.

Perkins uses a similarly active metaphor for what happens when we get smarter — we 'learn our way around'.[179] Clearly, the teacher as subject expert is not ruled out in this formulation, but the outcome for students must be seen as the ability to apply what is learned in new contexts, not simply the capacity to regurgitate facts and theories.

It follows that formally trained teachers are not the only ones who can help students learn. While the status of teachers cannot be mandated from the top, by edict or by improving salaries or by educating the public, it could be enhanced by recognising teachers' special skills, preserving their time for the specialised tasks of guiding students through their discipline, leaving much of the less complex work to teacher assistants and other mentors, and outsourcing much of the complex social work to those trained to deal with such problems.

This, of course, challenges the monopoly of the teaching unions over education, but if they could agree that using human resources other than teachers in the schools might enhance teacher status and improve their effectiveness, opposition might be less vocal. By analogy, doctors do not do all the work required in hospitals — we have nurses, nursing aides, technicians and administrators — with no resultant loss of status for the doctors.

Thus the roles of adult workers in the schools would be reconfigured. The school principal should be a key master teacher, the leading professional in the school. The principal would work in partnership with a professional school manager, qualified to administer financial and bureaucratic systems. Teacher promotion could lead to being a master teacher, guiding the work of other teachers and teacher trainees towards better learning effectiveness. Assistant teachers could work under the supervision of teachers, paid less, but offered formal professional development opportunities to move up the system as they become more expert at guiding the learning process. Professional development could take the form of industry sabbaticals outside the schools; outside workers could become portfolio teachers seconded from industry or elsewhere as consultants, while much secondary school teaching could be contracted out to TAFE and other training institutions.

Small schools could join together in consortia/clusters to share their administrative infrastructure, in preference to the closing down of locally responsive small schools. Such initiatives could be worked through with teacher unions, in an effort to improve the range of adult resources available to students, improve the effectiveness of teachers, and enhance the status of teachers as knowledge navigators essential to the future lives of children in our schools.

Primary schools as family resource centres

The early years of schooling lay the foundations for later life, not just in terms of basics such as literacy and numeracy but also in terms of encouraging curiosity and creativity, learning how to learn, the habits of the inquiring mind. Primary schools move children beyond the particularistic bias of parents and towards a more objective, detached evaluation of achievement. They bring children into a comparative framework of peers rather than older or younger siblings, where they can test themselves out and develop a sense of competence, learning with and from others their own age.

But primary schools are still very close to the home, both geographically and also in the sense that teachers are more like substitute parents than strictly objective assessors of performance. Primary schools draw from a locality of families usually similar to one another in terms of socio-economic status and ethnicity. At this age, children are still learning about social standards, what is acceptable behaviour and what is not, and the culture of middle-class teachers is often at odds with what has been learned at home. Indeed, many teachers complain that no standards have been taught or enforced at home, so that they have to spend more of their time on discipline and emotional counselling than on the formal school curriculum.

Rather than complain that they cannot cope with such demands, teachers in primary schools should be encouraged to work more closely with parents, to use them as mentors, or as tutors in the basic skills, drawing them into discussions about parenting, child development, managing behaviour, even the curriculum itself. They should bring into the schools a whole range of outside experts — parent educators, counsellors, social workers, older people — who can do the social-emotional work better than they can.[180]

Every teacher needs training in the development of what is called emotional competence or emotional intelligence, and the school as an organisation must be imbued with the ethos of fostering social-emotional health.

But an additional step, as I have already outlined, would be to draw on other, more appropriate resources — childcare, youth and ethnic community services, non-government welfare agencies, business human resource managers — to work with them in the cause of helping those most in need, insisting that government departments dealing with sectors such as human services, police, health, aged care and so on work more closely with the schools and use them as a community hub for more effective intervention in the social-emotional and learning difficulties experienced by many students.

While the central government bureaucracy needs to remove barriers to such collaboration, integrating all of the human service related departments, it would be preferable for each school or cluster to develop its own unique links with external agencies, since each school and area will have its own mix of social needs. Schools with a high Aboriginal or other ethnic population, for example, would work with linked agencies in different ways from schools where there is more of a multicultural or socio-economic mix. Such links cannot be mandated from the top; they must develop generically from careful negotiation in the local area.

School resources reflect another emerging problem: the increasing divide between regions in terms of job opportunities, social disadvantage, parental stress and dysfunctional student behaviour. Disadvantaged regions are readily identifiable from ABS statistics, and additional resources could be devoted to them. In particular, attention needs to be paid to early childhood readiness for school, with special provision of childcare, parenting education and family counselling, based on policies of community inclusion and connectedness. Infant health and welfare, like pre-school programs, should focus on readiness factors.

The state systems are losing enrolment share, particularly at the pre-school level, many parents recognising that these early years are a vital foundation for learning and that the state system under-resources this stage of childhood development. There is hardly a better-researched and documented aspect of education than these significant early childhood years, including the long-term cost-benefits of quality childcare/pre-school programs and the long-term disadvantages for children without access to quality early childhood programs. Historically, provision has been bedevilled by the false distinction between childcare and pre-school, the reluctance of kindergarten experts to focus on education as compared to play.

The clear need is for education to seize the day, cut through the theoretical and academic niceties, recognise that investment in children at this level will pay off in myriad ways, helping to prevent child abuse, lack of thriving, ill-health, school failure, early dropout, poor job chances, delinquency and crime in later life, and ensure that every child has access to quality childcare and pre-school programs. The government and community must recognise that quality childcare (even without specific educational programs), playgroups, parent education programs, creative playgrounds, and mobile children's book and toy libraries are all part of preparing children for schools — absolutely essential in disadvantaged areas where parental resources are lacking.

Unless children are ready to learn when they start formal schooling, much of the teachers' time is wasted and the cost to the general community is huge. Briefly, the literature suggests the following qualities that define a child who is ready to learn and already learning effectively: confidence, curiosity, intentionality and persistence, self-control, relatedness, capacity to communicate and cooperativeness.[181] These are the qualities one would hope every child and every adult citizen has developed through their educational experience and their personal life, but the foundations must be laid early in life.

Australia does not need another study to investigate which form of childcare leads to what sort of positive versus negative outcomes as proposed by the Howard Government but, rather, the establishment of a readiness to learn inquiry, to highlight what is known and to indicate ways in which early childhood services can be better integrated into the pre-school and early primary school years.[182]

Clearly, such readiness cannot be achieved without the parents of every child understanding best practice and cooperating as partners in the education process. This is crucial in the primary school years, where a more family-like atmosphere in the school can and should be encouraged. This requires open encouragement for parents to participate in the life of the school, assisting teachers as aides in classroom learning, not just slicing oranges or as schoolyard watchdogs. The present control mentality of some schools has to be broken down in order for this to occur.

The schools are a community resource, funded by the state from public tax revenue, and all members of the community, not just parents, have a right to be involved and to use school resources. Especially in new areas, school facilities could be shared with community welfare groups, sporting groups, and a range of youth, arts, elderly and ethnic clubs, and it is the duty of central government to remove legal and bureaucratic impediments to such school–community interaction. Public liability concerns are too often used as an excuse to exclude others from using these costly publicly provided facilities.

State governments should therefore consider as suggested in the preceding chapter designating every primary school a family resource centre, responsible for far more than just the teaching/learning of primary school students. The pragmatic and doubtless cost-effective integration of much of the work of human service providers, both statutory and non-government, could be centred on the primary schools as community hubs. Kindergartens, infant health centres, childcare centres and after-school programs could be more closely linked, perhaps co-located, with primary schools. Funds currently allocated to central bureaucrats could be diverted to these community hubs, and used to finance coordination workers and spaces allocated to the school's broader work in family education/support. Funds might also be needed to assist the development of computerised links between area cluster schools, childcare centres, libraries and so on, to allow information sharing across all access points.

In particular, parent-education programs could be centred round the primary schools, not conducted by school staff but by experts seconded from outside and funded by other departments. But they would work cooperatively with teachers to share their knowledge of family and community problems/needs, as partners in the education provided by the primary school. The starting point should be a clear understanding of the family and community background of the pupils, the wishes of their parents, and a knowledge of the foundations required for lifelong learning.

Cognitive psychology makes it clear that every child has the potential to develop several forms of intelligence, not merely the two on which schools have traditionally focused: linguistic and logical-mathematical intelligence. Gardner identifies eight sets of competence or intelligence, which are inter-linked, and need attention if children are to develop even those two. Each child has a different blend of the eight, so his/her route to understanding will vary with their unique balance of intelligences.[183] Gardner does not argue that schools should have separate curriculum areas pursuing the other six forms of intelligence (spatial, bodily-kinaesthetic, musical, interpersonal, intra-personal and naturalistic), but he does argue that every child should be challenged to develop all forms as far as is possible.

Other researchers describe this variety of abilities differently. For example, Bentley emphasises the child's practical ability to adapt to varying contexts and situations, and the ability to display creative intelligence by creating routines for familiar activities and becoming better able to deal with novelty.[184] Ceci and Cole both insist on the importance of the child's varying environment and context to the way intelligence develops.[185] Writers such as Salovey and Mayer, and Goleman, highlight the importance of emotional intelligence or emotional competence in determining success in life, whether that success be in handling family relationships, school learning, peer-group interaction or workplace tasks.[186] This ends the rigid distinction between reason and emotion, and is a crucial advance in thinking about education for the global information age, where communication, adaptability and working with diversity are the crucial skills.

Perkins, like all the others, stresses the fact that the capacity for intelligent behaviour can be learned; it is not something only inherent in our genetic make-up, surely a lesson every teacher needs to comprehend in terms of both methodology and assessment.[187] There are, he says, three foundations for intelligent life performance: neural, experiential and reflective, the last two coming from experience and mastery in certain areas, plus the internal control system that allows self-review and strategic thinking. Most of these theorists stress the centrality of active practical learning as opposed to the passive learning of facts, theories and categories of information. Gardner, in particular, calls for 'apprenticeships to excellence', while Bentley describes numerous examples of learning in practice that go well beyond the confines of the school or classroom.[188]

It is therefore important that teacher education and all curriculum discussion relating to primary school be informed by the new psychology of intelligence. While linguistic and logical-mathematical skills will continue to be important, perhaps even more important, in the digital world, foundations must be laid in all aspects of potential competence if we are to educate the whole child.

The middle school as a surrounding organisation

The middle school years need to be given special consideration in the structure of education. Transition from primary school and the onset of puberty bring special needs and problems, and the school structure should deal with these directly and positively. Though, often, too much is made of the turbulence of the adolescent years, it is clear that facing the future as an adolescent today is somewhat more insecure than it was some decades ago.

How those middle school years are defined may vary state by state, but it is probably wise to separate teens aged 11 to 14 from young people aged 15 to 18, who are more adult-oriented and better able to control their own learning program. Because at this stage of their lives many students' mothers are re-entering the paid workforce, while their fathers are at the peak of their careers, working longer hours and feeling less secure in their jobs, it is important for the middle school to serve as a surrounding organisation, ensuring that its rules are worked out democratically with students; that every student is included and valued in the school community; that learning is relevant to the real world, and project-based whenever possible; that physical activity is encouraged; that every aspect of the school's program values effort, academic rigour and high achievement; that school-structured experiences both within and outside the school enhance competence and thus self-esteem on the basis of real achievement, not phoney praise; and that resilience, gaining confidence, and involvement with a widening circle of adult mentors is facilitated. A greater emphasis on learning how to learn, on problem-solving, on analytic and synthesising skills, rather than on fixed subject-matter content, might well lay the foundations for the more focused academic demands of the senior secondary years.

A particular need during the middle school years is to expose students to as wide a variety of work experiences and potential career paths as possible, to ensure that their future life choices and curriculum are not narrowed down. This is linked, of course, with the point made above about reducing the dominance of school curricula by university entry requirements. Close networks with local employers and TAFE colleges should be built, and credit given for student work in community services and workplaces. As Bentley points out, the knowledge economy is based not just on flows of information, but on the creation and application of human knowledge, and adding value. This is a fundamental shift from wealth generation through land, labour and physical materials. In the future, he says, wealth will derive from ideas, creativity and knowledge.[189]

He lists the core skills demanded by the new work context as being orientation to change adaptability and self-reliance; interpersonal skills as hierarchical work structures erode and teamwork and fluid work roles take over; analytical skills including seeing the broad picture, applying knowledge to new situations, and the capacity to sort information effectively; and problem-solving, rather than the repetition of functionally defined tasks. Mulgan describes the future workplace as a 'more intensively social model of labour', in which productivity is determined by the quality of relationships rather than by the rules of organisations.[190]

The need is for the middle schools, therefore, to rethink their old focus on individual achievement, individual assignments and individual competition in assessment. Most of the world of paid work involves teams of people combining their different skills to produce a jointly valued outcome. Working cooperatively, valuing the different but essential contributions of others, knowing how to add value to the group's effort, are important to later life success. While individual assessment may be required for the transition from final schooling to university entrance, the primacy of shared knowledge and jointly developed understanding and the application of knowledge to shared tasks should be a valuable focus of all student learning in the middle years of high school.

These years are also the years when students are coming to terms with sexuality and adult gender relationships. Particular attention needs to be given to how boys and girls are managed and taught to respect one another. Parental involvement is desirable, but the school has a wider responsibility to ensure that the values of self-respect, equality, empathy and respect for others are taught. Human-relationships education might be given a stronger focus at this level.[191]

Senior high schools as community colleges

The senior high school years also need to be rethought in light of the varied life prospects facing students in the new century. In general, the message is skills, skills, skills, but certainly not just narrowly defined academic skills, or vocational skills suited to one area of work alone.

Senior high schools need to consider several new ways of operating. For example, students could spend much less time in the school itself and more time engaged in self-directed home-based work or in activities in other community agencies or workplaces. Senior students need to be treated as responsible adults, taking the consequences for their own choices, decisions and actions.

Each student needs to develop at this stage a systematic portfolio of skills.[192] Such a portfolio would describe all assignments — whether individual or group — completed both within and outside the school, the skills involved, outcomes achieved and assessment reports. It would be important for every student to have gained credit for workplace experience, community service, hobbies, and interests outside the school curriculum itself, such as music, drama or sports.

All of this implies a completely different school workplace culture, where teachers are knowledge navigators, not information disseminators, where clothing and rules are appropriate to the age group, relying on student self-management, and with leisure and study spaces apart from formal classrooms. It would involve active encouragement by the school of adult mentors and assistant/portfolio teachers from the world of business and the wider community.

There is, in fact, no reason why senior high schools could not develop an ethos of adult lifelong learning, a place where students aged 16 to 19 complete their formal schooling, but to which they will return as adults needing updating of skills, further education or advice on career choices and to which they might later offer their time as adult mentors. Better links with local businesses and with TAFE colleges would transform senior secondary schools into community learning centres, or community colleges, open at all times to learning adults as well as to secondary students.

The special needs of youth need to be met in a more integrated fashion than they are at present, but integration does not mean standardisation; it means easier transition from one path to another. As the Victorian Kirby report argues, we need multiple pathways for youth, removing the boundaries between school, TAFE colleges and work experience, so they can gain a sense of reality and purpose from their education experience.[193]

The best qualified teachers would be employed in senior high schools/ secondary colleges/community learning centres, but their qualifications would include a willingness and demonstrable capacity to guide students in self-directed learning within the more independent, adult-oriented school environment.

The overall purposes of education identified in community consultations seem to point to the sort of pragmatic approach I am suggesting here.[194] Parents and the public appear to understand that education has social purposes, not just narrow economic ones, and that education for life, citizenship, community development, social cohesion and respect for diversity, are of more importance than narrow vocational training for jobs that may or may not exist by the time students complete their formal schooling.

There is expressed interest in quality, challenge and excitement as characteristics of the good school but, it seems, not a very clear understanding that such qualities depend on encouraging diversity and innovative experiment in the schools instead of insistence on a standard core curriculum.

But there is also a recurring theme in the public consultations — a theme relating to education for action, active planning, active learning, involving the development of skills that can be applied by children to life situations, their future work and their active citizenship in a democracy.

There is also a recognition that quality involves nurturing the best in every student, not processing them through a standard sausage factory. People agree that schools should be child-focused, not just system-driven, with children seen as active participants in the learning process, not just passive recipients. In fact, there is apparent consensus that a state-specific education system is meaningless in today's world, since each individual in future will have to operate in a national and global context, not just within one state, region or neighbourhood. The concern expressed for students suspended or expelled for behaviour problems is just one element of this. The public appears to want the state school system to deal decently with every child, not exclude anyone who might be a problem for teachers or for the system as a whole.

There is a clear recognition among these consultation participants of the changed nature of work in Australian society. They stress generic skills; vocational education for life rather than vocational training for specific jobs; the need to develop entrepreneurial, self-directed skills; the significance of education for relationships, and for equitable access to computer literacy; and the reality of lifelong education for every future worker.

There is also an understanding that education is more than what takes place in the schools. Calls for better resourcing of early childhood programs, for closer school links with family support agencies in the community, for seeing students not as individual learners but as part of a family and a community, which influence the learning process, are all indicators of a broader view of education, in which the schools play a key but not exclusive role.

However, there seems to be a high level of scepticism about school-based management, and little understanding that separate government departments could operate in a more holistic way. People say they want some stability and an end to fads, but they are not completely happy with the status quo. In my view, this is where state education departments can and should take a leadership role.

Despite much talk of a whole-of-government approach, no federal or state government has yet moved beyond the outmoded structure of functionally separate departments, largely because of bureaucratic inertia and a silo-mentality resistance to changing the power balance through pooling resources. But it is not beyond the realms of possibility, representing a logical extension of the impossibility of managing complexity from the centre. Whilst it may be dangerous to suggest that governments could further save money through closer integration of separate departments, when it is in the interests of a more holistic, developmental and preventative approach to children it cannot be dismissed lightly.

No grand, utopian reform program from the top will work. Instead, the message is that the system must allow greater experimentation, innovation and control at the local level. In that way, schools might regenerate trust and respect from the public whose taxes fund their important work.

Schools have to find new ways of helping students understand the complexity and unpredictability of life in the knowledge society. Schools must themselves become learning organisations in the fullest sense, open to new ideas and drawing upon a wider range of learning resources in their communities and beyond.

Schools will have to shift emphasis away from the old industrial models on which they were based — the model of the factory, transforming raw materials into a product that met standardised quantity and quality requirements; the model of the prison, taking young people off the hands of other adults, controlling pupils' behaviour rather than cultivating knowledge, skills and understanding; — and away from the metaphor underlying both these models, that of the machine — well-oiled, efficient, with a clear purpose and measurable outcomes, everything controlled hierarchically from the top.

This is a task of organisational culture change, never easy when people feel threatened and misunderstood, and made particularly difficult by the weight of common knowledge about education and schools and the vested interests of institutional structures that have survived long past their use-by date.

Lasting culture change involves changing organically the taken-for-granted habits of an organisation — the way we do things around here — not simply preparing a new mission statement and calling for a change in attitudes. Workplace culture is a lived thing. Usually, that involves change in work processes across all levels. Culture change cannot be imposed from the top, it has to be experienced as a better way of achieving desired goals than the old way.[195]

Both teachers and the wider public are weary and rightly mistrustful of the grand plans to reform the education system that seem to emanate from each new government taking over the reigns of power. So it would be unwise for any system to announce yet another restructure unless it involves adaptable change to be initiated at the school and regional level.

But culture change can be facilitated and encouraged by leadership at the top of the system, not in the form of new commandments to be followed and enforced, but by modelling the new forms of behaviour desired. For example, the central administration could demonstrate such a new culture through its structures and actions by adopting the following values framework:

- greater trust and respect for teachers;
- a recognition that the individual child is the key unit in education, not the school as an organisation, and that the school is a more important component of education than is the central bureaucracy;
- acceptance of the diversity of student backgrounds and needs at different schools in different localities, and encouragement of flexibility and autonomy in the way separate schools arrange the learning process;
- closer integration of services across the departments of health, education and human services, to improve the wellbeing and learning outcomes of children as well as to reduce costs;
- equitable provision of essential support services for schools, particularly workable computer networks, to facilitate student learning, the sharing of best practice, and cross-referencing of community resources that could be drawn into the education process;
- a marked reduction in central bureaucratic demands on schools in relation to reporting, accountability and student assessment;
- a clearer recognition of the differing purposes, needs and learning cultures of schools catering for early childhood, middle childhood and later adolescence, with encouragement of their differentiation; and
- determination to make the state school system one of quality and innovation.

Tertiary/university education facing a global challenge

At the tertiary level, we must move towards more generic skills instead of narrow specialisation. We might follow the British initiative and develop what are being called foundation degrees, establishing active links between a student's work experience and their academic studies through the involvement of employers and regional development agencies. Such foundation degrees might replace short-term certificate courses in TAFE, comprising a minimum of two years' credits, but not having to be completed within a two-year continuous block of time, with much simpler transition pathways to complete a standard university degree over a further one or two years' study. The foundation degrees would subsume the present jungle of qualifications at the undergraduate level. They might also be designed so that students could cover components taught at different colleges, which could work together as a consortium rather than engaging in the present wasteful duplication and competition for student enrolments.

At their best, such foundation degrees would link our current TAFE colleges and universities, but they might also involve components taught by industry within a region or area. Many companies are now facing an ageing workforce in need of a skills upgrade. They have difficulty recruiting young people from within their own region, but find local mature adults to be willing and intelligent learners. Running such foundation degrees across companies, colleges and universities, making their times and requirements flexibly responsive to both the special needs of business and the diverse family and work circumstances of adult employees, might well generate the sort of regional economic and social development governments are seeking at every level.

The long-standing domination of the school curriculum by universities should be addressed. So, too, must the detailed prescription of VET options. Schools should not deny alternate student destinations and pathways that are equally legitimate to that of achieving university entry. In fact, much of the alienation of students and parents from the education system probably stems from this narrow framework of achievement. Much more flexibility for schools to arrange learning in meaningful ways is required. Hargreaves attacks as a myth the proposition that final-year examination results are 'qualifications'. 'One cannot simply be qualified tout court: one is qualified *as* something in order *to do* something. So far as I can see, success in the HSC/VCE qualifies one as or in very little: it qualifies one to take an examination at the next level — on the path to — guess where? — the universities. We dupe ourselves by calling them qualifications rather than educational and academic achievements.'[196]

Each State could replace its university-oriented Board of Studies with a new Core Curriculum Board, which would develop a minimum core of educational outcomes to be achieved in each school, in whatever way schools choose, leaving substantial room for additional specialist and innovative areas of study to be determined by the schools themselves, based on community needs and staffing strengths. This core curriculum would include what is called above the public language of citizenship, civic and social education essential to the functioning of a multicultural democratic society.[197] It would be left to universities themselves to develop entry tests and requirements.

Too many of our universities are still stuck in the old British mode, scorning applied knowledge and insisting on outmoded academic standards. We did away with Colleges of Advanced Education and allowed them to become imitation universities, neither academic nor practical, having lost their original purpose of advancing broadly vocational education. We established TAFE colleges and virtually destroyed the old apprenticeship system, allowing mickey mouse training to take place in courses too narrow to prepare students for anything, often in disciplines totally removed from the real needs of industry, particularly those at the regional level who might become the employers of graduates.

Adult and further education is still funded poorly, as the Cinderella of a supposed lifelong learning continuum.[198] Teachers are among the most poorly paid semi-professionals in the nation, which drives down the quality of those teaching attracts, while university salaries are pegged in a way that contradicts the government's stated aim of making universities more autonomous and competitive.

As a result, Australia is falling behind in the race to become a knowledge economy.

In a recent article, Deidre Macken reported on the loss of Australia's intellectual elite. 'Globalisation is prompting skilled labour to behave like capital, flowing across the world to the centres that offer the best returns and the best future. In corporate circles, this flow tends to be two-way traffic, with professionals and managers moving in and out of Australia, benefiting themselves and local businesses with worldwide expertise. But for those who work in Australia's depleted academic and research institutions, the flow has been one-way.'[199] In fact, migration from this country has risen 17 per cent, to

82,860 a year, in the past three years; the number of returning Australians has fallen 15 per cent, to 68,000. Most of those leaving indefinitely are key knowledge workers — 46 per cent professionals, 12 per cent managers, 10 per cent academics and teachers, 8.5 per cent associate professionals and 3.6 per cent computing professionals. Of 1100 PhD graduates from the Australian National University over the past decade, 40 per cent have taken their first job overseas. Typically, no-one is monitoring whether or not they ever return.

Top talent finds Australian universities and research institutes a poor cousin to their overseas counterparts. Government funding of universities here is 75 to 80 per cent of that in Canada and the UK, and only one-third of what many US and Japanese universities receive. A top scientist in the USA will earn a minimum of $160,000 a year, compared with $92,000 in Australia. Australian universities do not encourage negotiated salary packages to attract the best talent, preferring every professor to be on the same rate — a guarantee of mediocrity. And there has been resistance until very recently to business-university partnerships, endowed chairs and corporate-funded programs, again a benighted approach to what is now a world-competitive industry, the very heart of the global knowledge industry. The energy level and teamwork of overseas talent banks is matched by low morale in the Australian context, and top talent recruited over the Internet means a loss of leadership among research teams here. Academic teaching loads have increased as administration diverts reduced funds from teaching and research. Australia is losing specialists in the very areas most likely to be crucial to economic development — information technology and biotechnology, with the IT and telecommunications industries haemorrhaging at a time when they will need to double their workforce over the next five years.

The Industry, Science and Resources Committee of the House of Representatives, in its September 1999 report 'The Effect of Certain Public Policy Changes on Australia's R & D', allocates the blame for Australia's lag broadly.[200] It suggests that the 1996 scrapping of the research and development (R&D) syndication scheme, criticised as being open to rorting, had cut research spending; the cut in the tax concession for R&D from 150 per cent to 125 per cent had exacerbated the drop in business investment; competition policy in itself had had a potentially negative effect, by breaking up public utilities and thus leaving them less able to undertake research and development, abdicating their responsibility for often important, if commercially unattractive, long-term and public-good R&D activities. Moreover, the policy shift towards outsourcing government services was discouraging long-term research projects and favouring overseas R&D providers — a clear example of free-market ideology damaging Australia's chances of being competitive in the global marketplace. As a result, Australia's research expenditure for the financial year 1999–2000 was only 0.8 per cent of GDP, compared with an OECD average of 1.27 per cent.[201]

Federal government expenditure on universities has plateaued ($5.723 billion in 2000, compared with $5.510 billion in 1997), while student numbers have soared (from 441,000 in 1989 to about 686,000 in 1999). As a percentage of total federal expenditure, higher-education funding has dropped from 3.1 per cent in 1994–95 to an estimated 2.2 per cent in 2001–02. On a per-student basis, expenditure has fallen from $11,032 in 1989 to $10,060 a decade later, while the staff-student ratio has deteriorated from 14.4 in 1989 to 18.5 in 1998. The federal government now provides less than half of all university funding, the rest coming from private student fees, the HECS fee and other sources. Pleas for deregulation from federal control have been defeated by political bungling and opportunism.

Present government policy on higher education suggests even further challenges to existing research and development within universities. The 1999 Green Paper 'New Knowledge, New Opportunities' points in the direction of rewarding a greater concentration on industry research and commercialisation, plus a system of portable postgraduate research places.[202] Of particular significance is the intention to make the government's $700 million operating grant money, which includes the research training component of operating grants and the proposed institutional grants scheme, open to both public and private providers. Public funding for research and postgraduate student support would be available to any institution that completes a research management and training plan and that offers courses recognised through the Australian Qualifications Framework. This could destroy the university monopoly on research training and encourage other agencies such as CSIRO or Telstra to provide competing research education programs funded by the government's operating grant money.

There is probably nothing wrong with this, if it stirred universities into more innovative and high quality programs, but under our international trade treaty obligations, we would have to extend the same rights and privileges to foreign companies and universities providing they comply with foreign investment laws, thereby losing the stimulus of having R&D programs contributing to our own stock of knowledge. One might argue that the students thus trained will still benefit the Australian economy, but given the brain drain described above, they are more than ever likely to be recruited to jobs offered by the foreign providers. The problem lies less in this form of open competition than in the level of Australia's public investment in R&D — $700 million is very little, given the need for advanced training, creative development and research investment.

Universities are set to undergo a further review at government initiative, partly along the lines of the West Report, with the Minister of Education foreshadowing full fee-paying, with student loans carrying commercial interest. A student-centred funding mechanism in the postgraduate area foreshadows a form of undergraduate voucher system that would provide a fixed government subsidy per student (to be spent wherever the student chooses), allowing the universities to set top-up fees. The dismay of academics denotes a still-entrenched resistance to change; instead, they should be coming up with their own, more sensible reforms.[203] The Labor Party under Kim Beazley is standing firm against the deregulation of fees, arguing that such a move would favour the older universities and reduce equality of opportunity for lower income and middle-class families, damaging the smaller regional universities. But innovation is hamstrung by the federal department's control of subsidised student places, and Peter Karmel is doubtless right in arguing that the university's role as conscience and critic of society is hampered by being an arm of government policy. The sensible way to go would be a full range of scholarships, the application of HECS loans to all students with payback starting time restored to Dawkins' original level of average weekly earnings, or what David Kemp called in his rejected cabinet submission, 'universal entitlement to higher education for all who can meet entry qualifications'. Total deregulation and competition might remove much of the unnecessary duplication and poor quality of teaching in the lesser universities, with the government relying more on student assessment of value for money than on a centralist, Canberra-controlled subsidy.

In any event, as Professor Lachlan Chipman suggests, most of the universities as we know them will probably disappear in the next decade, because they will be unable to compete.[204] At present, we have 37 public universities, all offering a comprehensive, but not necessarily high quality, range of undergraduate and postgraduate courses, plus research and other scholarly activity. Chipman argues that we can sustain only about six or seven full-coverage universities, with the rest having to narrow down their activities to niche courses in order to contain costs and remain viable. This might improve quality, but it would certainly reduce access to a broad-based student population, especially in regional Australia, unless other things change as well.

The seeds of such change lie in the West Committee report on higher education, which recommends a shift away from institutional grants and towards student-centred funding, a type of voucher that students can trade for any course, anywhere, at any time. Students would thus be able to stitch together the equivalent of a degree, using several sources, not relying on any one campus, not conforming to any one university's rigid coursework requirements.

The Internet already offers several university courses and degrees from overseas, and it remains to be seen whether Australian students would be permitted to use their voucher money on them rather than at Australian universities. Students are likely to choose the best courses on offer anyway, as public funding is reduced and top-up fees make them look for more competitive options. Coles-Myer is talking of providing university-level e-courses, possibly linked with universities outside Australia itself. Already, Rupert Murdoch's Newscorp has moved to form a joint venture with 18 leading universities to tap the global higher education market. Universitas 21 includes the universities of Melbourne, Queensland and New South Wales, along with Birmingham, Singapore, Michigan, Hong Kong, Toronto and Peking. Britain's Open University has now spread to the USA; the University of Phoenix has campuses in rented buildings for 56,000 students in 13 states and in Puerto Rico; California State University's 22 campuses are connected on a fibre-optic network, funded by Hughes Aircraft, Microsoft, Fujitsu and MCI; Stanford's engineering faculty offers 100 courses worldwide; and Duke University charges $485,000 for its Global Executive MBA Program. Australia's old-fashioned, comfortably complacent academics valiantly hanging onto their turf will have little hope of surviving in such a global environment.[205] Labor's proposed e-university is at a disadvantage before it starts.

Resistance will be strong as already evidenced by the rapid backdown of the Howard Government from Education Minister Kemp's leaked proposals in November 1999, but if Australia does not get this central knowledge industry working more effectively, we may as well all give up and become white slave service-providers to the rest of the world.

Clearly, the processes and structures of education in Australia will have to change. Though the global economy seems to be the main driving force, my argument is that education is the key to a more active democracy, a more civil society in which individuals can achieve their own goals while not forgetting the value of the community which supports them.

Chapter 14

Conclusions — driving culture change and linking the future

MOST OF THE ESTABLISHED WAYS OF doing things, that is, our culture depend upon continuing to meet the reality tests of everyday life. This book argues that the ways we have been doing things in the workplace, in the schools and in the wider community no longer meet the reality tests of life as it is lived by many people in Australian society.

The drivers of change are already putting pressure on those institutions that grew out of the industrial era. For Australia to survive and thrive in this century, we have to forge new links that make better sense financially, personally and socially.

There are several challenges for governments. They must continue to set the framework for Australia's competitive development in the new world economy. That means, inevitably, open markets, free trade, and the encouragement of competition and innovation in Australian industry. It means, also, avoiding a return to the rigidities of union demarcation disputes, or awards that went beyond a sensible set of basic human conditions for employees, and refining rather than removing the flexibility that has come from individual workplace agreements and enterprise bargaining. Maintaining minimum wages and reasonable working conditions is essential to an equitable democratic society, as is maintaining an adequate and non-punitive welfare safety net for those who are the victims of structural change or individual misfortune. But governments of whatever persuasion have to accept that society is ever more complex, people's life courses ever more varied, and that they cannot dictate from the centre how people should live their lives or what choices they are allowed to make.

Rather, the task of government is to use its revenue and power to ensure an equitable distribution of resources to its citizens, through its systems of health, education, family support and care; a safe and positive environment in which people can pursue their own life goals; and opportunities for paid employment in ways that match people's personal responsibilities. Government has to talk less about costs and more about investments — investments in education, skills, know-how, health, family support, child development, community networks, human capital and social capital.

I have argued that community-building is the central task of an intelligent government. This implies a holistic view of economic and social development, not an approach that puts the economy first and relegates the community sector to third place, an afterthought. It also implies a radical shift in the culture of government, the culture of what has become an overweening bureaucracy, with the domination of central managerialism over those whose lives are directly concerned with the way government funds are spent.

It calls for a reinvention of institutions such as schools, community health centres and family support agencies so that they are directly responsible to and directly run by regional and local communities. Government policies would spell out the broad parameters, the priority areas for action, but there would be no army of central bureaucrats poring over submissions, devising useless performance indicators and report forms, and interfering with the diverse and creative ways in which different regions would apply those policy guidelines.

My vision of the new, intelligent government would involve a massive decentralisation of administrative staff, a further reduction in the numbers sitting in central offices, and an extensive retraining and redeployment of those staff as on-the-ground community development workers. Just as e-business is doing away with middle men, intelligent government would do away with those who run interference between government and its citizens. It would send a clear message to the bureaucrats that they alone do not know best, that a democratic government wants to hear from and be guided by its citizens, and that democracy depends on the practice of decision-making across the whole community, not the passive conformity of citizens to the dictates of capital city mandarins and their lackeys.

Government can do this without my provocative tone. They could invest more in on-the-job training, insisting on apprenticeships, and on sabbaticals for all bureaucrats to give them up-to-date experience of the reality of their field outside the central office. One year out, two years in might be a sensible formula. It would guarantee sufficient support for the development of those new structures I have described, Family Resource Zones, Community Health Committees, New Links Workplace Teams, Education Area Committees, and it would transform the culture of administration from one of control to one of support and guidance. It might even restore morale and a depth of expertise to a bureaucracy decimated by mindless downsizing over the past decade.

The new institutional structures needed for the future will be flexible, adaptable, self-managing and entrepreneurial. They will be designed for and will change according to the unique economic and social conditions of their region. They will be linked, not acting as separate silos making decisions and administering programs in isolation from one another. The new regional processes would involve police and social workers working closely with teachers and parents; employers working closely with local government, schools and community services; and community agencies monitoring closely the circumstances of families across their whole community, not merely servicing the ones brave enough to ask for help or those forced in by child-welfare officers. Funds would be provided for broad policy purposes and within certain parameters to ensure equity and to guard against tribal takeovers, but no central office would dictate how that money might be spent or insist on rigid procedures unsuited to that community's needs and circumstances.

As I have also outlined, workplaces need much more active involvement in the work of schools and training institutions, indeed, across the whole range of community services. They depend on the quality of their social environment, the skills and life satisfaction of their employees, and their ability to influence change in directions that suit their needs, both for the viability of their business and for the security of the surrounding regional community. Business philanthropy should become an archaic term, replaced by business responsibility, business involvement and business partnerships with their communities, inside and outside the workplace. Programs such as work–family, work–life and equal opportunity should become incorporated into a workplace culture that optimises the productivity of every worker, designing work to get the best effort out of those employed, at times that allow workers to meet their other private and public responsibilities as well.

No intelligent employer can expect to have full attention paid to the tasks at hand when workers are distracted by family concerns or burnt out by overwork and stress. The intelligent organisation will learn from and with its employees, not see them as expendable commodities to be cast aside. Their skill levels will not be left to outside training or qualifications; they will be integrated within the workplace acting in concert with universities, TAFE colleges and the schools. The catch cry would become valuing diversity or building new links for greater productivity. Business would see itself as a partner with other businesses in their region, developing networks and sharing information with each other and with local government, state and federal departments, schools and community agencies.

In this endeavour, government would increase the funding of the present Area Consultative Committees (ACCs), set up to stimulate just the sort of activity described above. The problem with ACCs at present is that many of them lack the depth and skills necessary to work effectively, with some members not used to funding large projects or to dealing with more holistic solutions to local problems. You cannot expect regionalism or community development to work without adequate resourcing and training. It takes time.

My own experience with the Country Education Project and the New Links Workplace Project taught me that you can change the culture gradually, that you can build up trust by helping people think things through to a new level, by resourcing community-building properly and showing people that the funding body is serious about the devolution of power. As the Commission on Civil Society puts it: 'In pursuit of these goals, we must be both modest and tenacious. Modest because ... the institutions of civil society are organic, not mechanical, and can at best be nurtured, not engineered.'[206]

But I believe government can engineer without being too dogmatic. There is nothing so effective as giving people control of the money that is to be spent. Give them guidelines about addressing educational disadvantage, or about ensuring readiness for school, or about giving teenagers a stake in their local community, or about building a sense of connectedness between families and support agencies and schools, and let them go. They will be creative and reliably accountable in regard to how the money is spent.

You don't get community involvement out of altruism, or exhortation, or setting up committees for volunteers to have a say. The new public policy approach has to be very place-specific and issue-specific. People will volunteer if they see a benefit to themselves, their children or their immediate community. And they will argue over the use of scarce resources in a constructive way, provided they are actually resourced and then trusted to spend the money in the way they see fit. The engaged citizen is the key to change in building up a community.[207]

So government and its bureaucrats have to learn to trust those local processes of engagement. They have to learn to live with risk, expecting neither neat outcomes nor a lack of conflict and procedural messiness. Government has to become governance — increasingly, self-governance — because the days of top-down, one-size-fits-all solutions are gone. Just as business in the future will rely increasingly on networks and interlocking partnerships, so the new approach to intelligent government will become polycentric, adept at resourcing networks that may well become relatively autonomous from the state.[208]The job of government is to provide the stitches that link the patchwork, not to prescribe the colour, shape and texture of every separate piece of the quilt.

The best of the new links will be created by people who rely on their own practical, tacit knowledge of what is needed and who harness their own anger and frustration into a new and positive energy.[209] They may well be uncomfortable for politicians and bureaucrats alike, but that is what democracy is all about. People problems are not neat and tidy packages to be handled by experts at the centre. Indeed, the best and only solutions to people problems are those on which they work actively themselves. We know that when we think of children, top-down authoritarian treatment simply drives resistance underground, with self-control developing from experiencing authority gradually as they get older. Yet we still suffer the hangover of authoritarian, centralist government control that treats citizens as naughty children, telling them what to do instead of encouraging them to work out what to do by themselves.

The way forward has to shift that culture of control — has to actively resource that famous adaptability of Australians as a nation of immigrants in a strange land. Aussie disrespect for authority has always sat oddly with our reliance on central decision-making, but that stemmed largely from the tyranny of distance. The information revolution removes that tyranny, and permits a much more diverse, adaptable approach to governance by communities themselves. Intelligent government will aim at linking the future, through a whole range of new networks that are financed, perhaps guided and nurtured by retrained bureaucrats, but run by local citizens themselves, acting in their own interests but at the same time building social capital.

Those networks will operate at a variety of levels, not be fixed by central planning, because the needs and interests of communities differ across time and place and because engaged citizens will not trust any imposed solution in the new age of tribalism. Instead, they might turn their tribal interests towards the common good and the national interest, if they are resourced to build adaptable communities that can thrive and prosper in the global future we all face. The modern patchwork nation is one that benefits from and nurtures diversity, difference and innovation.

Equity comes from equitable resourcing and equal opportunity, not from uniform solutions and centrally controlled programs. That will be an enormous culture shift for a Labor movement used to distrusting the forces of freedom and sadly captive to the elitism of the centre. It may be less of a shift for the Liberals and Nationals, though they, too, have been deceived by their own propaganda on smaller government and have fallen into the trap of central managerialism coupled to incompetence at the practical level. I advocate smaller government at the centre, not smaller government in terms of its active building of linked communities and the networked economy.

The future demands a more active level of democracy, a more diverse and open approach to the way policies are applied at the local or regional level, a more place-oriented, citizen-oriented way of handling government responsibilities. Government is not politicians and central bureaucrats — it is of the people, by the people, for the people. By resourcing those people to build new links across the whole range of their interests and fields of action, we might restore that sense of trust and reciprocity on which a truly civil society depends.

Notes

Introduction

Saul, John Ralston (1995), *The Unconscious Civilization*, Penguin, London.

Etzioni, A. (1993), *The Spirit of Community*, Simon & Schuster, New York.

Interestingly, we are developing new Internet communities of interest that have no location in space or time and these can be used for both good and evil. In the new cyber age, many relationships will be virtual ones. Indeed, the most active networks in the cause of the common good now appear to be those between activists against big corporations mindlessly pursuing profit regardless of its impact on the physical and social environment. Many work contacts are maintained via the computer or by telephone and never become face to face. But they require interpersonal skills, tolerance, restraint and compromise in the same way as do our daily physical interactions. Thousands of people already play out a range of persona via the Web, hiding their true self, or testing the limits of self in a way not possible in their own family situation. Such activities are no less genuine or human than what we have always done through our vicarious enjoyment of life in dramatic plays, novels and films. They expand the potential range of self-exploration and human contact.

Jefferson, Thomas (1820), Letter to William Charles Jarvis, Sept. 28, 1820, quoted in People Together Project (2000), *The Power of Community, A Report of the Initiatives Reinvigorating Victorian Communities*, People Together Project and Victorian Local Governance Association, Melbourne, p. 28.

Chapter 1: Transforming the industrial economy

Several writers tackle the transition of Australia from an economy reliant on primary produce, then on minerals, to one where manufacturing began to develop under government protection, only to be opened up to world competition as economic nationalism gave way to economic rationalism and the free market ideology of neo-liberalism. Perhaps the clearest account is given by Capling, A., Considine, M., & Crozier, M. (1998), *Australian Politics in the Global Era*, Longman, Melbourne. Other versions are given by Brain, P. (1999), *Beyond Meltdown: The Global Battle for Sustained Growth*, Scribe Publications, Melbourne; Kelly, P. (1992), *The End of Certainty*, Allen & Unwin, Sydney; Latham, M. (1998), *Civilising Global Capital*, Allen & Unwin, Sydney; and Tanner, L. (1999), *Open Australia*, Pluto Press, Melbourne; etc.

Durkheim, E. (1893/1964), *The Division of Labour in Society*, Free Press, New York.

Kellner, Peter (1998), *New Mutualism: The Third Way*, Cooperative Party, Victory House, Leicester Square, London.

Owen, Robert (1991/1827), *A New View of Society and Other Writings*, Penguin Classics, London.

See MacFarlane, A. (1978), *The Origins of English Individualism: The Family, Property and Social Transition*, Basil Blackwell, London, for a detailed examination of this historical process.

9   There is now a vast and growing literature on globalisation.

       For me, the best analysis remains the three volumes by Manuel Castells (1996), *The Information Age: Economy, Society and Culture*, Blackwell, London, especially Volume 1, *The Rise of the Network Society*.

       Fukuyama, Francis (1999), *The Great Disruption: Human Nature and the Reconstitution of Social Order*, Free Press, New York, offers a better analysis of social trends than he does of possible solutions to the social problems of uncertainty and inequality that have arisen. But see also:

       Offe, C. (1996), *Modernity and the State: East, West*, MIT Press, Cambridge Massachusetts.

       Ohmae, K. (1990), *The End of the Nation State*, Harper Collins, London.

       Reich, R. (1991), *The Work of Nations: Preparing Ourselves for 21st Century Capitalism*, Vintage Books, New York.

       Strange, S. (1996), *The Retreat of the State*, Cambridge University Press, UK.

       de Alcantara, Hewitt (ed.) (1996), *Social Futures, Global Visions*, Blackwell, London. See Chapter by A. Giddens, 'Affluence, poverty and the idea of a post-scarcity society'.

       In Australia http://www.Bootwatch.com.au reviews much of the literature on globalisation, the impact of technology, sustainable environments, etc.

10   Pierre Pettigrew (1 June 2000), address to the National Press Club, Canberra, ABC TV.

11   Bagnall, Diana (9 May 2000), 'The influence epidemic', *The Bulletin*, Australia.

12   O'Rourke, K. & Williamson, J. (1999), *Globalisation and History: The Evolution of a 19th Century Atlantic Economy*, MIT Press, Harvard, Boston.

13   *New York Times*, 26 December, 1999.

14   Colebatch, Tim (23 November 1999), 'The West won the 20*th* century, but what of the next?', *The Age*, Melbourne.

15   Many of the writers on globalisation address the issue of the so-called service economy, variously emphasising networks, the shift from information to knowledge, the decline of traditional manufacturing jobs, insecurity, and the need for adaptability. See for example:

       Rifkin, J. (1995), *The End of Work: The Decline of the Global Labor Force and the Dawn of the Post-Market Era*, Putnam Books, New York;

       Letcher, M. (1997), *Making Your Future Work*, Pan Macmillan Australia, Sydney;

       James, P., Veit, W., & Wright, S. (eds.) (1997), *Work of the Future: Global Perspectives*, Allen & Unwin, St. Leonards;

       Davidson, J.D. & Rees-Mogg, Lord W. (1997), *The Sovereign Individual: How to Survive and Thrive During the Collapse of the Welfare State*, Simon & Schuster, New York, is one of the most interesting (if extreme) books on how the information revolution is likely to transform the place of the individual in relation to work and society as a whole;

       Menzies, H. (1996), *Whose Brave New World: The Information Highway and the New Economy*, Between the Lines, Toronto, is a Canadian take on 'the new cybernetics of labour';

       Neef, D., Siesfeld, G.A. & Cefola, J. (eds.) (1998), *The Economic Impact of Knowledge*, Butterworth/Heinemann, Woburn, provides an interesting set of essays on the new economies of knowledge;

       Hilmer, F. (1993), *National Competition Policy: Report by the Independent Committee of Inquiry*, Australian Government Publishing Service, Canberra.

Chapter 2: The impact of structural change on Australian society

16   This section draws heavily on the work of Australia's Productivity Commission, always better on the objective economic analysis than on any analysis of its social impacts. For example:

       Productivity Commission (1998), *Aspects of Structural Change in Australia*, Research Paper, Melbourne;

Productivity Commission (1999), *Productivity and the Structure of Employment*, Staff Research Paper, Melbourne.

[17]   Colebatch, Tim (30 May 2000), 'The tariff cuts that may boil this frog', *The Age*, Melbourne.

[18]   Colebatch, Tim (19 March 2000), 'Manufacturing work slumps', *The Age*, Melbourne.

[19]   Australian Bureau of Statistics (1996), *Australian Social Trends*, ABS Cat. No. 4102.0.

[20]   ABS figures quoted in *The Australian*, 23 June 2000.

[21]   Richard Sennett, quoted in David Leser, 'The lost men', *Age Good Weekend*, 25 March 2000.

[22]   Hilmer, F., (1993), *National Competition Policy: Report by the Independent Commission of Inquiry*, was the key foundation point of many recent reforms in industrial relations and monetary policy, though the reduction of tariffs, opening up of our markets and floating of the Australian dollar had begun in the Whitlam Labor Government years and were consolidated by the Hawke-Keating Labor Government;

   Kenwood, A. (1995), *Australian Economic Institutions Since Federation: An Introduction*, Oxford University Press, Melbourne, is a useful starting point on structural change. Pusey, M. (1991), *Economic Rationalism in Canberra*, Cambridge University Press, Sydney, gave one of the first detailed accounts of how the culture of neo-liberal economic policy had permeated the Canberra bureaucracy.

[23]   Norris & Wooden (1996, p. 2), quoted in Productivity Commission (1998), *Aspects of Structural Change in Australia, Research Paper*, p. 52.

[24]   See details in Productivity Commission (1998), *Aspects of Structural Change in Australia: Research Paper*, Section 4.2.

[25]   Phil Ruthven (1998), paper presented to VicHealth Conference on 'The Healthy Workplace', Melbourne.

[26]   Productivity Commission (1998), *Aspects of Structural Change in Australia: Research Paper*, p. 64.

[27]   ABS (1998), Labor Mobility in Australia, Cat. No. 6209.0.

[28]   Kelly, Paul (1992), *The End of Certainty*, Allen & Unwin, Sydney.

[29]   Leser, D. (25 March 2000), *The Age Good Weekend*, op cit.

[30]   Brain, P. (1999), *Beyond Meltdown: The Global Battle for Sustained Growth*, Scribe Publications, Melbourne, p. 63. Brain puts a convincing case for further restructuring Australian industry and education in order to make the nation more competitive. He is particularly good on Australia's links with and the weaknesses of the Asian economies, urging new economic policies for Australia in a coming period of low growth.

[31]   For further reading on the workplace changes brought about by technology and restructuring to meet global demands, see Bagnall, Diana (1999), 'All work, no jobs', *Bulletin*, 2 February, pp. 13–15; and Letcher, M. (1997), *Making Your Future Work*, Pan Macmillan, Sydney;

   Hilmer, F. G. (1989), *New Games New Rules: Work in Competitive Enterprises*, Angus & Robertson, North Ryde, is an early introduction to the potential impact of competition policy and industry restructuring. Hilmer was the architect of reform in Australian industrial relations, via the report Hilmer, F.G., Rose, J., Macfarlane, D. & McLaughlin, P.A. (1989), *A Better Way of Working: Enterprise-Based Bargaining Units, Report to the Business Council of Australia by the Industrial Relations Study Commission*. Of historical interest in the Australian business context also is the book by Blandy, R. et al (1985), *Structured Chaos: The Process of Productivity Advance*, Oxford University Press.

Chapter 3: The growing complexity of family life

[32]   There is also a vast literature on the modern transformation of family life and the nature of intimate personal relationships. See for example:

Giddens, A. (1992), *The Transformation of Intimacy: Sexuality, Love and Eroticism in Modern Societies,* Polity Press, Cambridge, a sweeping analysis of the way sexuality has become 'plastic', leading to a demand for more open and mutual disclosure between men and women in their relationships;

Edgar, D. (1997), *Men, Mateship, Marriage,* Harper Collins, Sydney, outlines how the nature of Australian marriage and family life has changed, in particular in relation to the involvement of men in family life and women's participation in the paid labor force;

De Vaus, D. & Wolcott, I. (eds.), *Australian Family Profiles: Social and Demographic Patterns,* Australian Institute of Family Studies, Melbourne, gives a factual description of Australian families which is useful in countering many of the common and mistaken assumptions about Australian families;

Silva, E. & Smart, C. (1999), *The New Family,* Sage, London, gives an up-to-date European perspective on changing family patterns, as does Commaille, J. & F. de Singly (eds.) (1997), *The European Family,* Kluwer Academic Publishers, Dordrecht. (See Chapter by Edgar, D. 'The Australian family as an expression of modernity', pp. 121–32.);

Hartley, R. (ed.) (1995), *Families and Cultural Diversity in Australia,* Allen & Unwin/AIFS, is the most comprehensive and up-to-date outline of the diversity of family values in Australia, making it important not to generalise too easily about 'the Australian family';

Family Matters, the regular journal/newsletter of the Australian Institute of Family Studies, Melbourne, is an excellent source of the most recent research and analysis of family trends. Available by subscription from AIFS, 300 Queen St., Melbourne.

[33] Other readings of interest in relation to new family policy matters include:

Wilkinson, H. (1998), 'The family way: navigating a third way in family policy', in Hargreaves, I. & Christie, I. (eds.), *Tomorrow's Politics: The Third Way and Beyond,* Demos, London, pp. 111–25;

Relationships Into the New Millennium (1999), Relationships Australia, Sydney;

Weeks, W. & Quinn, M. (eds.) (2000), *Issues Facing Australian Families: Human Services Respond, 3rd. Edition,* Longman/Pearson, Frenchs Forest. (See chapter by Edgar, D., 'Families and the social reconstruction of marriage and parenthood in Australia', pp. 19–31);

Edgar, D. (1999), 'Families as the crucible of competence in a changing social ecology', in Frydenberg. E. (ed.), *Learning to Cope: Developing as a Person in Complex Societies,* Oxford University Press, Oxford, pp. 109–29.

[34] Saunders, P. (1999), 'Families, welfare and social policy', *Family Matters,* No. 54, Spring/Summer, pp. 4–11, quoting from Maley, B. (1996), *Wedlock and Wellbeing: What Marriage Means for Adults and Children,* Centre for Independent Studies, Sydney, p. 26.

[35] Maley, B. (1996), *Wedlock and Wellbeing: What Marriage Means for Adults and Children,* Centre for Independent Studies, Sydney, p. 26.

[36] Buckingham, J. (June, 2000), *Boy Troubles,* Report from the Centre for Independent Studies, Sydney.

[37] Giddens, A. (1992), *The Transformation of Intimacy: Sexuality, Love and Eroticism in Modern Societies,* Polity Press, Cambridge.

[38] McCallum, J. & Geiselhart, K. (1996), *Australia's New Aged: Issues for Young and Old,* Allen & Unwin, Sydney, is the best and most accessible summary of demographic trends and their social impacts.

Laslett, P. (1989), *A Fresh Map of Life: The Emergence of the Third Age,* Weidenfeld & Nicolson, London, was a seminal work in rethinking the value of age and experience in social and economic terms.

See also, for a state response to the problems of aging, Brinkman, H.R. (1993), *Will you need* me when I'm sixty-four?: A guide to the abolition of compulsory retirement in South Australia, Office of the Commissioner for the Aging, South Australia.

39 McDonald, P. & R. Kippen (1999), 'Aging: the social and demographic dimensions', in *Policy Implications of the Aging of Australia's population, Conference Proceedings*, Productivity Commission, Melbourne.

40 McCallum & Geiselhart, op cit.

41 Fine, M. (1999), 'Aging and the balance of responsibilities between the various providers of child and aged care: shaping policies for the future', pp. 263–92; and Briggs, L. (1999), 'Policies governing aged and child care', pp. 293–313, both in Productivity Commission *Conference Proceedings*, op cit.

42 Barnes, P., Johnson, R., Kulys, A. & Hook, S. (1999), *Productivity and the Structure of Employment, Staff Research Paper*, Productivity Commission, Melbourne.

43 Wooden, M. (1999), 'Discussion', Productivity Commission *Conference Proceedings*, op cit, p. 214–21.

44 *The Courier Mail*, Brisbane, 2 October 1999.

45 Bennington & Tharenou (1996), as quoted by M. Wooden, *Conference on Aging*, Adelaide, October, 1999.

46 Giddens, A. (1998), 'Equality and the social investment state', in Hargreaves, I. & Christie, I. (eds.), *Tomorrow's Politics: The Third Way and Beyond*, Demos, London, pp. 25–39. See also in this volume, D. Hargreaves & I. Christie, 'Rethinking retirement', pp. 40–9.

47 Ibid, p. 36.

48 Bentley, T. (1998), 'Learning beyond the classroom', in Hargeaves & Christie, op cit, pp. 80–95.

49 Johnson, P. (1999), 'Aging in the twenty-first century: implications for public policy', Productivity Commission *Conference Proceedings*, op. cit., pp. 11–32.

Chapter 4: The new nexus of work–family–community

50 For more detailed work on the ideas outlined in this chapter and the next, see Edgar, D. (1997), 'Developing the New Links Workplace: The Future of Family, Work and Community Relationships', in Dreman, S. (ed.), *The Family on the Threshold of the 21st Century: Trends and Implications*, Lawrence Erlbaum , New Jersey, pp. 147–66;

Bagnall, D. (2000), 'The child in time', *The Bulletin*, 20 June, pp. 32–8, outlines the dilemmas faced by women who want to combine career and family and the social implications of a declining birth rate.

51 See Edgar, D. (1998), 'The certainty of uncertainty: Let's aim for equity and live that', *The 3R's: Relationships, Rights, Responsibilities, Proceedings* , 7th National Family Law Conference, October, Canberra, pp. 1–18; and Edgar, D. (2000), 'The family, towards 3000', *Proceedings*, 9th National Law Conference, Sydney, pp. 891–3.

52 Richardson, S. (1998), 'Progress in the workplace', in Eckersley, R. (ed.), *Measuring Progress: Is Life Getting Better?*, CSIRO Publishing, Collingwood, pp. 201–22.

The number of hours worked is a good indicator of how much time parents have for family responsibilities and for leisure, for pursuing their own quality of life. In the last 20 years, total paid hours have increased from 221 million to 276 million per week (up 23 per cent). Forty per cent of that increase is due to women's paid work, and 25 per cent of it represents increased hours of part-time work. Though the average hours worked per person of working age have dropped by one hour since 1978, the hours worked are very unevenly distributed. Richardson reports on research showing that the number of people working 49 hours per week is up by 225 per cent; the number working 45 to 47 hours is up by 176 per cent; while the number of those working only 30 to 34 hours has halved. However, Richardson also reminds us that hours of work are, on average, shorter in Australia than in countries such as the USA, the UK, Japan, Germany, France, Sweden and New Zealand, reflecting the higher incidence of part-time work in Australia and also, perhaps, different work norms.

53   Leser, D. (2000), 'The lost men', *Age Good Weekend*, 25 March, p. 19.

    Apart from hours of work and income earned, the degree of security people enjoy in their job has a major impact on family life and social participation. Whereas in 1989, some 73 per cent thought their job was secure, by 1994 only 57 per cent thought so. In 1995, 38 per cent of men and 31 per cent of women who left a job did so involuntarily, with two-thirds of the men being fired. The last decade has seen the number of men employed as casuals double, and one-third of employed women are in casual positions. In the decade of the 1990s, 3.4 million jobs had been snuffed out across Australia.

54   In the United States of America, a massive investigation and consultation on the problem of a declining civil society by the National Commission on Civic Renewal resulted in the report *A Nation of Spectators* (1998), now available on the web at http://www.puaf.umd.edu/civicrenewal/ finalreport/final_report_transcript.htm. There are several other reports on aspects of the consultation and public briefings by the Commission.

55   For the latest figures on Australian voluntarism, see *Voluntary Work*, ABS Cat. No. 4441.0, June 1995. The massive turnout of volunteers for the Sydney Olympic Games would suggest that, when a cause is seen as truly worthwhile (in this case in the national interest rather than a particular group interest), voluntary altruism can be regenerated, though even there many volunteers failed to turn up at the required times.

    The corollary of increased female workforce participation is supposedly the disappearance of women from the communal life of their neighbourhoods. They are no longer able to attend the church or school fêtes, do tuckshop duty, arrange the flowers, or organise lamington sales to raise money for local charities.

    Yet the facts on volunteerism do not bear this out. Older retired persons are most likely to be volunteers in churches and community groups, but it is the employed younger mothers and fathers who make up the bulk of voluntary workers on school committees, at sports and hobby clubs attended by their children, in professional groups and in political lobby groups in the community. Even in the USA, a 1998 report entitled *A Nation of Spectators*, based on a supposed decline in civic participation and trust in government, found that the average American belongs to 4.2 voluntary groups. There has been a shift from church involvement and membership of community service groups to active membership of professional and political organisations, and a marked rise in hands-on, community development activities, in 'the little platoons' of social life.

    Voluntarism is never merely driven by altruism; it is driven by personal and family interests in filling the gaps left by government in one's own quality of life.

56   Haas, L., Hwang, P. & Russell, G. (eds.) (2000), *Organisational Change and Gender Equity, International Perspectives on Fathers and Mothers at the Workplace*, Sage, Thousand Oaks, is the most up-to-date review of how different nations are handling the new work–family partnerships. See chapters by Glezer, H. & Wolcott, I., 'Conflicting commitments: Working mothers and fathers in Australia', and by Russell, G. & Edgar, D., 'Organisational change and equity: An Australian case study.'

    The most recent review of the state of play in Australia on workers with family responsibilities is that by Russell, G. & Bowman, L. (2000), *Work and Family: Current Thinking, Research and Practice*, Department of Family and Community Services, Canberra. The Work and Family Unit of the Commonwealth Department of Workplace Relations and Small Business publishes a regular newsletter on work and family issues and has an active website for exchange of information and ideas. Their many publications are obtainable through http://www.dewrsb.gov.au.

Many publications of the Australian Institute of Family Studies address the growing complexity of juggling work and family responsibilities. These include:

VandenHeuvel, A. (1993), *When Roles Overlap: Workers with Family Responsibilities*, AIFS, Melbourne;

Wolcott, I. & Glezer, H. (1995), *Work and Family Life: Achieving Integration*, AIFS, Melbourne;

Ochiltree, G. & Edgar, D. (1995), *Today's Child Care, Tomorrow's Children*, AIFS, Melbourne;

A special edition of the *Australian Bulletin of Labour*, Vol. 25, No. 3, September 1999, focused on 'Work and Family in Australia', with articles by D. Edgar, P. Reith, G. Russell & J. Bourke. *The Australian Financial Review*, 17 September 1999, also featured a Special Report on Work and Family, titled 'The new world order is here'.

[57] Sennett, R. (1999), *The Corrosion of Character: The Personal Consequences of Work in the New Capitalism*, WW. Norton & Co., New York.

[58] For an interesting analysis of how work affects the family life of men, see Russell, G. et al (1999), *Fitting Fathers into Families: Men and the Fatherhood Role in Contemporary Australia*, Department of Family and Community Services, Canberra. An American equivalent is Levine, J.A. & Pitt, E.W. (1995), *New Expectations: Community Strategies for Responsible Fatherhood*, Families & Work Institute, New York.

[59] Bowen, G.L. (2000), 'Workplace programs and policies that address work–family and gender issues in the United States', in Haas, Hwang & Russell, op cit, pp. 79–98 (quote from p. 83). See also:

Aldous, J. (1969), 'Occupational characteristics and males' role performance in the family', *Journal of Marriage and the Family*, 31, pp. 707–12;

Bowen, G. (1991), *Navigating the Marital Journey: Map: A Corporate Support Program for Couples*, Praeger, New York;

Kanter, R. (1977), *Men and Women of the Corporation*, Russell Sage Foundation, New York;

Orthner, D., Bowen, G. & Beare, V. (1990), 'The organisation family: A question of work and family boundaries', *Marriage and Family Review*, 15 (3/4), pp. 15–36;

Sussman, M. (1977), 'Family, bureaucracy, and the elderly individual: An organisational linkage perspective', in Shanas, E. & Sussman, M. (eds.), *Family, Bureaucracy and the Elderly*, Duke University Press, Durham, pp. 2–20.

[60] Pleck, J. (1992), 'Work–family policies in the United States', in Kahne, H. & Giele, J. (eds.), *Women's Work and Women's Lives: The Continuing Struggle Worldwide*, Westview, Boulder, pp. 248–75.

[61] Yankelovitch Partners (1996, June), *The Impact of Workplace Changes on Families and Children*, Paper presented at Family Reunion V: Family and Work, Nashville, Tennessee.

[62] Galinsky, E., Bond, J. & Friedman, D. (1994), *Highlights: The National Study of the Changing Workforce*, Families and Work Institute, New York; Hammonds, K. (1996), 'Balancing work and family: Big returns for companies willing to give family strategies a chance', *Business Week*, September 16, pp. 74–80; Bond, J.T., Galinsky, E. & Swanberg, J.E. (1997), *The 1997 National Study of the Changing Workforce*, Families and Work Institute, New York.

[63] Bjornberg, U. (2000), 'Equality and backlash: Gender and social policy in Sweden', pp. 57–76; and Haas, L. & Hwang, P., 'Programs and policies promoting women's economic equality and men's sharing of child care in Sweden', pp. 133–62, in Haas, Hwang & Russell, op cit.

[64] Glezer, H. & Wolcott, I. (2000), 'Conflicting commitments: Working mothers and fathers in Australia', pp. 43–56 in Haas, Hwang & Russell, op cit.

[65] Robertson, R. (1998), 'The pregnancy trap', *Australian Financial Review*, 4 December.

[66] *Work and Family, State of Play (1998)*, Work and Family Unit, Dept. of Employment, Workplace Relations and Small Business, Canberra.

67   Wright, S. & Sheridan, A. (1998), 'The Mummy Track', *Asia-Pacific Journal of Human Resources*, Spring, pp. 22–5.

68   Bjornberg, in Haas, Hwang & Russell, op cit, p. 72.

69   Haas & Hwang, in Haas, Hwang & Russell, op cit, p. 152.

70   Semler, R. (1993), *Maverick: The Success Behind the World's Most Unusual Workplace*, Arrow, London. As well, France's much maligned experiment of bringing in a 35 hour week has in fact reduced unemployment and is seen as positive by 80 per cent of French workers (*The Age*, 2 January 2001).

71   Quoted in Haas & Hwang, op cit, p. 151.

72   *Relationships into the New Millennium* (1999), Relationships Australia, Sydney.

73   Bellah, R. (1990), 'The invasion of the money world', in Blankenhorn, D., Bayme, S., & Elshtain, J. (eds.), *Rebuilding the Nest: A New Commitment to the American Family*, Family Service America, Milwaukee, pp. 227–36.

74   Littleton, C., Friedan, B., Auerbach, J., Resnik, J., & Geller, L. (1994), 'Rethinking the values of work and economic measures of costs and benefits: What realities of family and work for women and men must now be taken into account in the workforce?', *American Behavioral Scientist*, 37, pp. 1074–89, quoted in Bowen, G.L. op cit, p. 91.

Chapter 5: A business paradigm shift

75   Several critiques of the failure of economic theory are drawn on here, for example:

  Ormerod, P. (1997), *The Death of Economics*, John Wiley & Sons, New York.

  Handy, C. (1999), *The Hungry Spirit: Beyond Capitalism, A Quest for Purpose in the Modern World*, Hutchison, London; Korten, D. (1999), *When Corporations Rule the World*, Berrett-Koehler Publ., New York.

  Bessis, S. (1995), *From Social Exclusion to Social Cohesion: A Policy Agenda*, Management of Social Transformations (MOST) Project, UNESCO, Paris, puts a strong case for rethinking the links between economics and social order.

  Stretton, H. (1999), *Economics, A New Introduction*, University of New South Wales Press, is an Australian attempt to change the paradigm in economics teaching.

  The slowly rising field of behavioural economics (see *New York Times*, 11 February 2001, Money and Business Section) has finally recognised that human behaviour is not entirely a matter of rational choice.

76   Davidson, K. 'Why Reith's reforms are out of this world', *The Age*, 5 June 2000; see also Hugh McBride, in the Winter 2000 issue of *Dissent*.

77   For a review of the literature on discretionary effort, see Edgar, D. (1995), *Whose Cost, Whose Benefit? Measuring the Outcomes of Work–Family Changes*, New Links Workplace Project Working Paper, No. 3, July, Monash University Key Centre in Industrial Relations.

78   McBride, H. (2000), 'The productivity of unionised and non-unionised companies', *Dissent*, Winter.

79   Yunus, M. (1998), *Australian Financial Review*, November 12, pp. 6–7.

80   Argy, F. (1998), *Australia at the Crossroads — Radical Free Market or Progressive Liberalism*, Allen & Unwin, Sydney.

81   Argy, F. (1998), 'All for one under free marketeers', *The Age*, 5 May; and 'Australians need to fight hard liberalism', *The Age*, 6 May.

82   Henderson, H. (1996), *Building a Win-Win World: Life Beyond Global Economic Warfare*, Berrett-Koehler Publ., New York.

83   Macken, J. (1998), 'A futurist with fire power', *Australian Financial Review*, 2 December.

84   Alan Wolfe's (1989) book, *Whose Keeper: Social Science and Moral Obligation*, University of

California Press, Berkeley, makes a strong case for renewed business ethics and an active role for academics in arguing for social equity.

The Center for Living Democracy, Vermont, USA, is one of a growing number of Internet-connected groups pushing for change in business ethics and the way the global market operates. Their website is http://www.livingdemocracy.org.

See also:

Simon, J.L. (ed.) (1996), *The State of Humanity*, Blackwell, London.

Christie, I. (1998), 'Ecopolis: Tomorrow's politics of the environment', in Hargreaves, I. & Christie, I. (eds.), *Tomorrow's Politics: The Third Way and Beyond*, Demos, London, pp. 96–110.

Elkington, J. (1996), *Cannibals With Forks: The Triple Bottom Line of 21st Century Business Conscientious Commerce*, New Society Publ., New York.

[85] Bartholmeusz, S. (2000), 'Onus on institutions to improve voting record', *The Age, Business*, 30 May, p. 3.

[86] Uren, D. (2000), 'Unions hit campaign trail', *The Weekend Australian*, 27 May, p. 37.

[87] Batt, C. 'Ethics link boosts profit for investors', *The Sunday Age*, 14 May 2000, and Gullifer, B. (1999), 'When corporate philanthropy pays', *The Age*, 3 May. See also reports by Kitney, G. (1998), 'Red-green future for Germany', *The Age*, 29 September; Gittens, R. 'The folly of appeasing capitalist gods', *The Age*, 16 September 1999; Wood, L. 'Bountiful BHP cuts its social dividend', *The Age*, 5 May 1999; Gettler, L. 'Corporate bridge to citizenship sways over murky waters', *The Age*, 18 June 1999 and 'Corporates going from caring, sharing to give and take', *The Age*, 27 August 1999; Macken, J. 'There's money in morality: The rise and rise of ethical investments', *Australian Financial Review*, 24 June 2000; Strauss Einhorn, C. 'Corporate reputations at real risk', *Australian Financial Review*, 1 September 2000; Johns, G. 'Corporations are not citizens', *Australian Financial Review*, 1 September 2000.

Bole, W. (1998), 'Dissident shareholders win louder voice at corporate annual meetings', *American News Service*, Article No. 438, 30 March, refers to several groups pursuing better business ethics, such as the Investor Responsibility Research Center, Washington, DC (http://www.irrc.org); United for a Fair Economy (http://http://www.stw.org/home.html); Interfaith Center on Corporate Responsibility, New York, (Tel: 212–870–2296).

One of the most incisive comments on the debate about corporate ethics and the failure of corporate citizenship is by John Carroll, 'Rise of the corporate carnivores', *Australian Financial Review*, 6 October 2000.

[88] Berreby, D. (1999), 'The hunter-gatherers of the knowledge economy', *Strategy & Business*, 16, pp. 52–64; and Nevins, M.D. & Stumpf, S.A. '21st century leadership: redefining management education', pp. 41–51.

[89] Googins, B. (1994), 'Redefining the social contract', in Heuberger, F. & Nash, L. (eds.), *A Fatal Embrace? Assessing holistic trends in human resources programs*, Transaction, New Brunswick, p. 210.

[90] Friedman, M. (1970), 'The social responsibility of business to increase its profits', *New York Times Magazine*, 13 September, pp. 32–3, 122–6.

[91] Wheeler, D. & Sillanpaa, M. (1997), *The Stakeholder Corporation: A Blueprint for Maximizing Shareholder Value*, Pitman Publishing, London.

[92] Murphy, J. & Thomas, B. (2000), 'Developing social capital: a new role for business', in Winter, I. (ed.), *Social Capital and Public Policy in Australia*, Australian Institute of Family Studies, Melbourne, pp. 136–64.

[93] The most comprehensive and convincing analysis of how information technology has transformed the nature of modern business remains that by Manuel Castells (1997), *The Information Age: Economy, Society and Culture, Vol.1: The Rise of the Network Society*, Blackwell,

Oxford. His three-volume work is compulsory reading for anyone wishing to understand globalisation and its social impacts in the Information Age.

Drucker, P.F. (1993), *Post-Capitalist Society,* Butterworth/Heinemann, Oxford, is still one of the most lucid accounts of the transformation of work as we move towards a knowledge society, better (in my view) than Richard Sennett (op cit) on the negative impact of teamwork, flexibility and responsibility in the modern workplace on personal and social morality.

On the way intellectual networks operate within a geographic area to enhance business development, Peter Brain (1999) op cit, refers to the need for Australia to develop the equivalent of the 'global city' if it is to remain competitive in the world markets. He cites California's Silicon Valley, Seattle, Denver, and others as global cities with a concentration of skills, financial backing and active networks which facilitate the rapid spread of innovation. On Silicon Valley, see Saxenian, A. (1993), *Regional Networks: Industrial Adaptation in Silicon Valley and Route 128,* Harvard University Press, and his 1996 companion volume, *Creating Regional Advantage,* Harvard University Press, Massachusetts. The interesting point often made about such developments, including the rapid technological growth of countries such as Finland, Israel and Ireland, is that governments do form active partnerships with business and community leaders rather than leave it all to the so-called free market. The key to success seems to be the density of networks formed across the whole range of public and private concerns. See also:

Bodi, A. & Maggs, G. (1999), *Understanding Balanced Partnerships, Creating Balanced Partnerships in an Emerging Market,* Centre for Workplace Culture Change, RMIT, Melbourne, with the Office of Training and Further Education.

Mulgan, G. (1996), *Connexity: How to Live in a Connected World,* Chatto & Windus, London.

Leadbetter, C. & S. Martin (1999), *The Employee Mutual: Combining Flexibility with Security in the New World of Work,* Demos/Reed, London.

Sennett, R. (1998), *The Corrosion of Character: The Personal Consequences of Work in the New Capitalism,* W.W. Norton & Co., New York.

Gronovetter, M. (1973), 'The strength of weak ties', *American Journal of Sociology* 78, pp. 1360–80.

[94] The classic work is Bott, E. (1957), *Family and Social Networks,* Tavistock, London.

[95] Newspapers and industry journals are increasingly flooded with articles about B2B issues; see, for example: 'Potential vs. reality', *Honolulu Advertiser,* 22 May, 2000; special supplement on B2B in *The Australian,* 16 May 2000; Wilson, R., 'Jobs of the Future', *The Weekend Australian,* 22 August 1998; Parkinson, T., 'Mapping a global future for this wired country', *The Age,* 10 July 1999.

[96] Lynch, A. 'Survival rests on new customer alliance', *The Australian,* 30 May 2000, p. 18.

[97] Hochschild, A. (1989), *The Second Shift: Working Parents and the Revolution at Home,* Viking, New York.

[98] See also Inayatullah, S., 'Home alone — and stuck in the office', *Australian Financial Review,* 1 October, 1999.

Chapter 6: National identity and sense of place

[99] The recent book by Alan Oxley (2000), *Seize the Future,* Allen & Unwin, Sydney, is an upbeat account of Australia's growing self-confidence as a nation and the need to capitalise on it for both economic and social reasons. See also the 2001 Barton lectures organised by the NSW Centenary of Federation for a variety of takes on the concept of national identity.

Argy, F. (1998), *Australia at the Crossroads,* Allen & Unwin, Sydney, takes a more critical look at the failure to match economic policy with social responsibility issues.

Capling, C., Considine, M. & Crozier, M. (1998), *Australian Politics in the Global Era*, Longman, Melbourne, offers an excellent overview of Australia's shift from economic nationalism to a competitive market economy and the clash between individualism and citizenship.

Emy, H. (1993), *Remaking Australia: The State, the Market and Australia's Future*, Allen & Unwin, Sydney, offers another overview.

[100] The various opinion poll mappings by commentator Hugh Mackay offer some insight into these processes, e.g. Mackay, H. (1993), *Reinventing Australia: The Mind and Mood of Australia in the '90s*, Angus & Robertson, Sydney; Mackay, H. (1997), *Generations: Baby Boomers, Their Parents and Their Children*, Macmillan, Sydney. So too, did the outpouring of national pride and reassessment of Australian identity that followed the successful Sydney Olympic Games in September, 2000.

Scanlon, Chris (2000), 'The network of moral sentiments', *Arena Journal*, No. 15, p. 57–79, offers an insightful analysis of the role of place in defining community and national identity.

[101] The set of essays on wellbeing edited by Eckersley, R. (ed.) (1998), *Measuring Progress: Is Life Getting Better?* CSIRO Publishing, Collingwood, offers some interesting insights into the way Australians see their life priorities. In the UK, the influential think-tank Demos has addressed in various ways the meaning of wellbeing, e.g. Etzioni, A. (2000), *The Third Way to a Good Society*, Demos, London; and Christie, I. & Perri 6 (eds.) (1998), *The Good Life*, Demos, London.

[102] Edgar, Patricia (1995), *When Betty Grable Died — the Australian Cultural Experience*, Keynote Address to the Banff Film Festival, 19 June, Australian Children's Television Foundation, Melbourne; also *The Future of Children's Programs Beyond 2000 — the Technological Age*, address to the Asian Broadcasting Union 1999 General Assembly, Sydney, 30 October, ACTF, Melbourne.

Chapter 7: Globalisation and social movements

[103] This chapter also draws on the masterly analysis of Manuel Castells, particularly his second volume, Castells, M. (1997), *The Power of Identity*, Blackwell, Oxford, Section 2: The other face of the earth: Social movements against the new global order. Drucker, P.F. (1993), *Post-Capitalist Society*, Butterworth/Heinemann, Oxford, Chapter 7, 'Transnationalism, regionalism, tribalism', is also still useful.

[104] See the work of Gramsci and de Tocqueville.

[105] See the work of Marcuse and Horkheimer.

[106] Castells, M. (1997), Volume 2: *The Power of Identity*, Blackwell, Oxford.

Melucci, Alberto (2000), 'Social movements in complex societies', *Arena Journal*, No. 15, pp. 81–99, points out the self-reflexive contradiction between increasing options for action and the system's need for control and regulation, a contradiction which changes the nature of social movements in a global context.

[107] Etzioni, A. (1995), *The Spirit of Community: Rights, Responsibilities and the Communitarian Agenda*, Fontana, London.

[108] Scheff, T. (1994), 'Emotions and identity: a theory of ethnic nationalism', in Calhoun, C. (ed.), *Social Theory and the Politics of Identity*, Blackwell, Oxford, pp. 277–303.

[109] Touraine, A. (1995), 'La formation du sujet', in Dubet, F. & Wieviorska, M. (eds.) (1995), *Penser le Sujet*, Fayard, Paris, pp. 21–46.

[110] Beck, U. (1992), *Risk Society: Towards a New Modernity*, Sage, London.

[111] Drucker, P.F. (1993), *Post-Capitalist Society*, Butterworth/Heinemann, Oxford.

[112] Latham, M. (2000), 'If only men were angels: Social capital and the Third Way', in Winter, L. (ed.), *Social Capital and Public Policy in Australia*, Australian Institute of Family Studies, Melbourne, p. 214.

[113] Giddens, A. op cit.

[114] Castells, M., Vol. 2, op cit, p. 11.

[115] Klein, N. (2000), *No Logo: Taking Aim at the Brand Bullies,* Knopf, Canada, p. xix. See also:

Ostrom, E. (1990), *Governing the Commons: The Evolution of Institutions of Collective Action,* Cambridge University Press, UK.

Horsman, M. & Marshall, A. (1994), *After the Nation-State: Citizens, Tribalism and the New World Disorder,* Harper Collins, London.

[116] Richardson, S. (1998), 'Progress in the workplace', in Eckersley, R. (ed.), *Measuring Progress: Is Life Getting Better?,* CSIRO, Melbourne, p. 213.

[117] ABS (1997), *Australian Social Trends,* Cat. No. 4102.0, p. 115.

[118] *Participation Support for a More Equitable Society,* Department of Family and Community Services, Canberra.

[119] Saunders, P. (1998), 'The role of indicators of income poverty in the measurement of national progress', in Eckersley, op cit, pp. 223–38.

[120] Johnson, D.T., Manning, I. & Hellwig, O. (1995), *Trends in the Distribution of Cash Income and Non-Cash Benefits,* AGPS, Canberra. See also the chapter by Johnson, D. (1998), 'Incorporating non-cash income and expenditure in the measurement of inequality and poverty', in Eckersley, op cit, pp. 255–66. See also the papers in Edgar, D., Keane, D., & McDonald, P. (eds.) (1989), *Child Poverty,* Allen and Unwin & AIFS.

[121] See also the series of special articles in *The Australian,* June, 2000, on the topic 'Advance Australia Where?'

[122] ABS (1998), Cat. No. 6101.0.

[123] Colebatch. T. (2000), 'Rural Victoria has nation's lowest earners', *The Age,* 29 May.

See also the health report, 'Victorian Burden of Disease by Local Government Areas' released in January 2001 by the Victorian Government.

[124] Productivity Commission (1998), *Aspects of Structural Change in Australia: Research paper,* Melbourne.

[125] Kingston, M. (1999), *Off the Rails: The Pauline Hanson Trip,* Allen & Unwin, Sydney; and Stokes, G. (1999), *The Rise and Fall of One Nation and Pauline Hanson,* University of Queensland Press, St Lucia.

Atkins, C. & McCaughey, J. (1999), *Social Justice Report Card — Women: Balancing Social Justice with Economic Efficiency,* People Together project, Melbourne is just one example of how the public evaluated the Kennett Government's reforms in Victoria. See also Costar, B. & Economou, N. (eds.) (1998), *The Kennett Revolution,* University of NSW Press, Sydney for chapters on other policy areas.

The Bulletin, 5 October 1999, devoted much of that issue to 'After the Fall', an analysis of why Victorians turned against the Kennett Government.

[126] Costar, B. & Economou, N. (1999), *The Kennett Revolution,* University of NSW Press, Sydney.

[127] People Together Project (1999), *The Power of Community,* PTP with Victorian Local Governance Association, Melbourne.

[128] Mutuality is a Melbourne-based movement based on the ideas of mutual cooperatives that were strong in the post-War years. They also draw from the writings of British think-tank Demos about the Third Way adopted by Prime Minister Blair. See, for example:

Peter Kellner (1998), *New Mutualism: The Third Way,* Cooperative Party, Victory House, Leicester Square, London;

Patricia Hewitt (1998), *Is Mutuality the Third Way?* available on http://www.new-mutualism.poptel.org.uk/mutualism/msg00015.html;

Charles Leadbetter (1998), *Civic Spirit: The Big Idea for a New Political Era,* Demos, London.

Another attempt to regenerate community links is the Australia Connects: A People's Vision group, based on the efforts of Canadian Robert Theobald. Theobald, R. (1998), *Reworking Tomorrow: The Slim Book*, Institute of Workplace Training and Development, 36 Rose St., Wooloowin, Queensland 4030. See their Website: http://www.australiaconnects.net and their newsletter *Reworking Tomorrow Now*, available through jknapen@om.com.au.

See also:

Bagnall, D. (2000), 'The influence epidemic', in *The Bulletin*, May 9, pp. 26–33, gives a clear picture of how the Internet enables NGOs to influence governments in ways hitherto impossible;

Capling, M., Considine, M. & Crozier, M. (1998), *Australian Politics in the Global Era*, Longman, Melbourne, Part 3 on 'Political Culture'.

Matthews, R. (1999), *Jobs of Our Own — Building a Stake-holder Society*, Pluto Press, Sydney, draws on the Mondragon and other models of mutualism and cooperative distribution, for another Australian vision.

Chapter 8: Finding a more intelligent role for government

[129] Perhaps the most extreme examples of the view that globalisation will spell the end of national governments are by:

Davidson, J.D. & Rees-Mogg, Lord W. (1997), *The Sovereign Individual, How to Survive and Thrive the Collapse of the Welfare State*, Simon & Schuster, New York;

Rifkin, J. (1996), *The End of Work: The Decline of the Global Labor Force and the Dawn of the Post-Market Era*, Tarchner/Putnam Books, New York.

For Australian approaches to the changing role of government see:

Capling, A., Considine, M. & Crozier, M. (1998), *Australian Politics in the Global Era*, Longman, Melbourne, which offers an excellent overview of how the links between government, market and the civil society have changed throughout Australia's history;

Tanner, L. (1999), *Open Australia*, Pluto Press, Annandale, argues for a more integrated approach to the way government operates;

Latham, M. (1998), *Civilising Global Capital*, Allen & Unwin, Sydney, offers another Labor view of how modern governments should operate;

Queensland Government (1999), *Charter of Social and Fiscal Responsibility*, Dept. of Premier & Cabinet, Queensland.

Other approaches to government in the global age are advocated by:

Drucker, P.F. (1993), 'Really reinventing government', *The Atlantic Monthly*, Feb. 1993, p. 61;

Osborne, D. & Gaebler, T. (1996), *Reinventing Government: How the Entrepreneurial Spirit Is Transforming the Public Sector*, Addison-Wesley Publishing, Reading, Massachusetts;

Leadbetter, C. (1998), 'The digital age will mean the death of taxes', *The Australian Financial Review*, 24 July, p. 8;

Bessis, S. (1995), *From Social Exclusion to Social Cohesion: A Policy Agenda*, Management of Social Transformations (MOST) Project, UNESCO, Paris, puts a strong case for a renewed but different role for governments in the global age;

Ostrom, E. (1990), *Governing the Commons: The Evolution of Institutions of Collective Action*, Cambridge University Press, UK;

Beck, U. (1992), *Risk Society: Towards a New Modernity*, Sage, London.

[130] Several of the directions outlined in this section were stimulated by Martin Stewart-Weeks' chapter, 'Trick or treat? Social capital, leadership and the new public policy', in Winter, I. (ed.) (2000), *Social Capital and Public Policy in Australia*, AIFS, Melbourne, pp. 276–309. In my view, he has a better grasp of the location-based nature of social capital than others such as Mark Latham who still seem enamoured of top-down government control of every service.

The chapter by Eva Cox & Peter Caldwell, 'Making policy social', pp. 43–73, in that book is also valuable in thinking about the limitations of central versus local control; and Mark Lyons' chapter 'Non-profit organisations, social capital and social policy in Australia', pp. 165–191, is sceptical (as I am) of the virtues of non-government organisations versus government in taking notice of diversity and the needs of clients.

[131] Rifkin, op cit, p. 236.
[132] Ohmae, K. (1990), *The Borderless World,* Harper Collins, London; and Ohmae, K. (1995), *The End of the Nation State,* HarperCollins, London.
[133] Harding, A. (1999), National Centre for Social and Economic Modelling, University of Canberra, press release, June 23.
[134] Prime Minister John Howard, quoted in *The Australian,* 12 January 2000.
[135] Britain's Prime Minister Tony Blair, quoted in *Time Magazine,* 27 October 1997.

Chapter 9: Building human and social capital

[135a] The best reference on the differing meanings of social capital and problems with its measurement is the book edited by Ian Winter (2000), *Social Capital and Public Policy in Australia,* Australian Institute of Family Studies, Melbourne. Chapters by Winter, Cox & Caldwell, Latham and Stewart-Weeks discuss the conceptual confusion; chapters by Hogan & Owen, Baum et al and Hughes, Onyx & Bullen, Bellamy & Black give some of the first empirical data on the sources and active application of social capital in Australian communities. Some scepticism about the voluntary welfare sector is expressed by Mark Lyons, and Stewart-Weeks puts the strongest case for an active governmental role in building social capital.

Winter, Ian (2000), *Towards a Theorised Understanding of Family and Social Capital,* Australian Institute of Family Studies, Working Paper 21, is another attempt (only partly successful) to explain how changes in the nature of family life may affect the way Australia operates as a civil society.

The standard references in developing the concept of social capital (and commonly referred to in any of the growing literature on social capital) are Putnam, R. (1993), *Making Democracy Work: Civic Traditions in Modern Italy,* Princeton University Press; Coleman, J. (1988), 'Social capital in the creation of human capital', *American Journal of Sociology,* 94, pp. 95–120; and Bourdieu, P. (1986), 'The forms of social capital', in *Handbook of Theory & Research for the Sociology of Education,* Richardson, J. (ed.) Greenwood Press, New York, pp. 241–58.

Putnam's most famous essay, 'Bowling alone: America's declining social capital', published in the *Journal of Democracy,* Vol. 6, No. 1, pp. 65–78, and elsewhere, after taking into account all other factors such as working patterns, education and income levels, ethnicity, etc., traced the cause of America's decline in voluntarism to the advent of television as a time-filler in the life of busy families. The thesis has been disputed, but he makes a plausible case.

They all derive in part from the classic sociological work of Toennies, F. (1963/1887), *Community and Society,* Harper & Row, New York and Weber, M. (1947/1922), *The Theory of Social and Economic Organisation,* Free Press, New York.

Often overlooked by current exponents of the concept is the important work of Gouldner, A. (1979), 'The norm of reciprocity', *American Sociological Review, 25,* pp. 161–178, and Berger, P. & Luckmann, T. (1966), *The Social Construction of Reality,* Doubleday, New York. Berger, P. & Berger, B. (1983), *The War Over the Family,* Hutchinson, London, is a conservative exposition on the importance of mediating institutions. In the more recent overseas literature, perhaps the book by Francis Fukuyama (1995), *Trust: The Social Virtues and the Creation of Prosperity,* Penguin, London, has been the most influential. And Amitai Etzioni (1996), *The New Golden Rule,* Basic Books, New York, has been a busy exponent of communitarianism.

In Australia, the theme of social capital has been taken up most notably by Eva Cox in her ABC Boyer lectures, published as *A Truly Civil Society* (1995), ABC Books, Sydney, and Labor politician Mark Latham, in his book *Civilising Global Capital: New Thinking for Australian Labor* (1998), Allen & Unwin, Sydney. The edited book by Norton, A., Latham, M., Sturgess, G. & Stewart-Weeks, M. (1997), *Social Capital: The Individual, Civil Society and the State*, Policy Forum 14, Centre for Independent Studies, Sydney, is also a valuable source of ideas. Tanner, L. (1999), *Open Australia*, Pluto Press, Annandale, NSW, also takes up several of the issues in a different way.

In the United States of America, a massive investigation and consultation on the problem of a declining civil society by the National Commission on Civic Renewal resulted in the report *A Nation of Spectators* (1998), now available on the web at http://www.puaf.umd.edu/civicrenewal/finalreport/final_report_transcript.htm. There are several other reports on aspects of the consultation and public briefings by the Commission.

There is also a vast literature on the meaning of community, much of it romantic nostalgia for an age that never existed. For example, I prefer the realistic, conflict-based approach of Neuwirth, G. (1969), 'A Weberian outline of a theory of community: its application to the "Dark Ghetto"', *British Journal of Sociology*, Vol. 20, pp. 148–163, to the idealistic exhortations of Robert Theobald (1997), *Reworking Success: New Communities at the Millennium*, New Society Publishers. For an interesting commentary on modern attempts to recapture an idealistic suburban family-based community, see Pollan, M. (1997), 'Town-building is no Mickey Mouse operation', *The New York Times Magazine*, 14 December, pp. 56–88.

Some useful Australian minor publications on community include:

Sher, J.P. & Sher, K.R. (1993), *Beyond the Conventional Wisdom: Rural Development as if Australia's Rural People and Communities Really Mattered*, Report for the Commonwealth Department of Primary Industries & Energy, Canberra;

Rainbow Alliance (1997), *Community Participation in Local Government*, Fitzroy;

Bolton, R. (1987), *People Skills: How to Assert Yourself, Listen to People and Resolve Conflicts*, Sunar & Schusta, Australia;

Macleod, G. (1997), *From Mondragon to America: Experiments in Community Economic Development*, University College of Cape Breton Press, Sydney, Nova Scotia, covers a range of practical examples, particularly with indigenous communities. The closest Australia comes to these is in the Cape York Partnership program being developed between the Queensland Government and Aboriginal peoples and the various attempts to combine individual welfare payments into community development schemes.

See also:

Bodna, B., McCaughey, J. & Scott, D. (2000), *The Power of Community: Celebrating & Promoting Community in Victoria*, People Together Project & Victorian Local Governance Association, Melbourne;

Etzioni, A. (1993), *The Spirit of Community*, Crown Publishers, San Francisco.

[136] Quoted in Gettler, L. 'New economy unearths hidden asset — human capital', *The Age*, Business Section, 2 June 2000.

[137] Bourdieu, P. (1986), 'The forms of capital', in Richardson, J. (ed.), *Handbook of Theory and Research for the Sociology of Education*, Greenwood Press, New York, pp. 241–58.

[138] Coleman, J. (1988), 'Social capital in the creation of human capital', *American Journal of Sociology*, Vol. 94, pp. 95–120.

[139] Putnam, R. (1993), *Making Democracy Work: Civic Traditions in Modern Italy*, Princeton University Press, New Jersey; and Putnam, R. (1995), 'Bowling alone: America's declining social capital', *Journal of Democracy*, Vol. 6, No. 1, pp. 65–78.

[140] Oxley, A. (2000), *Seize the Future: How Australia Can Prosper in the New Century*, Allen & Unwin, Sydney.

[141] Taylor, M. (2000), 'Tackling social exclusion at local level: Neighborhood management', Summary Paper (Ref. 310), *Top Down Meets Bottom Up: Neighborhood Management*, Joseph Rowntree Foundation, London.

Chapter 10: Redefining regionalism — the way forward

[142] ACOSS (1999), *Common Cause: Relationships and Reforms in Community Services*, Paper 102.

[143] Oxley (2000), op cit.

[144] ACOSS (1999), op cit, p. 62. Labor leader Kim Beazley has flagged (February 2001) a review of competition policy and its negative impact on small communities.

[145] McKinsey & Co. (1994), *Lead Local Compete Global: Unlocking the Growth Potential of Australia's Regions*, Report for the Department of Industry, Transport and Regional Development, Canberra, ACT, p. 18.

[146] Putnam, op cit; Ostrom, op cit; Brain, op cit.

[147] For further arguments in favour of a more regional approach to managing Australia, see:

Hornby, F. (1999), *Working Together to Develop Our Communities: Good Practice and Benchmarking in Local Government Community Development and Community Services*, Local Government Community Services Association of Australia, Inc., Townsville;

Hodge, G. (1996), *Contracting Out Government Services: A Review of the International Evidence*, Montech, Melbourne;

Victorian Council of Social Services, in collaboration with Swinburne University of Technology (1998), *The Citizenship Project: A National Project to Establish National Benchmarks and National Indicators of Social Wellbeing*;

Johnstone, P. & Kiss, R. (1996), *Governing Local Communities — The Future Begins*, The Centre for Public Policy, Carlton;

Time Running Out: Shaping Regional Australia's Future (2000), House of Representatives Standing Committee on Primary Industries and Regional Services, Canberra, ACT;

Collitts, P. (1998), *Up-skilling local and regional leaders and economic development practitioners: a survey of current issues and possible future directions*, NSW Department of State and Regional Development, conference held at Tanunda, SA;

O'Neill, D. (1999), *Infrastructure: The Challenge*, paper given at the Regional Australia Summit, October;

Productivity Commission (1999), *Impact of Competition Policy Reforms on Rural & Regional Australia*, Report No. 8, September, Canberra;

Jobs for the Regions: A Report on the Inquiry into Regional Employment and Unemployment (1999), Senate Employment, Workplace Relations, Small Business and Education References Committee, Canberra.

Chapter 11: Workable models of community-building

[148] A more recent review of the Country Education approach is contained in the Proceedings of the October 1998 conference held in Ballarat on the theme *Rural Community Partnerships — Education for the 21st Century*, published by the School of Mines & Industry, Ballarat, Victoria.

[149] Lyons, M. (2000), 'Non-profit organisations, social capital and social policy in Australia', Ch. 7 in Winter, op cit, p. 177.

[150] The first outline of the New Links Workplace Project is contained in Edgar, D. (1994), *Connecting Family, Workplace and Community Resources*, Working NLW Project Working Paper No. 1, National Key Centre in Industrial Relations, Monash University, Melbourne. Also outlined

in Spearritt, K. & Edgar, D. (1994), *The Family-Friendly Front,* National Key Centre in Industrial Relations, Monash University, Melbourne. Later references include Edgar, D. (1997), 'Developing the New Links Workplace: The future of family, work and community relationships', Ch. 9 in Dreman, S. (ed.), *The Family on the Threshold of the 21st Century,* Lawrence Erlbaum Associates, New Jersey, pp. 147–166; Russell, G., Holmes, B. & Edgar, D. (1999), *Guide to Evaluating Work and Family Strategies,* Work & Family Unit, Department of Workplace Relations and Small Business, Canberra; and Russell, G. & Bowman, L. (2000), *Work and Family: Current Thinking, Research and Practice,* Department of Family and Community Services, Canberra.

For a glossy attempt by a big company to address the notion of corporate citizenship, see Rio Tinto's booklets *Education with Communities, Business with Communities* and *Partnering to Support Environmental and Cultural Research* (1999).

The Peter F. Drucker Foundation has set up an Australian equivalent called the Australian Forum on Nonprofit Management (1999). The contact point is Martin Stewart-Weeks (e-mail: martinsw@ozemail.com.au).

Philanthropy Australia Inc. is closely involved with the Prime Minister's Business and Community Partnerships Initiative (e-mail: pa@philanthropy.org.au).

151 Handy, C. (1994), *The Empty Raincoat: Making Sense of the Future,* Hutchinson, London.

152 Wolcott, I. (1991), *Work and Family: Employers' Views,* Australian Institute of Family Studies, Monograph No. 11, Melbourne.

153 Bodie, A. & Maggs, G. (1999), *You have to go to Melbourne if you want a good job...,* Centre for Workplace Culture Change, RMIT, outlines briefly the findings of this regional development project and the cultural difficulties in changing the way education, training and community development might interact. The longer version of this study is *Understanding Skill Gaps – A Regional Perspective,* Regional Labour Market Project, Stage 1 Report, CWCC, Melbourne.

154 People Together Project (2000), *The Power of Community,* Melbourne.

155 For other overseas examples, see Shuman, M.H. (1998), *Going Local: Creating Self-Reliant Communities in a Global Age,* Free Press, New York.

Another excellent model for basing services round more integrated local and regional frameworks is that produced by Victoria's Department of Justice, outlined in *Safer Cities and Shires: A Guide to Developing Strategic Partnerships,* 1997. It has been implemented in several locations, most notably via Banyule City Council and Heidelberg Secondary College.

The City of Port Philip, Melbourne, has published a Work Book for Staff, titled *Improving Community Participation in the City of Port Philip* (1999*).*

Chapter 12: Servicing the community patchwork

156 OECD report 'Literacy in the Information Age', cited in *The Age,* 15 June 2000.

157 A more detailed exposition of the approach outlined in this chapter is contained in my report for Deakin Human Services, titled *Promoting the Positive: Family–Community Resourcing as a Model for Family Services* (1999), Deakin University, Melbourne. Both a long version and a summary version are obtainable through their website. The reference list in the longer report is extensive and not repeated here.

Several of the state governments are renewing attempts to diversify regional support services and break down the barriers between departments that have common goals. For example, Victoria under its new Bracks Labor Government has initiated a review of economic rationalist approaches. The Health Department has published a 'Partnerships in Health' document aimed at regionalising health services, and the Department of Human Services has published the Jan Carter *Community Care Review* (2000), which recommends an approach similar to that espoused in this chapter.

Queensland's Departments of Education and Human Services have combined efforts to make schools more central as a point of contact and information about family support services and to encourage regional and local diversity in provision.

See also the paper by Paul Smyth and Brendan O'Connor (2000), *Welfare Reform in Australia and the Concept of Welfare Dependency*, School of Social Work and Social Policy, University of Queensland, for the Department of Families, Youth and Community Services, Queensland.

See also Queensland Chamber of Commerce & Industry (2000), *The Problems of Marginalised Youth in Australia — An Industry Perspective*, Brisbane, for an interesting industry approach to social issues via a more decentralised, regional framework built around the schools system.

The Commonwealth Department of Family and Community Services has also published its *Stronger Families & Communities Strategy* (1999), with extensive funding for new community-building initiatives.

In the United Kingdom, several attempts are being made to change the way services are managed: the Education Action Zones, attempts to encourage entrepreneurial activity in the welfare sector, and neighbourhood management of programs tackling social exclusion. See Taylor, M. (1999), 'Tackling social exclusion at local level: Neighborhood management', Joseph Rowntree Foundation, Ref. 310, London; and Speak, S. & Graham, S. *Service Not Included: Social Implications of Private Sector Restructuring in Marginalised Neighborhoods*, Findings, Ref. 230, Rowntree Foundation, London.

[158] For an extended critique of how competitive tendering has affected the role of welfare organisations, see ibid; ACOSS (1999), *Common Cause*, op cit; and Carter, J. (2000), *The Community Care Review*, Department of Human Services, Melbourne.

[159] Leadbetter, C. & Goss, S. (1998), *Civic Entrepreneurship*, Demos, London.

The first Australian conference on 'Social entrepreneurs' was sponsored by Mutuality in Sydney in February 2001

[160] Carter, op cit.

[161] The research on toxic social environments is central to any policy of prevention and universal family support services. See in particular, Garbarino, J. (1995), *Raising Children in a Socially Toxic Environment*, Jossey-Bass, San Francisco; and Hawkins, J.D., Catalano, R.F., Morrison, D.M., O'Donnell, J., Abbott, R.D. & Day, L.E. (1992), 'The Seattle Social Development Project: Effects of the first four years on protective factors and problem behaviors', in McCord, J. & Tremblay, R.M. (eds.), *Preventing Anti-Social Behavior: Interventions from Birth Through Adolescence*, Lawrence Erlbaum Associates, Hillsdale, New Jersey.

Homel, R. et al (1999), *Pathways to Prevention: Developmental and Early Intervention Approaches to Crime in Australia*, National Crime Prevention Unit, Attorney-General's Department, Canberra, is one of the best and most comprehensive reviews of the literature on preventive support services for families and communities. It goes far beyond a narrow focus on crime as such, and could serve as a model for a range of local and regional initiatives.

See also the report (January 2001) 'Victorian Burden of Disease by Local Government Areas' for another take on toxic social environments.

Chapter 13: Education — the driving force

[162] A more detailed version of the views put forward in this chapter is contained in my reports to the Queensland Ministry of Education: Edgar, D. (1999), *Social Trends and Their Impact on Queensland Education*, and Edgar, D. (1999), *Options for Schooling*, both available through Queensland Education, Brisbane.

Schofield, Kaye (1996), *Think Local and Compete: An Analysis of the Role of Adult and Community Education in the Implementation of a National System for Vocational Education and Training,* Australian National Training Authority, Canberra, argues a similar position.

[163] Cuttance, P. & Stokes, S. (2000), *Reporting on Student and School Achievement,* University of Sydney.

[164] Ben-David, J. (1963), 'Professions in the class system of present-day societies', *Current Sociology,* 12, pp. 247–330, is still the best analysis of why universities in the USA, modelled on Germany, were much more innovative than the British elite university system.

[165] Bentley, T. (1998), 'Learning beyond the classroom', in Hargreaves, I. & Christie, I. (eds.), *Tomorrow's Politics: The Third Way and Beyond,* Demos, London, pp. 80–95. See also the longer exposition of the new place of schools in Bentley, T. (1998), *Learning Beyond the Classroom: Education for a Changing World,* Demos/Routledge, London and New York.

[166] Hargreaves, D. (1994), *The Mosaic of Learning: Schools and Teachers for the Next Century,* Demos, London; and Hargreaves, D. (1998), *Creative Professionalism: The Role of Teachers in the Knowledge society,* Demos, London.

[167] Gardner, H., (1983), *Frames of Mind,* Fontana, London; Gardner, H. (1991), *The Unschooled Mind: How Children Think and How Schools Should Teach,* Basic Books, New York; Gardner, H. (1993), *Multiple Intelligences: The Theory in Practice,* Basic Books, New York; and Gardner, H. (1999), *Intelligence Reframed: Multiple Intelligences for the 21st Century,* Basic Books, New York.

[168] Illich, I. (1971), *Deschooling Society,* Calder & Boyars, London.

[169] For other international approaches to linking schools and businesses, see OECD (1998), *Review of the Transition from Initial Education to Working Life, Interim Comparative Report,* OECD, Paris, and *The Problems of Marginalised Youth in Australia — An Industry Perspective* (2000), Queensland Chamber of Commerce & Industry, Brisbane. See also:

Tedesco, J. (1997), *The New Educational Pact: Education, Competitiveness and Citizenship in Modern Society,* UNESCO, Paris;

Levin, B. & Riffel, A. (1997), *Schools and the Changing World: Struggling Toward the Future,* Falmer Press, New York;

Delors, J. et al (1998), *Learning: The Treasure Within: Report to UNESCO of the International Commission on Education for the Twenty-First Century,* UNESCO, Paris;

Kellahan, B. et al (1993), *The Home Environment and School Learning: Promoting Parental Involvement in the Education of Children,* Jossey-Bass, San Francisco;

Steinberg, L. (1996), *Beyond the Classroom: Why School Reform Has Failed and What Parents Need to Do,* Simon & Schuster, New York;

Clark, D. (1996), *Schools as Learning Communities: Transforming Education,* Cassell, London;

White, J.N. (1997), *Schools for the 21st Century: Educating for the Information Age,* Leonard Publishing, Harpenden;

Baldwin, P. (1997), *The Lighthouse: Towards a Labor Vision for the Learning Society,* Sydney.

[170] Matathia, I. & Salzman, M. (1998), *Next: Trends for the Future,* Pan Macmillan, Sydney.

[171] Letcher, op cit.

[172] Matathia & Salzman, op cit, p. 249.

[173] Edgar, D. (1995), 'Connecting family, workplace and community resources: The New Links Workplace Project', *Journal of the Home Economics Institute of Australia,* Vol. 2, No. 3, pp. 15–25; Russell, G. et al (1999), *Fitting Fathers into Families,* Department of Family & Community Services, Canberra; Petre, D. (1998), *Father Time,* Macmillan, Sydney; Glezer, H. & Wolcott, I. (1999), 'Conflicting commitments: Working mothers and fathers in Australia', in Haas, Hwang & Russell, op cit, pp. 43–56.

[174] Qvortrup, J. (ed.) (1993), *Childhood as a Social Phenomenon: Lessons from an International Project*, Eurosocial Report No. 47, European Centre, Vienna.

[175] Leach, P. (1994), *Children First*, Michael Joseph, London.

[176] Gardner (1985), op cit.

[177] Hargreaves (1994), op cit, pp. 32ff.

[178] Gardner (1991), op cit, p. 18.

[179] Perkins, quoted in Bentley (1998), op cit, p. 129.

[180] The Full-Service School model has been developed in various ways, both here and overseas. In Australia, the Health-Promoting Schools Movement is strongest in the ACT, which combines its Departments of Education and Human Services. The Newsletter of the ACEE/NSN Full Service Schools Research Circle is called *The Circle*, coordinated through the Victorian Independent Education Union, e-mail: mbuckley@edunions.labor.net.au, and other details are available from Stephen Kemmis on e-mail kemmis@sx.com.au. In the USA the National Network of Partnership Schools is accessible through http://www.csos.jhu.edu/p2000.

[181] NCCIP (1997), *The Emotional Foundations of School Readiness*, National Center for Clinical Infant Programs, Arlington, Virginia.

[182] See also: Boyer, E.L. (1991), *Ready to Learn: A Mandate for the Nation*, The Carnegie Foundation for the Advancement of Teaching, Princeton, New Jersey; *Focus on the First Sixty Months: A Handbook of Promising Programs for Children Zero to Five Years of Age* (1987), National Governors' Association Committee on Human Resources, USA; and Homel, R. (1999), *Pathways to Prevention: Developmental and Early Intervention Approaches to Crime in Australia*, National Crime Strategy, Canberra, ACT.

[183] Howard Gardner's books, passim; and Bentley, op cit, p. 23.

[184] Bentley, op cit.

[185] Ceci, S.J. (1996), *On Intelligence: A Bioecological Treatise on Intellectual Development*, Harvard University Press, Cambridge, Mass.

Cole, M. (1996), *Cultural Psychology: A Once and Future Discipline*, Belknap Press, Cambridge, Mass.

[186] Salovey, P. & Mayer, J.D. (1990), 'Emotional intelligence', *Imagination, Cognition and Personality*, 9, pp. 185–211.

Goleman, D. (1996), *Emotional Intelligence: Why It Can Matter More than IQ*, Bloomsbury, London.

[187] Perkins, D. (1995), *Outsmarting IQ: The Emerging Science of Learnable Intelligence*, Free Press, New York.

[188] Gardner (1993), op cit, and Bentley (1998), op cit. See also Edgar, D. (1992), *Multiple Intelligences as a Framework for 'Lift Off'*, Australian Children's Television Foundation, Melbourne.

[189] Bentley, op cit, p. 101.

[190] Mulgan, G. (1996), 'The new 3Rs', *Demos Quarterly 8: The New Enterprise Culture*, Demos, London: and Mulgan, G. (1997), *Connexity: How to Live in a Connected World*, Chatto & Windus, London.

[191] For an excellent overview of recent Australian research on Australian teenagers and sensible approaches to their socialisation, see Fuller, A. (2000), *Raising Real People: A Guide for Parents of Teenagers*, ACER Press, Melbourne.

[192] Handy (1994) op cit; and Letcher (1997), op cit.

[193] Kirby, P. (2000), *Moving Out: Schools, Training and Jobs*, Victorian Dept. of Education, Employment & Training, Melbourne.

[194] Schofield (1999), op cit.

[195] Hargreaves (1994), op cit, p. 10.

196 ibid.

197 Boyer, E.L. (1995), *The Basic School: A Community for Learning*, Carnegie Foundation for the Advancement of Teaching, Princeton, New Jersey.

198 The importance of adult further education was made clear in my report to the Victorian Government (1987), *Focus on Adults: Towards a Productive Learning Culture (The Edgar Report)*, Ministry of Education. Many of the changes recommended were implemented, but governments still seem unaware that informal adult pathways into further education and training are more effective than fixed courses aimed at specific skills.

199 Macken, D. (1999), *Australian Financial Review*, 28 September.

    See also the controversy over online tertiary courses between Dale Spender (*The Age*, 15 January 2001) and Janet McCalman (*The Age*, 17 January 2001); and Spender, D. & Stewart, F., 'Short and Sweet Learning Deals' *The Australian*, Higher Education Supplement (17 January 2001).

200 House of Representative Committee on Industry, Science and Resources (1999), *The Effect of Certain Policy Changes on Australia's R & D*, September, Canberra, ACT.

201 Adams, W. (1999), 'Sharp drop in R & D spending', *The Australian*, 22 September.

202 Department of Education, Training & Employment (1999), Green Paper, *New Knowledge, New Opportunities*, Canberra, ACT.

203 Kelly, P. (2000), *The Australian*, 17 May.

    Though note that Mark Latham has more recently suggested a similar scheme of lifelong learning vouchers as Labor Party policy (January 2001).

204 Chipman, L. (1999), *The Australian*, 8 September.

205 See Peter Appleyard (1999), 'The campus of tomorrow', *New York Times*, 4 April.

Chapter 14: Conclusions — driving culture change and linking the future

206 As quoted in Stewart-Weeks, Chapter 11, in Cox (2000), op cit., p. 289.

207 Schorr, L. (1997), *Common Purpose: Strengthening Families and Neighborhoods to Rebuild America*, Anchor Doubleday, New York, as quoted in Cox (2000), op cit, p. 291.

208 Rhodes, R. (1997), 'From marketisation to diplomacy: It's the mix that matters', *Australian Journal of Public Administration*, Vol. 56, No. 2, June, pp. 40–53.

209 Botsman, P. (2000), as quoted in Stewart-Weeks, op cit, in Cox, op cit, p. 295.

INDEX

Aboriginal & Torres Strait Islanders 78, 80,173
Adams, W. 214
adult education 40, 84, 214
The Age 196, 197, 199, 202, 203, 214
ageing 26–7, 35–41, 68, 198, 201
Alcoa Australia 121–31
altruism 200
Amnesty International 11
Area Consultative Committees 192
Arena Journal 204, 205
Argy, Fred 61, 202, 204
Appleyard, Peter 214
Asia 12, 21, 63, 80, 197
Atkins, C. 206
Aum Shinrkyo Cult 85
Australia Post 61, 132–6
The Australian 204, 214
Australian Assistance Plan 107, 114
Australian Bulletin of Labour 200
Australian Bureau of Statistics (ABS) 196, 205
Australian Council of Social Services (ACOSS) 11, 104, 109, 209, 211
Australian Council of the Ageing (ACOTA) 11
Australian Financial Review 200, 202, 203, 214
Australian Institute of Family Studies (AIFS) 197
Australian Journal of Public Administration 214
Australian productivity Commission Ch.2 *passim*, 196, 197, 198, 199, 206, 209
Australian Workplace Agreements (AWAs) 55

Baby Boomers 27, 33, 204
Bagnall, Diana 11, 197, 199, 206

Baldwin, Peter 213
Bartholomeusz, Stephen 202
Beazley, Kim 209
Beck, U. 205, 207
Bellah, Robert 201
Ben-David, Joseph 212
Bennington, R. 37
Bentley, Tom 39, 176, 199, 212
Berger, Peter 208
Berreby, D. 203
Bessis, S. 202
Bjornberg, Ulla 201
Blandy, Richard 197
Bodi, Anna 204, 210
Bodna, Ben 206, 208
Body Shop 71
Bole, W. 203
Bolton, R. 209
Botsman, Peter 215
Bott, Elisabeth 204
Bourdieu, Pierre 208, 209
Bowen, G.L. 201
Boyer, E.L. 213
Bracks Government 211
Brain, Peter 30, 195, 197, 203
Bretton Woods 13, 62
Buckingham, Jennifer 198
The Bulletin 206
bureaucracy 8
business ethics 59–68, 70, 96, 202–4
B2B 29, 73

Cairns Group 95
Caldwell, Peter 207
Campbell Inquiry 62
capitalism 5
Capling, Ann 195, 204, 206, 207
carers/caring 35–6, 174–5

Carnegie Foundation for the Advancement
   of Teaching, 213
Carroll, John 203
Carter, Jan 144, 211
Castells, Manuel 195, 203, 205
casual work 199
Ceci, S.J. 213
Center for Living Democracy 202
Centre for Workplace Culture Change
   137–8, 204, 210
child care 50, 198, 200
child neglect/protection xiii, 143–5
children's television 205
Chipman, Lachlan 214
Christie, Ian 202
City of Port Philip 211
civic entrepreneurship 143, 212
civil society xiv, 83, 101–5, 207
Clark, D. 213
Cole, M. 214
Colebatch, Tim 196
Coleman, James 209
Collitts, P. 209
common good xii, 57, 96, 205
community xiii–xv, 42–5, 83, 178–82, 195
community colleges 178–82
community services xv, Ch.12 passim, 200,
   209
competence 198
Competition Policy (National) 25, 108–9,
   142–3, 196, 211
connectedness xi
competitive tendering Ch.12 passim, 211
Considine, Mark 195, 204, 206, 207
contracting out 20, 209
coping xii, 198
Corporate Work & Family Awards 53
corporate responsibility xiii, 70
corporate philanthropy 203
Costar, B. 206
Country Education Project 113–20
Courier Mail 199
Cox, Eva 207, 208
cultural capital 32, 102
culture change xvi, Ch. 4 passim, Ch. 14
   passim
curriculum 163–7, 183–4
Cuttance, P. 212

Davidson, James 195, 196, 206
Deakin Human Services 211
De Alcantara, H. 196
Delors, J. 213
democracy xii, xiv, xvi, 7
demography 35, 197
Demos 91, 202, 214
Department of Workplace Relations and
   Small Business 200, 201
Department of Family and Community
   Services 211
Depression, the Great 47
De Vaus, David 197
divorce 32
Drake Management 38
Dreman, Solly 199, 210
Drucker, Peter 54, 203, 205, 207, 210
Durkheim, Emile 7, 195

East India Company 12
Eckersley, Richard 204, 205
economic rationalism ix, 75
economic nationalism 195
economic theory 59–64
Economou, N. 206
Edgar, Don 197, 199, 200, 206, 210, 212,
   213, 214
Edgar, Patricia 205
education 16–17, Ch. 13 passim, 212–14
Education Action Zones 211
Elkington, J. 202
emotional intelligence 214
employment 21–4, 81, 87–8
Emy, Hugh 204
engagement xvi
environment xvi, 57, 102, 202
equity xii, 86–7, 194, 201
ethics 59–68, 70, 202–4
EthicScan Canada 66
Etzioni, Amitai 195, 204, 205, 208
European Centre, Vienna 213
exclusion xi, 202, 207, 209

family xv, 31–41, 61, 72–3, 197–9
Family Matters 198
Family Law 199
family policy 46–58, 141–4
Family Resource Zones 150–4, 172–6

family support services 140–54
family values xiv, 32, 50, 96, 103, 202
fathers/fatherhood 9, 213
Federation 197
flexible work 43, 68
free market/free trade ix, xiv, 14, 59 ff
Friedman, M. 203
Fukuyama, Francis 196, 208
full service schools 213

Galinsky, Ellen 201
Garbarino, James 212
Gardner, Howard 212, 214
GATT 13
GDP/GNP 14, 16
gender equity 200
Generation X 27, 45, 67
Gettler, L. 209
Giddens, Anthony 38, 196, 197, 198
Glezer, Helen 200, 201
globalisation ix, 10–15, 42, 83ff, 110–11,
        184, 196, 202–4, 206–7, 209
Goleman, Daniel 214
Googins, B. 203
Gouldner, Alvin 208
government, role of 10, 69, 89, 93–8
Grameen Bank 61
Greenpeace 11
Gronovetter, M. 204

Haas, Linda 200, 213
Handy, Charles 202, 210, 214
Hanson, Pauline see One Nation
Harding, Anne 207
Hargreaves, David 169, 198, 212, 213
Hawke, Robert J. 96
Health-Promoting Schools Movement 213
Henderson, Helen 202
Hewett, Patricia 206
Hilmer, Fred 196, 197
Hochschild, Arlie 204
Hodge, G. 209
Homel, Ross 212, 213
Honolulu Advertiser 204
Hornby, Frank 209
Horsman 205
House of Representatives Committee on
        Industry, Science and Resources 214

Howard, John 80, 96, 103
human capital 19, 32, 100–1, 207–9
human resources 54, 62

identity xii, 33–4, 78–84, 204–5
Illich, Ivan 212
International Labor Organisation (ILO)
        47, 56
International Monetary Fund (IMF) 10,
        13, 63
Inayatullah, S. 204
individualism 195, 196, 206
industrial economy 4ff
industrial relations reform 25, 51, 197
Industrial Revolution 5ff
inequality xii, 86–7, 194
Information Age/technology xi, 43, 195,
        203, 212
intelligences, multiple 176, 212
interdependence 7, 11
Internet xv, 74, 195
intimacy/relationships 33–4, 197, 201

James, P. 196
Japan 199
Jefferson xvi, 195
Johnson, D.T. 205
Johnson, P. 199
Johnstone, P. 209
Joseph Rowntree Foundation 211

Kanter, Rosabeth Moss 201
Keating, Paul 80, 107
Kellahan, B. 213
Kellner, Peter 8, 195, 206
Kelly, Paul 195, 197
Kelty, Bill 108
Kennett Government xiv, 24, 90, 206
Kenwood, A. 197
Kingston, Margo 206
Klein, Naomi 205
knowledge economy/service economy 3,
        15–20, 62–4
knowledge worker 17

Laslett, Peter 198
Latham, Mark 103, 195, 207, 208, 214
Leach, Penelope 213

Leadbetter, Charles 204, 206, 207,
    211
Leser, David 28, 197, 199
Letcher, Marcus 196, 197, 213, 214
Levin, B. 213
lifelong learning 40, 184, 214
Luckmann, Thomas 208
Lyons, Mark 207, 210
Lynch, A. 204

Mackay, Hugh 204
Macken, Dierdre 202, 214
Maggs, Glenn 204, 210
managerialism x, 142
marriage 198
Maley, Barry 33, 198
Matathia, I. 213
mateship xii
Matthews, Race 206
Melucci, Alberto 205
men/masculinity 197, 200
Menzies, Heather 196
Microsoft 13
migrants/migration 79
mobility 27–8, 170, 197
Mondragon 206
Mulgan, G. 204, 214
mutualism/Mutuality 8, 91, 106–7, 195,
    204, 206

McBride, H. 202
McCalman, Janet 214
McCallum, John 198
McCaughey, Jean 206, 208
McDonald, Peter 206
McKinsey & Co. 209
Macfarlane, Alan 195

National Crime Prevention Unit 212
nation state 10, 94
national identity xii, 78–84, 204–5
Ned Kelly 78
Neef, D. 196
neighbourhood 209, 211
neo-liberalism 6, 59–60, 195, 197
networks/links xiii, 72–5, 152–4
Neuwirth, G. 208
New Economy 17, 28

New Links Workplace Project 120–37, 199,
    210, 213
New Radical Centre 91
New York Times 14, 196, 203, 214
Norris, D. 26, 197
Norton, A. 208

obligations, reciprocal 96
Ochiltree, Gay 200
Organisation for Economic Development
    (OECD) 16, 21, 211, 212
Offe, C. 196
Ohmae, K. 94, 196, 207
One Nation Party xiii, xvi, 4, 25, 81, 88–9
O'Neill, D. 209
organisational change 200
Ormerod, P. 202
O'Rourke, K. 196
Orthner, D. 201
Osborne, D. 207
Ostrom, E. 205, 207
outsourcing 20, 209
Owen, Robert 195
Oxfam 11
Oxley, Alan 109, 204, 209

parents/parenting 46–58, 157–60, 167–9,
    212, 214
participation xii, xiv
partnerships 30, 69, 120–37, 169
patriarchy 2
People Together Project xvi, 90, 138–9,
    206, 211
Pettigrew, Pierre 10–11
Petre, D. 213
philanthropy 203, 210
place, sense of Ch. 6 passim, 204
Pleck, Joseph 201
population trends 35
portfolio workers 39, 43, 85
postmodern xi, 2, 203, 205
professionalism x, 212
progress 204
public sector Ch.8 passim, Ch.10 passim,
    Ch.12 passim
Purple Sage Project 90
Pusey, Michael 197
Putnam, Robert 208, 209

Queensland Chamber of Commerce and
    Industry 211, 212
Queensland Education 168ff
Qvortrup, Jens 213

Rainbow Alliance 209
Ralph Report 64
reciprocity 7, 208
reconciliation 80
Rees-Mogg, Lord William 196
regionalism x, 24–5, 87–90, 106–12, 203–4,
    209–10
Reich, Robert 196
research funding 185–6
Rhodes, R. 214
Richardson, Sue 199, 205
Rifkin, Jeremy 196, 207
Rio Tinto 210
risk society 84, 146, 205, 207
Robertson, R. 201
rural 113–20, 209, 210
Russell, Graeme 200, 210

Saul, John Ralston 195
Saunders, Peter (AIFS) 32, 198
Saunders, Peter (SWRC) 205
Saxenian, A. 203
Scanlon, C. 204
Scheff, T. 205
Schofield, Kaye 212
schools 39, 41, 151–2, 155–82
    primary 172–6
    middle 177–8
    senior 178–9
Schools Commission 114
Schorr, L. 214
Seattle Social Development Project 212
security, job 199
Semler, Ricardo 201
Sennett, Richard 44, 197, 200, 204
service economy 196
sexuality 33–4, 197, 201
shareholders 70, 202, 203
Sher, Jonathon 209
Silicon Valley 73, 203
Simon, J.L. 202
Singles (Solo) Generation xvii, 27
Smart, Carol 198–9

social capital xiv, 62, 69–72, 101–2, 111,
    203, 207–9
social movements 83–92, 205–6
Speak, S. 211
Spearritt, K. 210
Spender, Dale 214
Steinberg, L. 213
Stewart-Weeks, Martin 207, 208, 214
stock market 14
Strange, S. 196
Stokes, G. 206
Stretton, Hugh 202
Sussman, Marvin 201
Sweden 49, 52, 199

Technical & Further Education (TAFE) 24,
    177
Tanner, Lindsay 103, 207, 208
tariffs 197
taxation 10, 48, 207
Taylor, M. 209, 211
teachers 170–1, 212
teamwork 44
Tedesco, I. 212
Theobald, Robert 206, 208
Third Age 198
Third Way 3, 8, 97, 103, 198, 202, 205
Toennies, Ferdinand 208
Touraine, A. 205
toxic communities xv
trade unions 60, 202
tribalism xvii, 25, 78, 82, 83–92, 113,
    205
triple bottom line 66, 70, 202, 203
trust 208

unemployment 21–4, 81, 87–8, 201
United Nations Educational & Scientific
    Organisation (UNESCO) 213
unions 60, 202
universities 183–8, 212
University of the Third Age (U3A)
    40

VandenHeuvel, Audrey 200
Victorian Council of Social Services
    (VCOSS) 209
voluntarism xii–vi, 100–5, 192, 200

weak ties 204
Weber, Max 208
Weekend Australian 203
welfare reform 211
welfare state ix, 47, 95–6
wellbeing xi
White, J.N. 213
Wilkinson, Helen 198
Winter, Ian 203, 207, 208
Wolcott, Ilene 197, 200, 201, 210

women & labour force 26, 34, 50, 199
work–family balance xiii, Ch. 4 *passim*
work–family policies 46–58, 199–202
World Bank 10, 13, 63, 85
World Economic Forum (WEF) xv, 85
World Trade Organisation (WTO) xv, 85

Yankelovitch Partners 201
youth xv, 177–8, 211, 214
Yunus M. 202

www.ingramcontent.com/pod-product-compliance
Lightning Source LLC
Chambersburg PA
CBHW032132020426
42334CB00016B/1134